The Accounting Wars

BY THE SAME AUTHOR:

The Big Eight
Land Rush
Model
How to Run Your Own Business Successfully
Like No Other Store in the World

MARK STEVENS

The Accounting Wars

Collier Books
Macmillan Publishing Company
New York

Copyright © 1985 by Mark Stevens

Excerpts on pages 147–48 from an article by Howard Rudnitsky with John Heins, *Forbes*, December 19, 1983, reprinted by permission of *Forbes* magazine.
© Forbes Inc., 1983.

All rights reserved. No part of this book may be reproduced or transmitted in any form or by any means, electronic or mechanical, including photocopying, recording or by any information storage and retrieval system, without permission in writing from the Publisher.

Macmillan Publishing Company
866 Third Avenue, New York, N.Y. 10022
Collier Macmillan Canada, Inc.

Library of Congress Cataloging-in-Publication Data
Stevens Mark, 1947–
The accounting wars.
Includes bibliographical references and index.
1. Accounting firms—United States.   I. Title.
[HF5616.U5S74   1986]   338.7′61657′0973   86-14713
ISBN 0-02-025540-6 (pbk.)

Macmillan books are available at special discounts for bulk purchases for sales promotions, premiums, fund-raising, or educational use. For details, contact:
Special Sales Director
Macmillan Publishing Company
866 Third Avenue
New York, N.Y. 10022

10 9 8 7 6 5 4 3 2 1

Designed by Jack Meserole

Printed in the United States of America

First Collier Books Edition 1986

The Accounting Wars is also published in a hardcover edition by Macmillan Publishing Company.

To Lee and Irv

CONTENTS

Foreword, *ix*

1. From Wall Street to Beijing, *1*
2. Main Hurdman + KMG = The Big Nine, *17*
3. Passage to China, *57*
4. Bulls, Bears, and CPAs, *92*
5. The Great American Tax Shelter: Where "the Name" Is the Name of the Game, *130*
6. Too Big to Be Small, Too Small to Be Big: Competing with the Big Eight, *177*
7. Book Cooking, Numbers Juggling, and Other Tricks of the Trade, *219*
8. Who Does What Best, *251*

Index, *254*

FOREWORD

Just a decade ago, the notion of "accounting wars" would have seemed preposterous not only to casual observers of the profession but also to those intimately involved in it. That practitioners of this conservative discipline would be assaulting each other with hit lists, press leaks, megamergers, talent raids, and hard-sell marketing campaigns—well, that would have seemed appropriate for mouthwash makers but not CPAs.

Times have changed. Today, the wars have spread beyond the first militarized zone, the audit market, to an evolving scope of services in a changing America, a changing world. And the combatants, once limited to the eight biggest accounting firms in the U.S.—the Big Eight: Price Waterhouse; Arthur Andersen; Arthur Young; Coopers & Lybrand; Deloitte Haskins & Sells; Ernst & Whinney; Peat, Marwick, Mitchell; Touche Ross —now includes increasingly competitive upstarts in the second tier: the likes of Main Hurdman; Laventhol & Horwath; Alex-

Foreword

ander Grant; Seidman & Seidman; Kenneth Leventhal; Oppenheim, Appel, Dixon, among others.

With specialized and entrepreneurial practices, smaller but in some cases more profitable (per partner) firms are proving to be tenacious competitors for the Big Eight. Even further down the size spectrum, lilliputian local practitioners are enlisting in the accounting wars, employing, on a limited scale, competitive techniques designed to take them to the next plateau in the accounting hierarchy. Whatever the outcome, whoever wins or loses, many believe the profession, for better or worse, will never be the same.

1
From Wall Street to Beijing

The place is the main dining room at Chicago's Ritz Carlton Hotel. The players are a Big Eight audit partner and his client, the chief executive officer of a 110-year-old midwestern manufacturer of building materials. The event is a luncheon called by the CEO. No one is smiling. No one is eating.

CEO: As you know, Bill, we're about to report our first profit after nine consecutive losing quarters.
PARTNER: Harry, you deserve all the credit in the world.
CEO: I'm not looking for credit.
PARTNER: Well, that goes without saying, but—
CEO: I've turned this thing around by cutting out the fat. Most of it. Now it's your turn, Bill. And I'm warning you, these days I'm a hard-nosed S.O.B.
PARTNER: You know the service we provide to your firm—as a long-standing and valued client—goes well beyond—
CEO: Spare me, Bill. I'll lay it on the line. We paid you a million-one for audit services last year. I want that cut to $600,000.

PARTNER: What? Christ, Harry, that's damned impossible. Okay, okay, you want to talk a 10 percent cut? If that's what you're getting at we can arrange something.

CEO: Bill, I'll pay $600,000. Period. If that's not profitable for you, I understand fully and we can terminate our relationship on the best of terms. I happen to know of several firms that are more than willing to take us on for that sum. Please call me by Friday with your answer. And I don't want any maybe's. Make it yes or no!

News of this showdown caused a hellstorm at Bill's firm, but the decision, made ultimately by the managing partner, was to accept the take-it-or-leave-it offer rather than let the client slip away to a competitor. Why this total capitulation? Bill explains: "Because our salad days as auditors are over. The very same clients that not only never nickel and dimed us, but actually took pride in paying premium fees to get the best possible audits, are treating us much as they do vendors of office supplies. The guy with the lowest bid gets the paper clip contract: In the same fashion the lowball CPA wins the audit engagement.

"This dollars-and-cents approach to selecting auditors isn't entirely new. No, what makes it alarming is that it's spreading. American business—especially the old industrial companies that make for the biggest names on our client list—is having its problems and is forcing its accountants to share the burden.

"Fortunately, some of the real war stories haven't gotten out yet. Many clients still don't know how easy it is to get wholesale cuts in their audit fees. They shoot for a ten percent to fifteen percent reduction and they're happy with that. But the very day my story—or others like it—makes the *Wall Street Journal,* we're going to get a thousand luncheon invitations by noon."

From Wall Street to Beijing

As the mid-1980s unfold, public accounting firms are stronger and weaker than at any time in their history. The future shock that has staggered American business—forcing a nation of basically inefficient smokestack industries to shift increasingly to a services- and high-technology-based economy—has caused seismic waves in national accounting practices. Most alarming, the Big Eight's traditional bread and butter market—audits of the *Fortune* 500 industrial corporations—shows evidence of continuing deterioration, prompting speculation of a precipitous decline in audit fees.

"We grew prosperous by serving what I call the Eisenhower companies," says a Chicago-based Big Eight partner. "By this I mean the TV makers and the tire companies and the steel mills that took off on long-term growth curves that started with Eisenhower's inauguration and continued unabated, save for occasional short-term dips, until the late seventies. I'm referring to the companies that mass-produced the cars, cameras, and televisions that were gobbled up nearly as fast as they were shipped from the assembly lines. The companies that made so much money on the basis of a seemingly foolproof formula, that of stamping out inferior merchandise engineered for rapid obsolescence, that they didn't perceive the threat from Tokyo or the end of the baby boom until these cataclysmic events suddenly changed their world and threatened their very survival."

The shift in emphasis from an industrial-based economy to one favoring services and technology—enormously difficult under any circumstances—was doubly difficult for the twentieth-century United States because it was forced into the change rather than having planned for it and because it was faced with an impossible deadline. With the gun of foreign competition at their heads, America's chief executives had to take one of two costly and essentially high-risk actions: to rapidly modernize a decrepit and inefficient physical plant to compete head-on with Tokyo or to shift the corporate vision to services or

3

The Accounting Wars

high technology, both of which are less sensitive to competitive pricing.

Corporate leaders could blame only themselves for this untenable position. For more than a decade, the best minds in American business focused not on producing better or more cost-efficient products, but instead on engineering intricate takeovers whereby one industrial giant acquired another and the combined entity was acquired by still a third. This corporate Pac Man shifted assets rather than creating them, and in the process simply produced fees and commissions for investment bankers, attorneys, and accountants. The era's most celebrated chief executives—Bendix's William Agee, Reliance Group's Saul Steinberg, and Gulf+Western's Charles Bluhdorn—were busy assembling acquired companies, committing billions in corporate capital and credit to asset-shifting takeovers while their Japanese counterparts were investing in sleekly modern steel mills and robot-driven auto plants.

"While American steelmakers clung to their open hearths and ingot casting, Japanese steelmakers were investing heavily in basic-oxygen furnaces and continuous casting. While American automakers toyed with style changes, Japanese automakers were investing in the new stamping technologies and experimenting with more efficient engines and pollution-control devices. In 1970, just two years after Motorola introduced solid-state circuitry, Japanese television manufacturers had fully commercialized the new technology. By 1971, 90 percent of Japanese-made color televisions were solid-state. And by 1979, the Japanese, unchallenged, were flooding the American market with video cassette recorders."*

In the U.S., the direction of capital to essentially nonproductive uses frustrated those remaining CEOs who hoped to keep America's entrepreneurial spirit alive.

---

* Robert Reich, "The Next American Frontier," *Atlantic Monthly,* April 1983.

From Wall Street to Beijing

Referring to the now infamous Martin-Marietta/Bendix/Allied Corporation/United Technologies takeover battle, in which Agee was a key player, Chrysler's Lee Iacocca complained that the corporate warriors had tied up $10 billion in credit between them without creating a single job. Although exceptional in its ability to resurface as a strong industrial competitor (primarily on the strength of its indomitable chairman), Chrysler was not alone in its search for capital and in its struggle to streamline and reposition itself. The bad news for the economy and for the Big Eight is that many of the beleaguered smokestackers have not fared as well.

"Many, more than I'd like to admit, of our clients have gone through a wrenching transformation, trying to adjust to the new demands of the marketplace," the Chicago-based audit partner continues. "Contrary to the impression conveyed by the national news shows, most are not going bankrupt, but they are being forced to prune away unprofitable divisions, lop off marginal subsidiaries, slash the work force, and generally tighten the fiscal belt. Things are changing out there—and it's only the beginning."

Accounting's senior executives are responding to this change. Thomas Holton, chairman of Peat, Marwick's international partnership, notes that there has been a "shift of our nation's economic foundation from manufacturing to services. Today, the services sector—banking, insurance, finance, law, accounting, real estate, and communications, as well as retailing and personal services—generates two-thirds of our gross national product. Services employ seven out of every ten Americans; between 1970 and 1980, services generated 14.3 million new jobs; and productivity in services increased at a rate twice that of manufacturing."

Price Waterhouse's chairman, Joe Connor, states: "It's a

truism that ours is increasingly a service economy and that the basic 'smokestack' industries, if not an endangered species, are at least undergoing radical changes that make their future profoundly uncertain."

The changes at American Can, one of the thirty blue chips that compose the Dow Jones Industrial Averages, are representative of the transformation. In recent years, this industrial mainstay has sold its paper operations and has purchased an investment brokerage firm, an insurance company, and a mutual fund. This must be seen as a defensive as well as an offensive move. One to counter the decline in its traditional markets.

"The basic industries which led our charge to world economic leadership are a mere vestige of their old selves," says Connor, adding, "We are squandering human and capital resources with often grossly inefficient methods of operation. . . . For this reason, I am calling for a national business agenda for the renewal of American enterprise.

"By renewal, I do not mean an inherently futile effort to resurrect a glorious past, but an effort that will allow what is timeless in our entrepreneurial spirit—the ethic of personal achievement, a profound individual commitment to risk-taking, and raw creative energy—to flourish in a radically new economic environment."

Connor's agenda, while built on valid proposals, also serves the interests of the major CPA firms by creating new profit opportunities for them. Connor proposes the following:

- An end to the adversarial relationship between business and government. "My plan is not a government giveaway; it is one of government getting out of the way." (What *Fortune* 500 client wouldn't toast to that?)
- The strengthening of the smokestack industries. How? With the aid of accounting firms designing and producing "finan-

cial and operating data, as well as data-gathering systems, necessary for these industries to evaluate their everyday needs and to develop effective long-term business strategies."
- Matching technology management to technology change. Basically, this means helping the private sector absorb new technologies in the office and the factory. (Again, a golden opportunity for venerable Price Waterhouse.) Says Connor: "As an illustration of what is being done to meet this challenge, my firm has been paying particular attention to developing the necessary data and information systems to support the operations of the 'company of the future.' We believe one of the most valuable is the computer-based manufacturing management system, which is designed to assist a company's management in the planning and control of its manufacturing process. Another valuable tool is a sophisticated cost-accounting system specifically geared to measuring the benefit of technological change."
- Enhancing public and private sector accountability, including the appointment of chief financial officers at all levels of government. (Public sector accounting has emerged as a tempting market for a smorgasbord of CPA services.)
- Encouraging small business growth. (Another target market for the Big Eight, made ever more attractive by the decline of the "Eisenhowers.")
- Aggressively promoting international trade and investment.

This relates directly to the expansion of PW's international practice, including an aggressive entry into the huge and virtually untapped market of the People's Republic of China. With the domestic market for *Fortune* 500 auditing services basically stagnant, opportunistic managing partners are stepping up practice activities overseas, especially in those emerging markets likely to experience the most dramatic growth, and are redirecting domestic marketing away from the slumping Eisenhowers to those fast-track service and high-tech ventures that have become America's premier growth companies.

While Price Waterhouse is focusing a major part of its efforts on China and overall geographic expansion, reversing what some observers regard as a decade of complacency in its overseas practice, Touche Ross is setting its sights on a dramatically different ideal of the eighties growth market: Wall Street. Just how the evolution of American industry is prompting the major accounting firms to scurry for new business and to reposition themselves for future growth is best illustrated by the fact that the Big Eight see promise in a capital of communism and a citadel of capitalism. Much as PW has thrown dollars at China, doing pro bono work for the PRC government, Touche Ross has invested heavily in a practice specialty geared to Wall Street's investment banking industry. TR's chairman, Grant Gregory (a master salesman in the manner of his mentor, former managing partner Russ Palmer*), is shifting his firm's marketing focus not geographically but industry-wise, hoping to build bridges to some of the most profitable businesses in America. With Manhattan now the unchallenged center of international finance, Gregory is betting that he can fatten Touche's treasury by selling tax, consulting, and in some cases auditing services to the prestigious investment banking houses of Lehman Brothers, Goldman Sachs, and Morgan Stanley. Gregory's gambit, which may turn out to be an extraordinary success or a colossal failure, is to respond to the industrial-to-services evolution by going where the dollars are. His plan is for Touche Ross, like the economy in general, to rotate on its axis, evolving from an in-

---

* Now dean of the Wharton School.

dustrial- and retailing-based accounting firm to one top-heavy with service clients.

Interestingly, the rise of the services economy that TR hopes to tap is mirrored in the changing landscape of the Manhattan real estate market. From the 1940s to the mid-1970s, New York's steel-and-glass office towers were a mecca to the corporate officers of such industrial heavyweights as Texaco and Union Carbide. Big Eight marketing partners, on the prowl for new business, could touch base with controllers and CEOs within walking distance of their own Manhattan offices. But beginning in the early seventies and accelerating throughout the decade, many of New York's most prominent corporate tenants responded to rising rents and sluggish business conditions by relocating their essentially boutique headquarters to less expensive suburban locations or to sites in closer proximity to online divisions in Ohio, Michigan, and the Sunbelt. At the height of their profitability, it had seemed only fitting that the Big Board's premier names should list as their residence of record a prestigious New York address, preferably Park Avenue or Avenue of the Americas. The most prominent figures in American management, the men and women at the helm of the industrial giants, took it as a symbol of their position in the nation's socioeconomic hierarchy to be elevated sixty floors into the clouds in a Manhattan tower 1,500 miles from the nearest manufacturing plant. New York's astronomical rents were accepted as the price of power and privilege.

But with the slowdown of growth in the industrial sector, rental costs of two to five times comparable space in less auspicious environs became increasingly difficult to justify. What's more, with red ink flowing at many of the once omnipotent Eisenhowers, the urge to paint one's corporate logo across the New York skyline was greatly diminished. As the blue chips departed for less pretentious digs, their exodus left Manhattan with recurring vacancies of one, two, or three million square feet of prime space. At first developers feared a collapse of the rental market. But in a commercial application of the law of physics that "every action has an equal and opposite reaction," Manhattan's fast-growing services sector rushed in to fill the void.

"Law firms, accounting firms, advertising agencies, investment banks, and financial institutions of all shapes and sizes have demonstrated a voracious appetite for New York's commercial space," says Simon Milde, a partner with Jones Lang Wootton, a prestigious, British-based real estate brokerage and consulting firm representing a coterie of Manhattan's most active landlords and developers. "These service firms are growing exponentially and are claiming a steadily increasing percentage of the available office space."

Count CPA firms among the city's most insatiable tenants. Although the decline of the Eisenhowers has reduced fees or slowed their annual growth in a number of hard-hit practice disciplines, redeployment of programs and personnel to more active markets (international, tax, bankruptcy, mergers and acquisitions, service industry specialization) has, in most cases, more than compensated for the shortfall. The truth is that CPA firms, from the multinational partnerships to the sole practitioners, have never been in a better position to sell their services. While being forced to change as America changes, most can do so from positions of strength. Two factors are responsible for this:

First: The reordering of the corporate establishment gives rise to enormously complex issues concerning taxes, accounting, asset valuation, depreciation, and net worth. Mergers and acquisitions, for example, which have accelerated significantly in an industrial sector more prone to shifting assets than creating them, are not singular events but intricate puzzles that must be meticulously pieced together. Accountants are indispensable to the process.

From Wall Street to Beijing

Second: Despite some dissatisfaction with their fees (primarily for audit work, which is often viewed as a commodity service), CPAs enjoy an enviable position as trusted, thoroughly professional confidants and advisers whose honesty and integrity is generally held beyond reproach. There is good reason for this. The caricature of the supercautious, nit-picking CPA who dotes endlessly over the veracity of a seemingly inconsequential figure is one stereotype that is more or less an accurate portrayal. Whether it be the rigors of their training or the bent of personality that first selects public accounting as a life's work, accountants are, for the most part, prudent men and women with an admirable, if curiously old-fashioned, predilection for playing it by the book. This close-to-the-vest quality distinguishes CPAs from stockbrokers, bond salesmen, financial planners, and assorted purveyors of the American dream. In a highly cynical society where learning to distrust, as a defensive safeguard, has become part of the national business curriculum, accountants are still viewed as relatively noncommercial and highly believable professionals.

Attribute this to the fact that CPAs—the aggressive marketing machinations of the giant firms are an exception—have kept their commercial instincts and aspirations (strong as they may be) from subverting professional standards. This is most evident on the local, independent practitioner level and is best seen by comparing the accounting and dental professions. While both started from positions atop the hierarchy of trust and respectability, dentists, by reversing the accountants' approach and allowing commercial objectives to supersede professional standards, have tumbled to a position somewhat above that of used car dealers but not much higher than TV repairmen. Quality work has been sacrificed for the sake of speed; advertising (including rock music radio jingles) has taken precedence over professional referrals, and the dentist's door is plastered with more credit card stickers than a Chinese restaurant. In an effort to maximize personal earnings and to merchandise $2,000 bridges and $500 root canals much the way appliance stores sell TVs and VCRs, dentists have adopted a full complement of modern marketing techniques. But in the process they have come to be seen as salesmen/professionals whose interests and those of their patients may be at odds. This has a devastating impact on the dentist's credibility. When a DDS recommends a course of treatment, the patient, consciously or subliminally, wonders if he isn't being sold more than he really needs.

CPAs rarely, if ever, elicit this response. In those cases where the sole practitioner's professionalism is suspect, in more cases than not he has reluctantly transgressed the lines of independence to satisfy the *client's* demands for additional services. Paradoxically, among the great challenges facing accountants in the 1980s and beyond is not only how to reposition their practices to reflect the changes in American business, but also how to limit the scope of their work. Because they are widely viewed as an endangered species, as rare sources of honest and dependable counsel, accountants are being called on to dispense a burgeoning list of services, some of which, like the dentists' radio jingles, may mar the image of objective independence that is their greatest asset. Consider this from an April 1984 report by the AICPA's Future Issues Committee: "The expansion of services and products is an issue of current significance. It does not appear to be an issue that can be put aside or resolved by proclamation, because it relates to a development that provides new opportunities to both CPAs and their clients.

"The issue is how should the profession adapt its practices and standards to allow firms to take maximum advantage of opportunities to expand services and products in a manner appropriate to the professionalism and integrity of CPAs.

"In today's environment, CPA firms are offering to their clients and others a wide range of nontraditional services and products, including: computer software and hardware, actuarial and appraisal services, educational programs, and service bureaus for various forms of record keeping. Seeking to expand significantly the range of services and products provided, CPA firms may expand in other nontraditional ways possibly including: establishing retail stores for the sale of computer hardware and software, developing venture capital and investment banking divisions, offering insurance (including insuring the financial stability of companies), offering telecommunication consulting and installations, operating subsidiary companies, and perhaps entering into commercial banking activities."

"We've got a very delicate balancing act to pull off here," says B. Z. Lee, chairman of the American Institute of Certified Public Accountants* and a partner with second-tier firm Seidman & Seidman. A thoughtful, soft-spoken Texan, Lee has settled into the role of accounting's elder statesman, having served as his firm's managing partner through some of its most tumultuous years (from 1974 to 1983).

"Let's explore this balancing act at the most fundamental level. Assume the CPA is serving his client, a small business owner, by maintaining his corporate books, handling his corporate and personal taxes, and doing his estate planning. That wide scope of responsibility involves the accountant in virtually every facet of his client's financial affairs, which is quite typical. If the CPA performs well in this influential capacity, the client comes to rely on him as his most trusted adviser and as such asks the CPA to add to his already substantial responsibilities. Typically, he'll press the accountant for investment advice, perhaps even asking the CPA to sell him shares in a limited-partnership tax shelter.

"On one hand, the accountant is tempted to deliver. Certainly, tax shelter programs are related to the accountant's func-

---

* Through October 1984.

tion. By selling them he can simultaneously satisfy his client and earn extra income. For this reason, many of my younger colleagues, as well as a good number of my peers, want to make room in their briefcases for tax shelter deals.

"But I think that's a mistake. Once you offer entirely subjective advice, once you sell products much like a stockbroker, you tamper with that image of independence that is so crucial to your special position as a certified public accountant. To my way of thinking, a CPA can make a very handsome living today without getting involved in questionable practices. So why should he be greedy? When you're a professional, you must temper commercial objectives with the standards that govern that profession. That's where the balancing act comes into play and it's a delicate balance indeed."

This is evidenced by the CPA's foray into microcomputer consulting. With millions of micros finding their way into corporate offices in the early 1980s, and with the introduction of computer technology causing widespread confusion concerning the selection and implementation of data processing systems, the major CPA firms christened practice units to tap this explosive market. Typically, microcomputer consultants brought in to man these units are non-CPAs recruited from digital equipment manufacturers, software houses, and independent consulting firms specializing in computer applications. Their services to the accounting firms' clients range from recommendations on hardware and software to the integration of computers into operating systems.

To say that this falls into the CPA's bailiwick is stretching the trousers to make them fit. Yes, computers are commonly used in financial management, but creating data systems qualifies as a technical rather than an accounting service. Questions of impropriety aside, the expansion to microcomputer consulting subjects the accountant's reputation to unnecessary and unacceptable risk. What if the recommended hardware or software performs below prescribed standards? What if the microcomputer manufacturer, as has happened with alarming regularity, goes belly up, leaving the owner with obsolete units and worthless warranties? These problems will be laid directly at the consultant's (read "CPA firm's") door.

By serving as microcomputer consultants, CPAs are providing a product they cannot control. This, in a nutshell, is the inherent risk in accepting the role of the all-knowing, multidisciplinary force that can help businesses negotiate the pitfalls of the evolving economy and a changing world. What's more, because the CPA firm's executive partners are not personally expert in microcomputer technology, they are in a poor position to evaluate the performance of their staff consultants. This lack of management control shows in the quality of microcomputer consultants now on staff at the major CPA firms. Interviews with computer consultants at Touche Ross, Seidman & Seidman, and Main Hurdman reveal a weak grasp of their alleged specialty, a tendency to make misleading and clichéd recommendations ("Select a user-friendly system") and a penchant for describing hardware in terms of its advertising slogans.

So we return to the fundamental question: How can CPAs adapt to the changes in American industry? Should they flatly refuse to offer novel services to cultivate new markets? Were it only that simple. What makes the commercial/professional balancing act so difficult is that every business (including accounting firms) must consciously move ahead. Management cannot simply hold its ground. Competition, attrition, and changing market conditions will not allow it. The business that chooses to stand in place inevitably falls behind.

This poses another question: Is the more cautious partner's aversion to opportunistic practices an anachronistic affectation or an effective check and balance on his more aggressive col-

The Accounting Wars

leagues? The answer probably lies somewhere in between. Only one thing is certain: As the accounting profession seeks to find its middle ground, to redirect but not debase itself in a tumultuous era, it will be haunted by questions that have plagued it for years and by new issues that will further test its mettle.

2

Main Hurdman + KMG = The Big Nine

Spend an hour in a senior partner's office and invariably the conversation turns to a whispered war story of a competitor's sloppy audit performance in a Third World trading outpost two time zones away from the New York headquarters.

It goes like this:

At Main Hurdman: "Price Waterhouse claims to have a worldwide practice, operating under the same standards from New York to London to Buenos Aires, but that's an exaggeration. Although Joe Connor likes to say that Price's client controllers can pick up their phones and get equally skilled handling of audit problems anywhere in the world, he's delivering more of a sales pitch than an accurate reflection of what's really going on out there. Like all the other Anglo-American firms, Price Waterhouse is heavily tilted toward the United States and the United Kingdom. The quality of their service declines the further they stray from their home bases. We recently had the opportunity to see some of their work on a South

The Accounting Wars

American audit and I've been told our partners found it to be below our standards."

At Price Waterhouse: "Look beneath the surface of what our competitors call their international firms and you find nothing more than a patchwork of basically independent firms loosely affiliated under a single brand name. That's all well and good for franchised real estate offices, but not for certified public accountants. I can tell you unequivocally that some of the work being done by KMG's member firms outside the United States is below the calibre of professionalism our clients would expect. And I'm not talking off the top of my head. We've gained some audit accounts that had been in the KMG system—one a very substantial European corporation that we snatched away from right under their noses. Precisely because KMG is an affiliation of separate CPA firms with individual histories and styles of practice, the quality of work varies from country to country. But with Price Waterhouse, clients are assured that our work conforms to uniform standards, uniform quality controls, and a single-engagement partner with global responsibility for that audit."

In multinational accounting, everyone seems to be pointing a finger at everyone else. In an effort to position themselves as the premier CPA firms worldwide, executive partners at some of the Big Eight consciously malign their competitors. The underlying strategy is to undermine client confidence in existing and sometimes long-standing relationships. Should the chief financial officer of a Houston-based multinational come to fear, thanks to the cocktail party caveats of a Big Eight partner, that his auditor is weak in Tokyo, he may, providing the corporation has substantial business interests in Tokyo, switch to a CPA firm with a stronger presence in that market. Or at least to one that projects a stronger image there. Thus the incentive to knock one's competitors.

This aggressive and fundamentally unethical practice, once limited to accounting's more ruthless competitors, is now rampant throughout the Big Eight. Even generally cautious, low-keyed firms are willing to denigrate competitors and vie for clients on the basis of smear tactics simply because there is so much at stake. Throughout much of the Big Eight, creating a strong multinational practice is now marketing mission number one. Although the urge to cultivate virgin territory, the likes of the People's Republic of China, is integral to this, there are far more compelling reasons for this global thrust. Consider this:

- Big business is increasingly multinational. Corporations confined exclusively to the U.S. as recently as a decade ago have since propelled themselves overseas to capitalize on cheap labor and growth markets worldwide. Coupled with this expansion have come production, distribution, and administrative facilities throughout Asia, Europe, and South America. The audit, once limited primarily to domestic borders, now requires complex coordination through an interlocking grid of nations, islands, and offshore tax havens. Competition among accounting firms reflects this growth in multinational business.

Peat, Marwick's vice chairman for international practice, Walter F. O'Connor, made this observation in a report to the PMM partnership: "As we all know, competition among accounting firms is becoming keener and keener as time goes on. I believe this will now move from the national level to the worldwide level. . . . One of the areas of tension in the U.S. market is the fact that the number of major companies seeking accounting services has not grown in the recent past. Consequently, the issue has been one of competing for a stagnant number of companies; however, on the international scene, more and more entities will become part of the public for whom we can render service, and for that reason I see a shift in the major competitive elements among the accounting firms on the international scene."*

- Chief financial officers (CFOs), once content to have their multinational audits conducted by a collage of foreign CPA firms all reporting to the "auditor of record," have come to favor, and in some cases insist, that the engagement stay within a single accounting firm "family." The consensus is that audits conducted under the auspices of a cohesive practice are more likely to conform to uniform standards and to meet a higher level of quality controls.

"Clients believe that they are better served if one accounting firm, or a group of firms sharing a single set of standards, conducts their audit worldwide," says Main Hurdman's Boston-born engineer-turned-marketing director, Dick Levine. "And they are increasingly disposed to act on that belief. Our firm lost a major account, Hewlett Packard, which we had served basically from its inception and which we took public, because we could not satisfy its needs as it developed into a sprawling multinational corporation."

Adds Main Hurdman's former chairman and now chairman emeritus, Richard Hickok, a Carroll O'Connor look-alike with an anachronistic penchant for boaters and boxy wool suits: "If you don't grow as your clients grow, you lose your clients. In this business, you cannot stand still. When clients expand beyond the domestic market, you must develop some facility for expanding with them. If you fail to do so, another firm that's made the investment in international capabilities will claim the client that was once yours."

* October 1981, Boca Raton, Florida.

Main Hurdman + KMG = The Big Nine

- Much as the early British accountants came to the United States to oversee their clients' stateside investments, American CPAs responded to domestic industry's burgeoning multinationalism by setting up practice units in the industrialized markets of Europe and the Third World. This was accomplished by both creating quasi-independent branch offices (generally run by U.S. or U.K. expatriates) and fusing existing national firms into an allegedly united worldwide organization. The competition among the firms, both for new clients and for PR points, now centers on the debate over whose international organization is stronger professionally, more extensive geographically, and subject to tighter quality controls. Because all of the major firms practice on a global basis, all are vulnerable to worldwide assaults on their client base. This is not new. But the growing concern for a uniform audit has made strength or weakness in even the smallest markets pivotal to the gain or loss of multinational audit clients. Should a major U.S.-based electronics manufacturer develop substantial interests in Seoul, South Korea, the competition for its global audit may be won by the CPA firm with the strongest unified presence in Seoul as well as in the corporation's standing markets in the U.S., U.K., and Germany. Should the current auditor be poorly represented in South Korea, it must consider bolstering its presence there or risk losing the client to a competitor. As CFOs place ever greater emphasis on single-firm audits, weak links in the accounting firm's international network expose it to competitive encroachment, to the loss of multinational clients with operations in those markets.
- In an evolutionary pattern similar to that of their Anglo-American counterparts, European CPAs are now extending beyond domestic borders in lockstep with the multinational march of French, Dutch, and German corporations. Once resigned to Big Eight dominance worldwide, European ac-

counting firms are now establishing global networks of their own, both to service home-based clients as they extend abroad and to defend against wholesale defection to the Big Eight. This emerging nationalism exposes the Anglo-American firms to aggressive competition on both their domestic and international flanks.
- The transformation of American industry, marked by the decline of the smokestack sector, gives new urgency to the search for profitable foreign-based clients not yet tainted by the American penchant for competitive bidding and drastic fee slashing.

"With European clients, price is rarely an issue," says Dick Hickok. "Thankfully, it is not standard practice among European corporations to solicit bids from every firm capable of handling their audit and to simply award the engagement to the lowest bidder. They want quality work coupled with strong market coverage and they're willing to pay well to get it. In many cases, the Europeans have a greater respect for professionalism and for the intangible benefits of long-standing relationships."

Hickok's views on the dynamics of international practice are especially interesting considering that his firm's foray abroad ranks among the most significant developments in multinational accounting. Main Hurdman's quick-strike strategy to strengthen its hand overseas reveals how one midsized firm, pressed to expand internationally or contract by attrition, opted for a novel approach that was at once offensive and defensive: It assured MH's long-term survival while laying the groundwork for its continued growth.

The story begins in 1899, when Geneva-born Ferdinand William Lafrentz—a colorful mustachioed accountant and sometime poet whose work included a book of verse on the Old West—teamed up with railroad auditor and native of Titusville,

Main Hurdman + KMG = The Big Nine

Pennsylvania, Frank Wilbur Main, to launch the American Audit Co. Soon after, Frederick Hurdman, a Canadian-born accountant only in his mid-twenties, launched a similar New York practice. From these humble origins sprang two successful and venerable firms—Main Lafrentz and Hurdman & Cranstoun—that roughly eighty years after their founding (September 1, 1979) merged to create the ninth-largest CPA firm in the United States, Main Hurdman & Cranstoun—a formidable domestic accounting organization with 475 partners, 2,500 professionals, respectable geographic coverage within major U.S. markets, and a substantial range of practice specialties. By combining their strength in personnel, market penetration, and industry specialization, the firms hoped to stay competitive at the very highest levels of the profession, to compete more effectively for new business, and to be in a position to service their fastest-growing clients.

An MH executive, Robert P. Putnam, put it this way: "There's an axiom in the accounting field that it takes a big firm to properly service a big client. Like all axioms, this one is a bit too pat, too simplistic—especially when it leads, by some perverse process of scrambled logic, to the conclusion that bigger is somehow better. Nonetheless, a firm's size—along with its organization, its standards of professional excellence, and its concepts of client service—is an increasingly vital factor in a world where multinational organizations continue to flourish and proliferate."*

One of the strongest proponents of the merger—a coterie of European accounting interests then exploring the feasibility of launching a multinational organization to compete head to head with the Big Eight—urged Main Lafrentz and Hurdman & Cranstoun to tie the knot. Although not the deciding factor, this transcontinental connection did provide additional incentive for

---

* *Viewpoint*, a Main Hurdman & Cranstoun publication, First Edition, 1980.

the American firms to unite. The merger, vital as it was to bolstering Main Lafrentz and Hurdman & Cranstoun's prominence in the domestic market, did little to improve the firms' international standing, their ability to succeed "in a world where multinational organizations continue to flourish and proliferate."* It may, in fact, have exacerbated the problem: The merged firms would be expected to service abroad the major domestic clients they'd positioned themselves to attract at home.

Enter the Europeans, led by Deutsche Treuhand and Klynveld Kraayenhof & Co., respectively Germany's second-largest and Holland's largest CPA firms. Enticed by the idea of creating, virtually overnight, an international accounting federation capable of competing with the Big Eight, Deutsche Treuhand's chairman, Dr. Reinhard Goerdeler, hoped to join together for this purpose a group of leading accounting firms around the world. The grand scheme hinged on recruiting the appropriate U.S. firm to serve as the American partner—the linchpin of the global organization. The challenge was to find a firm smaller than the Big Eight (all of which have their own international affiliations) but still large enough both to service European multinationals operating in the United States and, perhaps more important, to refer American multinationals to the federation's European members. The combined Main Hurdman & Cranstoun fit the bill.

On the same day the domestic merger of Main Lafrentz and Hurdman & Cranstoun became effective, and after only five weeks of negotiations with the European interests, MH&C joined forces internationally with nine semi-independent accounting firms.

"The merger of our United States firms was of critical importance to the process of putting together the international firm," said Main Hurdman's former director of international op-

---

*Before the merger both had marginal worldwide affiliations through McLintok, Main Lafrentz and Hurdman & Cranstoun International.

Main Hurdman + KMG = The Big Nine

erations, William H. Conkling.* "Negotiations in Europe had been underway for more than a year, but an international organization of the magnitude envisioned could not move forward without a really strong, competitive member firm in the United States. The combination of our two practices in the U.S. provided the impetus needed to move the international negotiations to a conclusion." †

The members were:

> Klynveld Kraayenhof & Co., largest in the Netherlands, and Perser Hamelberg Van Til & Co., of that country, which have since merged.
> Thomson McLintok & Co., seventh largest in the United Kingdom.
> C. Jespersen, largest in Denmark.
> Thorne Riddel & Co., largest in Canada.
> Fides Revision, one of the largest in Switzerland.
> Hancock and Offner, eighth largest of Australian firms.
> Deutsche Treuhand-Gesellschaft, second largest in Germany.**

The new entity, christened Klynveld Main Goerdeler (KMG), immediately took its place among the top CPA firms in the world, recasting the Big Eight on a global basis into the Big Nine and forcing Touche Ross, eighth internationally before the emergence of KMG, off the vaunted list.

Consider this from the October 13, 1980, issue of *Forbes*:

Corporation has several new positions . . . for individuals with two to three years of Big Nine audit experience," ran the ad for $945 million (sales) Harsco Corp.

Big Nine?

Yes, nine. Main Hurdman & Cranstoun is the ninth-largest account-

---
* Now retired.
† *Viewpoint*, First Edition, 1980.
** *Viewpoint*, First Edition, 1980, page 24.

The Accounting Wars

ing firm in the United States and is being increasingly referred to as a member of that exclusive group, formerly the Big Eight.

But why open the clubhouse? Next there'll be a Big Ten, and before you know it a Big Twenty, right? Wrong! Main Hurdman deserves inclusion because it's a member of the international firm Klynveld Main Goerdeler (KMG), the third-biggest firm in the world after Price Waterhouse and Coopers & Lybrand, which vie for the first two slots. So unless you want to have two Big Eights—domestic and international—you have to enlarge the group by one. Besides, if you do have two Big Eights, poor Touche Ross falls off the international list.

Public Accounting Report ranks the Big Nine (internationally) and the Big Eight (domestically) this way.

For KMG's United States firm, initially renamed Main Hurdman/KMG, membership in the federation served as a springboard to international practice under the auspices of a cohesive organization with the promise of uniform practice standards, joint quality controls, and limited income sharing. In effect, the newly created firm leapfrogged the slow, brick-by-brick prac-

Big Nine Ranking

FEES (IN MILLIONS)

	Y/E	1983	1982
Arthur Andersen	8/31	$1,238	$1,123
Peat, Marwick	6/30	1,230	1,150
Coopers & Lybrand	9/30	1,100	1,066
Price Waterhouse	6/30	1,013	946
Arthur Young	12/31	1,003	955
Ernst & Whinney	9/30	972	887
Klynveld Main Goerdeler	9/30	900*	970
Deloitte Haskins & Sells	4/30	894	852
Touche Ross	8/31	845*	800

Main Hurdman + KMG = The Big Nine

The Big Eight Firms Ranked by U.S. Revenue
(IN MILLIONS OF DOLLARS)

Firm	'83 Rev	'82 Rev	% Gwth	FYE	U.S. Ofcs	Prtnr	Prof Staff	Total Staff	SEC Audts
Arthur Andersen	$909	$809	12%	8/31	77	1,076	12,242	15,837	2,162
Peat, Marwick	810	741	9	6/30	96	1,284	9,905	13,016	1,095
Coopers & Lybrand	644*	570*	13	9/30	93	890	8,117	10,673	1,197
Ernst & Whinney	638	567	13	9/30	118	936	8,209	10,533	961
Price Waterhouse	493	475*	4	6/30	84	587	6,461	8,499	1,032
Arthur Young	438	410*	7	9/30	82	714	5,576	7,379	590
Deloitte Haskins & Sells	430	390	10	5/31	103	795	5,669	7,546	1,715
Touche Ross	380*	350	9	8/31	80	790	4,999	6,917	791

* Estimated

tice-building process that had occupied the Big Eight for decades. Overnight, it was out competing for clients with the established powers.

But how does KMG function? Is it the Century 21 of accounting (with a single name applied to diverse and essentially independent firms) or a truly cohesive entity? The answer is a bit of both.

At the heart of the system, an executive office in Amsterdam establishes accounting procedures, marketing programs, and audit standards for Klynveld Main Goerdeler's worldwide operation.

To assure clients that international audits are conducted under centralized controls, the engagement partner for the KMG member firm hired to conduct the audit retains worldwide responsibility for it. He plans the scope of the audit, selects the participating partners at each of the federation members involved in the engagement, and decides on the review procedures.

27

How the group is organized

ORGANIZATIONAL STRUCTURE:

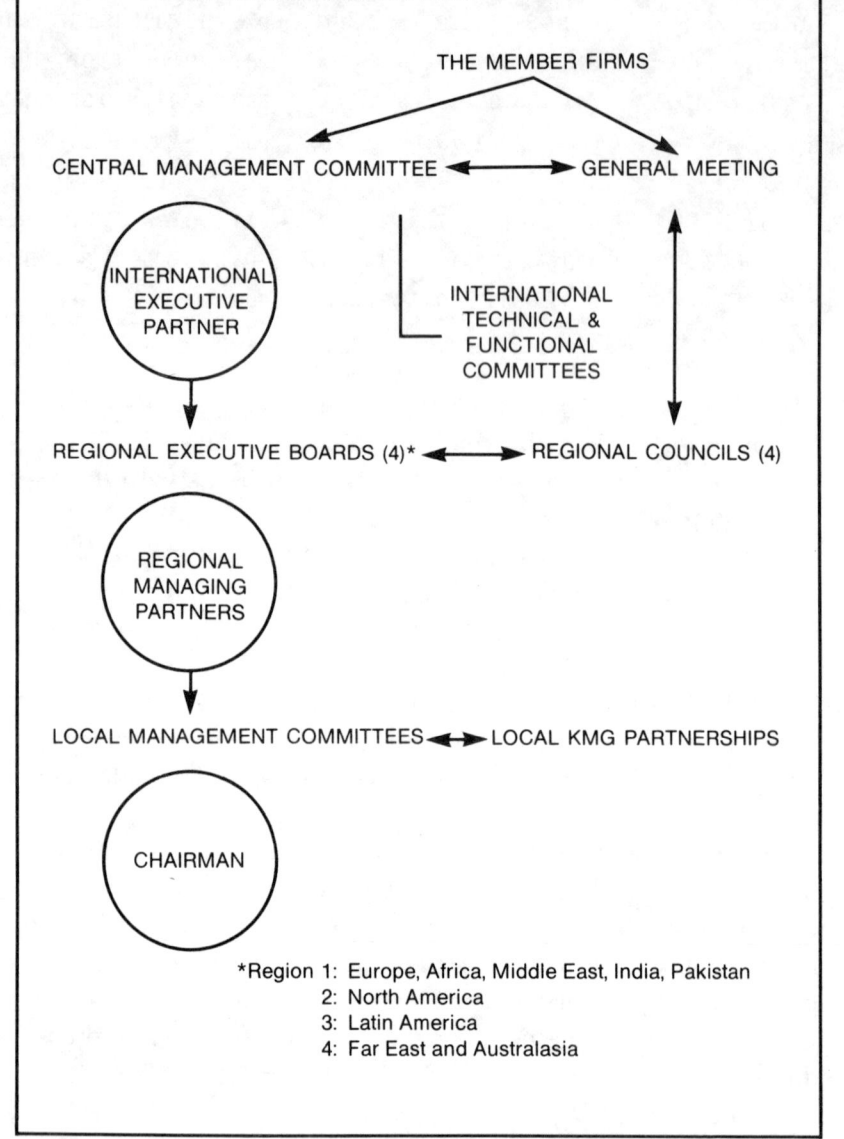

THE MEMBER FIRMS

CENTRAL MANAGEMENT COMMITTEE ⟷ GENERAL MEETING

INTERNATIONAL EXECUTIVE PARTNER

INTERNATIONAL TECHNICAL & FUNCTIONAL COMMITTEES

REGIONAL EXECUTIVE BOARDS (4)* ⟷ REGIONAL COUNCILS (4)

REGIONAL MANAGING PARTNERS

LOCAL MANAGEMENT COMMITTEES ⟷ LOCAL KMG PARTNERSHIPS

CHAIRMAN

*Region 1: Europe, Africa, Middle East, India, Pakistan
2: North America
3: Latin America
4: Far East and Australasia

Accountancy Age, March 28, 1980

Main Hurdman + KMG = The Big Nine

One step up, at the executive level, a central management committee (its members drawn from KMG's founding firms) oversees the firm's global practice. Senior officers represent the three heavyweight firms whose initials make up the KMG logo: chairman, Dr. Goerdeler; president, John A. Thompson of the United States (also Main Hurdman's chairman); and international executive Paul H. Boschma of the Netherlands.

Behind the organization charts and the stirring talk of professional cooperation, the KMG system functions on the old "you scratch my back and I'll scratch yours" arrangement. Specifically, a fee-sharing mechanism promotes the flow of engagements throughout the organization. Member firms accepting work beyond their domestic borders are obliged to make every effort to channel the multinational components to their KMG colleagues. This effectively traps engagements, regardless of where they are initiated within Klynveld Main Goerdeler's global system. Firms generating the heaviest volume of referrals are compensated through a sort of kickback mechanism administered by the Amsterdam headquarters. Members doing referral work must pay 10 percent of the fees to a KMG pool, which is then redistributed annually to the federation's member firms. Payments are based on a formula keyed to the relative percentages of international work referred to KMG by the member firms.

For Main Hurdman, the real benefit of the affiliation is not in referral fees—this was never the objective—but in the ability to offer American multinational clients an in-house global audit capability roughly equivalent to that of the Big Eight and to inherit the U.S. component of multinational audits emanating from Europe.

From a defensive posture, Main Hurdman has retained and apparently satisfied its largest multinational client, Union Carbide. A Hurdman & Cranstoun client since the early 1900s, Carbide's $9 billion sales in thirty-five nations outside of the

29

U.S. put it at the top of multinational accounting's client hit list. No doubt Carbide's senior managers have found themselves pursued by a host of Big Eight suitors. Whether they enticed Carbide to reconsider its audit relationship, or whether Carbide itself pressed MH to establish a more effective international capability, no one is saying. But Dick Levine admits that minus the establishment of KMG, Main Hurdman's days as Carbide's auditor were probably numbered.

"They never threatened us with a switch and they never told us that the KMG affiliation saved the account, but I'm convinced we would have lost Union Carbide as a client had we not made the move," Levine says. "They want one firm to perform the audit worldwide and we had to be in a position to do just that."

Lewis Peloubet, Carbide's controller, agrees. While he refuses to speculate on "what ifs," one gets the distinct impression that without the KMG association, Peloubet would have gone shopping.

"As we moved through the 1970s, it became clearer that with the plethora of rulings from the AICPA, the FASB,* and others—and the increasing complexity of international business—CPA firms needed a certain critical mass to be able to handle corporations of the size and complexity of a Union Carbide," he says. "Before the merger, there was some concern at Carbide and at Hurdman & Cranstoun that this critical mass was not being reached.

"But the mergers with Main Lafrentz and the KMG organization dispelled those concerns. Before, we had been using Big Eight affiliates to do our overseas work; now, most of it is under the KMG banner and that's been beneficial to us for a number of reasons. First, all of the work is performed according to uniform standards. Second, we have more clout within the audit

---

* American Institute of Certified Public Accountants and the Financial Accounting Standards Board.

Main Hurdman + KMG = The Big Nine

organization. If someone gets out of line, we can pressure the engagement partner to have the situation corrected. That's far more difficult to do when you're dealing with a collection of unrelated firms. Third, we find that there is better cooperation between the internal and the independent auditors. They just seem to work together more effectively."

Peloubet, a dream client because of his willingness to praise his auditors publicly, is also valued because he frowns on the lowballing that is now endemic throughout *Fortune* 500 land.

"The amount of money we spend with Main Hurdman, although not an inconsequential sum, doesn't amount to a drop in the bucket when viewed in light of the assurance they provide on the reliability of our numbers, the accuracy of our accounting entries."

Other multinationals likely to stay in the Main Hurdman camp as a direct result of the KMG affiliation include CPC International and Avon.

Retaining clients of this magnitude is clearly one of the federation's defensive plums. When asked if partners' earnings had climbed since the formation of KMG, Hickok paused momentarily, then quipped, "They would have declined without it."

On the offensive side, as the catch basin for foreign-based KMG multinationals with operations in the United States, Main Hurdman has gained numerous audit and tax engagements, including those from Daimler-Benz and Bavarian Motor Works (BMW) (both referred by Deutsche Treuhand), Grand Metropolitan (the owners of the Liggett Group), and Saatchi & Saatchi Advertising (both referred by Thomson McLintok).

Daimler-Benz is an interesting case. Audited in Germany by Deutsche Treuhand, whose chairman, Dr. Goerdeler, enjoys a personal relationship with the auto company's senior management, the United States engagement was for years farmed out to Price Waterhouse, which had the account from 1956 to 1982. Because Deutsche Treuhand did not have a United States practice, it was forced to refer the engagement to a firm it competes with in Germany, thus making the entire account vulnerable to competitive encroachment. But with the establishment of KMG, Deutsche Treuhand could ask Daimler to channel its entire audit within the Klynveld Main Goerdeler family. Because the Germans could now offer Daimler a uniform audit, they could keep the engagement in-house, collect referral fees for channeling the work to Main Hurdman, and most important, shield their large and prestigious account from competitors.

"The moment KMG was formed, we moved our U.S. audit work from Price Waterhouse to Main Hurdman," says Warner Bischoff, senior vice president, finance, for Daimler-Benz. "We wanted the guarantee that the principles followed in the mother country would be followed overseas. American companies have always had this philosophy. That's why Price Waterhouse set up practice in Germany.

"Although we were not displeased with Price Waterhouse, the new arrangement is far superior. A number of Deutsche Treuhand partners are now stationed at Main Hurdman in New York. Should there be problems with the consolidated balance sheet, currency translations, or the like, these representatives from Germany can help to smooth things out. The integration of the various components of our company and our audit is superb."

"The birth of KMG is most significant because it created, with a single stroke, a new organization that is large enough, strong enough, and damn cocky enough to compete for clients that require the services of a big accounting firm." Hickok boasts with a burst of enthusiasm that belies his normally low-keyed demeanor. A career auditor, first joining Hurdman & Cranstoun's New York staff in 1948, Hickok served as engagement partner for such heavyweight clients as Avon, and for more times than he'd like to remember was on the losing end of new business proposals that slipped away to Big Eight compet-

Main Hurdman + KMG = The Big Nine

itors. "The KMG affiliation put us in a position to win engagements from corporations that once thought us too small to meet their multinational requirements."

Changing the market's perception of Main Hurdman—convincing chief financial officers that the firm is now substantial enough to conduct global audits in-house—falls into Dick Levine's bailiwick and he absolutely relishes the challenge. A sixteen-year Touche Ross MAS (Management Advisory Services) veteran lured to Main Hurdman to build its consulting practice, Levine displays the kind of fiery zest for marketing* that is endemic at Touche but that has traditionally been absent at MH. A lanky, energetic man with a clipped New England accent and a propensity for talking in rapid, machine-gun bursts, Levine likes to dig his heels into Main Hurdman's conservative flanks, forcing what was once a stodgy firm to compete more aggressively for prestigious and profitable clients.

"We compile hit lists of major corporations we'd like to gain as clients and we go out and pitch our services to them," Levine says. "Our marketing strategy is to steer clear of the *Fortune* 50 —the GEs and General Motorses—because these giants rarely switch auditors and when they do usually insist on the Big Eight. So why knock on doors that won't open when there is ample opportunity, and in many cases more profitable opportunity, elsewhere? Our prime targets are the big corporations from *Fortune* 51 to 1,000. These names figure most prominently in our hit lists.

"But compiling lists is one thing and making contact with decision makers is another. That's where salesmanship comes in, and we're not bashful about being aggressive salesmen. One approach is to inject ourselves into existing relationships. Say we're friendly with a director of a client company and we learn that he's also on the board of one of our hit list targets. We'll

---

* He was named Main Hurdman's director of marketing in 1982 and is also director of management consulting.

33

have the appropriate Main Hurdman partner take him out to dinner, asking that he put in a good word for us with the targeted firm's senior management. We'll also host cocktail parties, receptions—what have you—always seeding the invitation list with executives from hit list companies. Once we have these guys on our turf, once they're a captive audience, our partners can spark a relationship, exchange business cards, extend an invitation to the golf club. The bottom line is that we want the opportunity to propose to new prospects. If we can do that, we're confident of landing a substantial share of new business.

"Typically, we'll hope to start with some tax or MAS work. Something to get our foot in the door. You can't expect to land major audit accounts over dry martinis and small talk at after-business-hours cocktail parties. No, the objective is to position yourself. To get that MAS engagement, demonstrate the calibre of your firm, build a close relationship with the client. Then, if a change of auditor is contemplated, you're in an excellent position to be among those asked to propose for the job.

"The KMG affiliation has vastly improved our chances of coming away with the prize. That's because we can now offer clients the services not of one firm but of an international family of CPA firms."

But is it really a family? Competitors carp that a truly global firm, as opposed to a collection of national firms loosely affiliated on the strength of three initials (KMG) added to their names, takes decades to establish.

"This isn't the hamburger business," says a partner active in Price Waterhouse's international practice. "You can't simply put the golden arches around a bunch of independent CPA firms stretched from here to Timbuktu and claim they're all selling accounting's equivalent of Big Macs. The hallmark of a strong international firm is not the fact that the practice offices use the same logo on their letterhead, but instead that they have a his-

Main Hurdman + KMG = The Big Nine

tory of working as a single firm, of applying the same standards, of implementing the same concepts of client service."

Says PW's Robert Jahrling, former engagement partner for the Exxon audit, "We are indoctrinating our people from the day they walk in the door, and even before that. The selection of the people that we hire plus the training that's given to them makes a difference. And we work very hard on developing the comparability and quality of work being done around the world. And to follow up on that, we have put into place a worldwide review program. Partners and managers selected more or less at random from different firms around the world review the work being done by other PW firms and critique it."

Jahrling's point is that a unified global firm, which PW claims to be, can respond quickly and decisively to the engagement partner's directives. This, he holds, is especially important in steering through the gray areas that run through multinational audits.

"In the seventies, when there was a great hue and cry about corporate bribes, illegal payments, and conflicts of interest, Exxon set up a strict code of ethics to guide its operating units around the world. Any and all questionable practices were forbidden. A control mechanism was put in place to monitor adherence.

"Price Waterhouse's role was to check for violations of the code and to report any and all questionable practices. I was personally responsible for reporting annually to the Exxon board on any and all cases of improper activities. A program of this magnitude could not have worked unless the engagement partner had his tentacles out to all of his staff people—people who shared a common set of standards and a sense of tradition."

Tradition may be the operative word. Certainly, it is in short supply at Klynveld Main Goerdeler. Although the member firms have distinguished histories within their domestic markets, the international entity has little collective experience to draw on. To some, this discredits KMG's claim to a position within the Big Eight—or to expand the vaunted list to nine. Should size, they ask, be the sole criterion for admission? By the same token, should Oral Roberts University be welcomed into the Ivy League if it manages to surpass Harvard in the number of labs, classrooms, or books in its library? Or are intangible factors the real measure of Ivy League or Big Eight membership? The issue is not academic. For KMG, the question is whether it will be recognized by clients as a Big Eight equivalent or a half-baked imitator. And more germane to current accounting trends, will it be viewed by the corporate community as a cohesive international organization or a collection of "golden arches around a bunch of independent CPA firms"?

KMG's marketing strategists are working to shape public perception in a way that will benefit the firm and simultaneously defuse its most vocal critics. Believing that a savvy offense is the best defense, they have positioned that aspect of the firm's structure most vulnerable to competitive assault—the individual character of its member firms—as a decided advantage over the Big Eight. Sneering at the latter's Anglo-American orientation, KMG sees itself as unique in international accounting: the first "transnational" CPA firm. This distinction plays to the emerging chauvinism of European corporations and in the process seeks to establish KMG as the most adept and locally connected practitioner worldwide.

Comparing the dynamics of today's international accounting market to previous periods of expansion when U.K. and U.S. firms pursued their clients to the States and the Continent, William H. Conkling, Main Hurdman's former director of international operations, says that "the important difference today is that no single nation can be considered preeminent in international business any more. What had been a one-way street dominated by two nations, each in its own turn, has become a

Main Hurdman + KMG = The Big Nine

multilane highway running in all sorts of directions. Given this change in the world economic situation, we feel that businesses originating in any nation are better served by the kind of truly multinational accounting firm we have created with KMG.

"After all, who is more capable of understanding accounting standards or economic conditions in any country than a leading national firm of accountants? Considering the changes that are taking place in the world economy, I feel that will be an increasingly important benefit that KMG can offer its clients. . . .

"The existing major international accounting firms grew to their present size over a long period of time, under basically Anglo-American direction. We've put together leading firms from a number of countries in what is truly a partnership, a combination of equals. . . ."*

A KMG position paper reveals management's strategy for selling the transnational concept: "The dynamics of world business have shifted dramatically, creating an economy that is much more multinational in scope and in operation:

"Nations such as Japan and Germany have outpaced the United States in GNP growth and have assumed leadership in key industry segments of the world market.

"Eurodollars, petrodollars, and the strengthening of other currencies have significantly altered international finance.

"Capital formation has become increasingly multinational, with significant invested capital now flowing from Western Europe, Japan, and the Middle East into the United States and other parts of the world.

"Although these new economic realities—the emerging transnational business environment—have made international accounting capabilities critically important, they have also made the concept of the Anglo-American-dominated international accounting firm, such as the Big Eight, obsolete because it does

---

* *Viewpoint*, ibid.

not suit the increasingly decentralized style of world business or the multinational corporation's need for superior accounting knowledge and service in multiple countries...."

To underline its transnational posture, KMG boasts a client list sprinkled with eight of *Fortune* magazine's fifty largest industrial companies in the world and fifty-four of the five hundred largest industrial corporations outside the United States. Major clients, by country, include:

Australia: Thomas Nationwide Transport
Canada: George Weston, Toronto-Dominion Bank, Stelco
France: Compagnie Générale d'Electricité, Compagnie Française des Petroles, Peugeot-Citroën
Germany: Siemens, Daimler-Benz, Mannesmann
Ireland: Cement Roadstone
Japan: Nissan Motor, Mitsui & Co.
Netherlands: Philips, Akzo, Royal Dutch Shell
South Africa: Anglo-American Corporation
Switzerland: Alusuisse, Pirelli, Grands Magasins Jelmoli

Whether one buys the transnational concept as a landmark innovation or dismisses it as so much advertising hype—in truth it is probably a bit of both—there is no doubt that the birth of KMG dovetailed with the growing nationalism on the part of European corporations and accounting firms and that this will help to attract and retain clients. In this environment, the dilemma for the Big Eight is to downplay their U.S. citizenship while retaining the image of global organizations capable of conducting uniform audits worldwide. In effect, they are being forced to imitate the KMG concept: that of an international force with strong national practices.

In his report to the partnership, Peat, Marwick's Walter O'Connor made this telling observation: "As time goes on, I see the international accounting firms competing to develop the most international of images in dealing with the multinational companies, while still maintaining the national image where that is appropriate, given the nationalism that is arising in some countries. It may be trying to carry water on both shoulders, but perhaps, to continue with that analogy, carrying a lot of water on one shoulder tends to tilt the person in an awkward direction. I believe, if anything, we are definitely looked at as being one of the preeminent international firms. As the growth potential of individual countries grows, however, the need for also developing strong national images will emerge. This is an area of challenge for all international accounting firms. . . ."

Arthur Andersen, perhaps the strongest Big Eight firm in Europe, recognized this challenge from the very beginning of its multinational expansion in the late 1950s. At that time, Andersen adopted a policy of appointing nationals to run its foreign offices and to consciously downplay the firm's American roots. "We sent Americans overseas to open offices, but we hired locals, raised them under the Andersen system, and sent the Americans back to the States," says William Hall, an Andersen partner and former director of its European accounting and audit practice. "We had a policy of Yankee go home."

Andersen has reaped enormous benefits from this approach, building strong and durable client relationships throughout its international practice. But even the seemingly harmless tradition of referring to itself as a "world firm" has suddenly become unacceptable in Europe. Société Cooperative*—Andersen's Swiss-based international umbrella unit established in 1977 for the promulgation of professional standards and the coordination of operating expenses—is now considered somewhat of a liabil-

---

* The Société serves as a conduit for balancing the costs of Andersen's international practice. Should the practice in one nation incur heavy start-up costs associated with the establishment of a small business unit, for example, part of those costs will be shared by the other members of the Andersen worldwide network.

ity by those who believe it creates the appearance of a centralized firm.

"We have become schizophrenic in accounting because we have to recognize the legitimacy of the desire to be strong internationally and also run by the nationals of the countries in which we practice," Hall says. "Accounting firms cannot be successful if they look as if they are entities that come from someplace else. Today, we all walk the line very carefully in this profession so as not to appear as a monolithic operation run from the U.S."

There is no denying that KMG has an advantage here, blessed as it is with member firms indigenous to key accounting markets and a rich lode of multinational clients nicely dispersed throughout the U.K., Europe, and the U.S. But does its "transnational" composition really make the Big Eight "obsolete"? Certainly not, and, more to the point, neither does it prompt all of Europe's nationalistic corporations to march into the KMG camp. Those accounting firms viewed as offering the most attractive mix of services and fees will often get the nod regardless of where they plant their flags. Examples abound. In one case —clearly a painful blow to KMG—Dutch-based multinational Thyssen-Bornemisza parted company with Klynveld Kraayenhof in 1983, awarding the engagement to Price Waterhouse. *International Accounting Bulletin*, which broke the story before the change of auditors was announced, noted that "the Thyssen-Bornemisza switch is likely to cause a sensation in Dutch accounting and business circles since it will be the first example in recent history of a major Dutch group dropping a national auditor in favor of an Anglo-Saxon international firm.

"Two of the firms that lost out described the PW appointment as historic, breaking a long tradition where Holland's big companies have kept their audits in the hands of big Dutch firms such as Klynveld Kraayenhof, Moret, Limperg, and Dijker en Doornbos."

Main Hurdman + KMG = The Big Nine

Certainly not the kind of precedent-shattering development KMG's founders had in mind when launching the transnational organization. The temptation, one might think, would be for the member firms to hold Klynveld Kraayenhof responsible for the loss, and although no one in KMG is willing to say so, perhaps they did. But the members' primary concern is not with the Dutch, the German, or the British partner, but instead with the biggest KMG member, Main Hurdman.

On this subject, the KMG national firms are ambivalent. The British, more than others, appear to resent the Americans' preeminent position in the federation. The old saying that "CPA firms are partnerships with some of the partners more equal than others" is also true of the KMG affiliation, but the gentlemen at Thomson McLintok find this hard to accept as it relates to the boys in the States. This probably relates to a conviction shared by many English CPAs that they are the supreme practitioners of public accounting.

"You can't help but pick up a sense of arrogance, a grudging suspicion, whenever you deal with London," says a New York–based Main Hurdman partner. "They're always calling to double-check on this or that fact when the matter doesn't seem to warrant such diligence. Or they'll foist their opinion on you when it's clear you don't want or need advice. This attitude doesn't exactly breed feelings of brotherhood or whatever the hell it is we are supposed to have for one another."

Paradoxically, KMG's overseas partners, including, oddly enough, the British, want Main Hurdman to be larger than it is. The paradox stems from the fact that the U.S. affiliate, though larger in terms of fees than all of its KMG brethren, is among the smallest founding members in its home market. While Klynveld Kraayenhof ranks number one in the Netherlands and Deutsche Treuhand-Gesellschaft is second in Germany, Main Hurdman weighs in as ninth-largest in the U.S. Although KMG pushes Touche Ross off the map internationally, Main Hurd-

41

man is much smaller than Touche in the U.S. This distinction is crucial because the United States is KMG's most important market. For the transnational affiliation to succeed, it must work that "two-lane highway" from power bases in both Europe and America. To attract multinational engagements to the KMG system, European members must convince clients that the American firm has the staff and geographic presence to handle audit work in the U.S. as effectively as the Big Eight. European CFOs, familiar with Price Waterhouse, Andersen, and Ernst & Whinney but not with Main Hurdman, may be skeptical. Exacerbating the problem is a festering resentment shared by KMG members that their U.S. practice is not a powerhouse in its domestic market. The bigger the affiliate, they believe, the more attractive it would be to Common Market clients and the more referrals it would export overseas.

Eager to squelch the grumblings from abroad and driven by their own ambitions, Main Hurdman's senior partners considered a number of options for bolstering the firm's presence in the United States, including opening new practice offices in traditionally weak markets and stepping up merger activities with small local firms. But a phone call placed to Hickok's office on a bitter cold January morning in 1982 put all of that on the back burner.

Robert Kleckner, chairman of Chicago-based Alexander Grant & Co., asked Hickok for an urgent meeting at Main Hurdman's New York office. The two prominent accountants, longtime colleagues who'd served together on AICPA committees, had never before met on each other's turf. Although Hickok hadn't an inkling of Kleckner's intentions, he knew this would be more than a social call.

"Accompanied by Howard Groveman, another senior Grant partner, Kleckner arrived at my office at the appointed time," Hickok recalls. "Quickly dispensing with the formalities, he got right to the issue at hand. Saying that Grant had explored a

Main Hurdman + KMG = The Big Nine

number of options for its long-term growth—some of which seemed promising, others which did not—he proposed a merger of our firms. This, he'd come to believe, would position both Grant and Main Hurdman for a strong and prosperous future. Although I hadn't even thought of a big merger ever since the Hurdman & Cranstoun/Main Lafrentz deal was consummated, Kleckner's proposal fired my interest."

Certainly the idea was tempting. For Main Hurdman and Grant, numbers nine and ten on the accounting hierarchy, the opportunity to pole vault from the ranks of the also-rans situated somewhere south of the Big Eight into clear domination of the second tier was heady stuff. Hickok agreed to a series of exploratory meetings involving senior people at both firms.

"But problems arose almost immediately," Kleckner remembers, a trace of lingering disappointment still evident in his voice. "Merging accounting firms is like putting together an extremely difficult jigsaw puzzle. In this case few of the pieces matched.

"Surprisingly, the greatest obstacles to a successful merger were in the administrative rather than the practice areas. It seemed that both firms conducted their internal affairs as differently as two similar-sized CPA firms could possibly do. For example, there were marked contrasts in virtually all of the key provisions of the Grant and Main Hurdman partnership agreements, including the rules for firm governance, the partner's capital requirements, the allocation of income, and the admission of new partners.

"I don't think we found a single major provision that was the same for both firms. In a partnership, this is a particularly difficult hurdle because the partners themselves have to approve the changes. Neither group was likely to agree to wholesale changes."

Discussions continued throughout the winter and spring of '82, but with little progress. The pivotal issues proved immune

The Accounting Wars

to compromise and both sides refused to make major concessions. Kleckner and Hickok—both earnest, slow-and-steady-wins-the-race types—were willing to remain at the negotiating table, grinding out the issues one by one, but the peculiar problems of managing partnerships once again bollixed the works. Word of the talks, which were intended to remain secret until and if substantive progress could be made, leaked to the press, to the profession's grapevine, and most damagingly to the MH and Grant partners, who expressed their displeasure at being kept in the dark. Even those who knew the talks were progressing resented having to learn the issues from unofficial sources. Aware of this growing impatience, the senior partners felt the time had come for decisive action culminating in a merger or a publicized end to the negotiations. Allowing the rumors and innuendos to continue unabated would be damaging to both partner and client relations.

"Our ultimate action was influenced by a coincidence of events," Kleckner recalls. "Each of us happened to have managing partners' meetings coming up; we schedule one every spring to bring our managing partners together for a two- or three-day session. I don't know whether they do it as a matter of course, but that particular year, they had one scheduled within about a week of ours. My plan was to inform our partners that we were having some talks, to run through the kind of issues we were discussing and to get any reaction. Just trying to take the temperature. We did that and we also asked the managing partners to talk with the partners in their respective offices. We asked them to please keep it confidential. . . .

"But public knowledge of the situation was spreading and we were getting numerous inquiries on the matter. I contacted members of our executive committee by telephone and said this was becoming an intolerable situation. You can't have meaningful discussions with someone and try to be responsive to your

Main Hurdman + KMG = The Big Nine

partners and the press simultaneously. It was undoubtedly a long shot anyway. I stated I would like to contact the Main Hurdman people and say let's call the discussions off. Our people said fine. I contacted them and said from our standpoint we simply can't function this way. They agreed and we ended the discussions."

Perhaps, but there is reason to doubt whether the negotiations were really severed or simply put on ice until the attendant publicity blew over. With a sideshow developing around what were to be secret discussions, and with the partnership growing visibly testy over the hodgepodge of leaks and rumors, Kleckner was likely frustrated with his inability to control the situation. A proposal to lie low until the smoke cleared would have appealed to both Kleckner and Hickok. Although it may never be known precisely what the press-shy senior partners decided amongst themselves, certainly the announcement to sever their talks did not quash the urge to merge.

"During the summer we had some internal discussions of the issues first identified in the spring," Kleckner says, "and in September we went back to the table with Main Hurdman. We developed some possible approaches to reconciling differing ways of doing things, and asked our respective executive committees to see if they were willing to expose the merger issues to the partners to get a reaction from them. Again, this was very important since we required two-thirds of our partners to approve a merger and they required an even higher percentage, three-fourths.

"Although our committee members had a number of reservations, they indicated a willingness to at least air the subject at our upcoming annual meeting. But their committee looked at the issues, suggested approaches thereto, and for whatever reasons said they did not want to expose it to their partners. That was the end of the discussions."

45

The Accounting Wars

Hickok's version of the on-again, off-again negotiations mirrors Kleckner's on the chronology and the basic points of contention, but another factor comes into play in his explanation of why the merger never materialized. The axiom "if there's a will there's a way" is important here. While Kleckner saw only administrative obstacles to the union, and was apparently convinced that these nuts-and-bolts issues could be solved through intense negotiations, Hickok questioned the merger's value from a marketing and strategic perspective. The more he analyzed the deal, the more he believed it would not add materially to Main Hurdman's market position at home or internationally. For a merger to be successful, two plus two must equal five. But no matter how Hickok fiddled with the calculator, four was the best he could do. That was not incentive enough to endure a year or more of internal disruption, the substantial expense of consolidating the two practices, and the resulting decline, albeit temporary, in partner earnings that generally follows a merger. While Kleckner remained firm in his conviction that a merger would assure the consolidated firm dominance in accounting's middle market, Hickok came away from the talks thinking that Grant's strength often duplicated rather than complemented Main Hurdman's.

"If you put an overlay of their offices on a map of ours, you'd see that they would not really add to our market presence where we needed it most," Hickok says. "Yes, their strength in Chicago was attractive, but they could do little for us in the key markets of Los Angeles and San Francisco. We found this hit-or-miss pattern repeated itself across the country."

In the final analysis, Hickok sized up the proposed merger as producing a larger entity, but one that was no greater than the sum of its parts. The extra dimension that comes part and parcel with truly synergistic mergers appeared to be absent here. Hickok called off the deal.

Main Hurdman + KMG = The Big Nine

From all indications, the principals parted amicably.* Although Main Hurdman's partners, having finally ironed out the kinks of their 1979 merger (Main Lafrentz and Hurdman & Cranstoun), were relieved not to be repeating the tumultuous process so soon after the first go-round, KMG's European executives were sorely disappointed, having lost the opportunity to work with a partner almost twice Main Hurdman's size. Even minus the synergy, the union would have impressed European multinationals and would have generated additional transatlantic referrals. Asked if Amsterdam had the legal right to force or block the merger, Hickok, measuring his words with utmost care says, "We informed them of our negotiations with Grant, as we were required to do, but they could not have made the decision on whether or not to proceed with the deal."

That a member firm could retain so important a prerogative adds fuel to the charges that KMG's international organization is more of a franchised setup than a cohesive entity. Naturally, Hickok refutes this, contending that Big Eight member firms also reserve the right to conduct their own merger activities.

"When the Big Eight apply their names to practices outside the United States, they are engaging first and foremost in a marketing tactic. The truth is that firms with Big Eight names around the world are really a collection of national partnerships simply using one name to present a unified image to the world. They have a more cohesive look than KMG, but they are not more cohesive firms."

Still, KMG's critics, some with vested interests in belittling their newest competitor, are undaunted.

"The issue of cohesiveness is not synonymous with struc-

* Kleckner, apparently hot for a merger, announced in September 1984 that discussions were under way with Denver-based Fox & Company to combine the two firms. As of November 1984, partners at both firms had voted to proceed with negotiations with the hope of effecting a merger by early 1985.

ture," says Walter O'Connor, "If the cohesiveness of a CPA firm is meant to be the same as a U.S. corporation with foreign subsidiaries, well, no one in the profession has that kind of cohesiveness. But if cohesiveness is the ability to respond to a client's problems anywhere in the world, that's what we have and that's what clients are asking for. They say 'If we have a problem in Buenos Aires, we want you to be able to get to that problem immediately, without hunting down the person to do it.' "

Asked if Arthur Andersen's organization, which through the Société Cooperative has the Big Nine's most effective cost-sharing mechanism, is more cohesive than Peat's, O'Connor returns to the theme of tradition—a popular rallying cry because it can only be measured subjectively.

"The operating components of industrial corporations such as General Motors or General Electric share a common profit fate, but there is still competition among the various executives. GM's people, and those at Andersen, don't necessarily walk hand-in-hand into the sunset. Just because someone in Spain is in the same profit pool as someone in Hong Kong doesn't mean they really have the same interests. In big, diverse organizations, the person in Hong Kong simply doesn't relate to the fact that helping his partner in Spain will put money in his own pockets."

O'Connor's remarks often echo those of the PW boys. "Peat, Marwick's strength as an international accounting firm can't be found on an organization chart or a profit-sharing pool. It stems from the fact that our firms around the world have worked together, with common goals and professional standards, for years. While KMG may look somewhat similar organizationally —we are both composed of legally independent accounting firms—they lack that all-important element of collective experience.

"But if you think about it, KMG had no other choice than to

Main Hurdman + KMG = The Big Nine

go the route they've gone. When they awoke to the fact that they needed an international practice network, they also recognized that it was too late to start one from scratch—as did our firm, Price Waterhouse, and Andersen. The only viable option at this stage of the game was to play catch-up ball—to assemble a federation of independent firms and hope like hell that they could weld it together into a cohesive practice."

O'Connor splits the Big Nine into three basic structural forms:

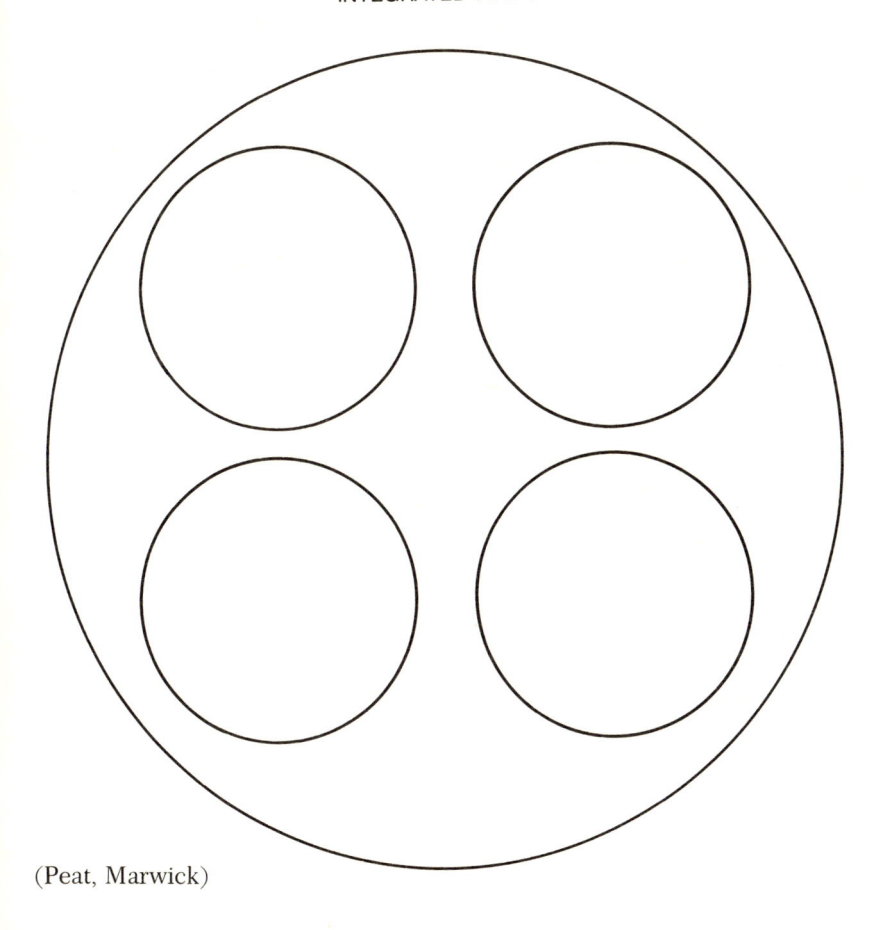

INTEGRATED FIRMS

(Peat, Marwick)

The Accounting Wars

"This structure—representative of Peat, Marwick, Price Waterhouse, and Arthur Andersen—is that of an integrated firm. While the practice units within the circle are independent, the wider circle represents Peat, Marwick's integration of those practices. This is expressed in the form of a common name, unified audit and training standards, services, and a history of working together.

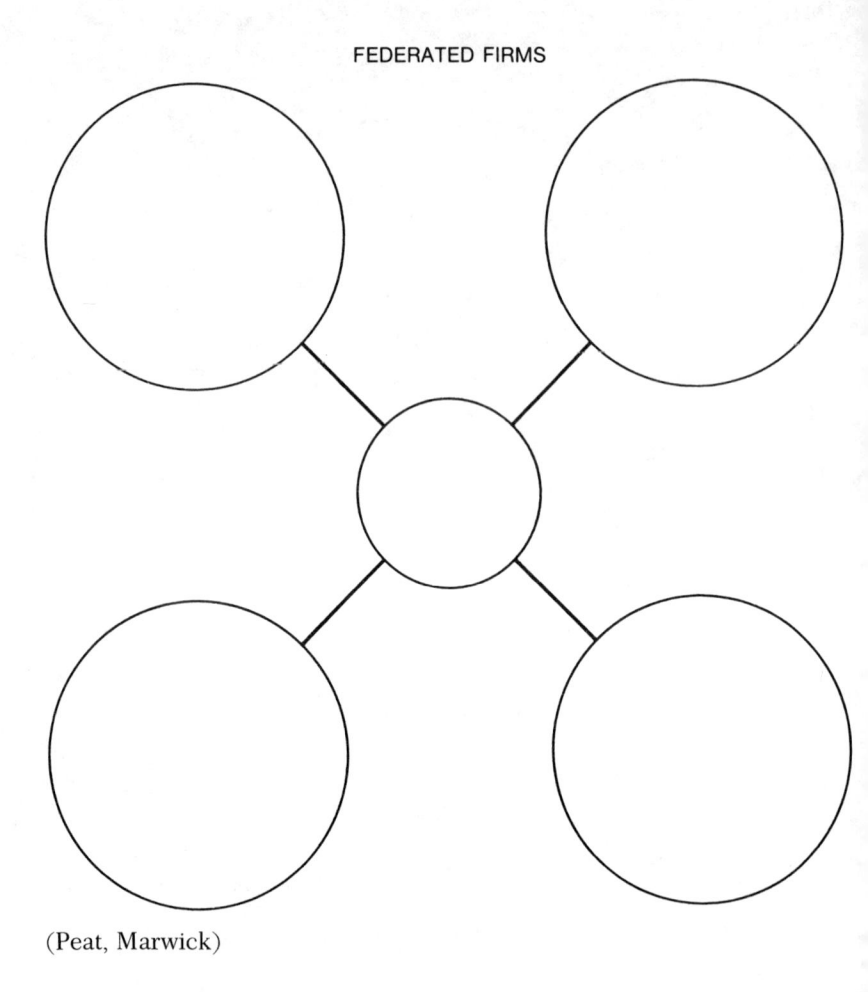

FEDERATED FIRMS

(Peat, Marwick)

Main Hurdman + KMG = The Big Nine

"KMG's structure is that of a federation. Although the organization seeks to bring some centralized controls to the independent firms, they are still far more autonomous than united. Over time, the inner circle should be able to expand to provide for a greater degree of interrelationship between the federation members.

NETWORK FIRMS

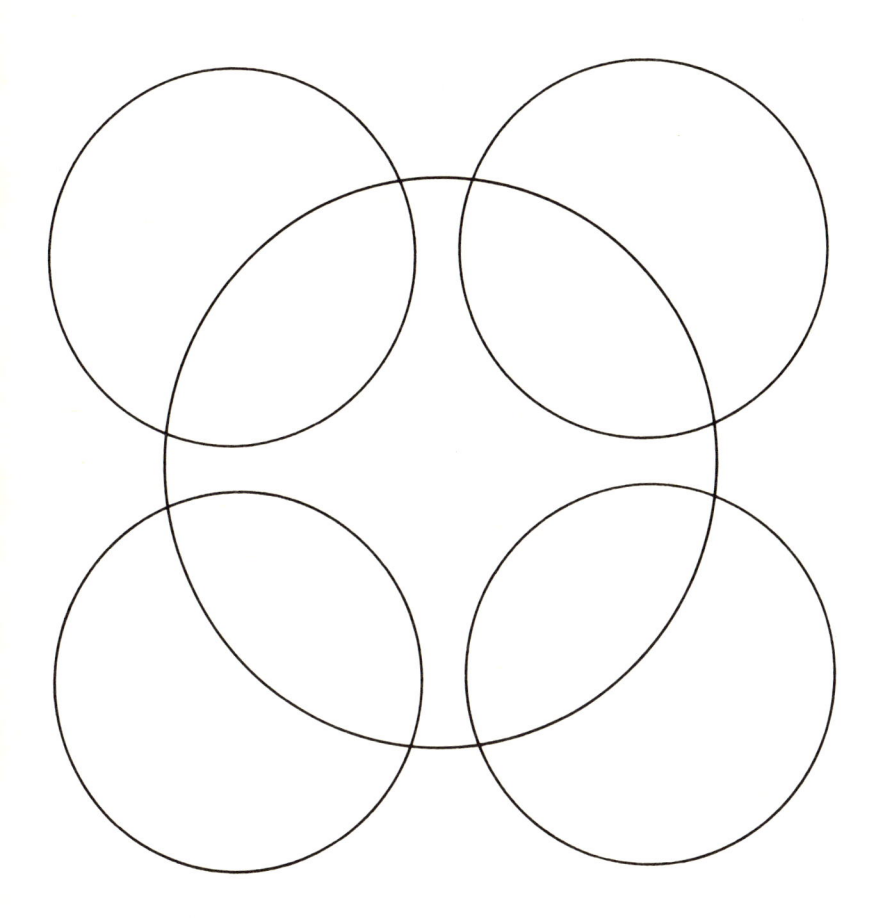

(Peat, Marwick)

"The type of network practice representative of the Arthur Young and Touche Ross organizations is basically a hybrid of the integrated and federated forms. The independent national entities use firmwide standards on international engagements, but adhere to their own standards for domestic work."

O'Connor holds that Klynveld Main Goerdeler's federated structure is little more than a marketing ploy designed to camouflage the member firms' lack of an integrated multinational practice. While admitting that KMG has scored some upsets in the marketplace—claiming a number of prized Big Eight clients—he insists that KMG does not provide the calibre of service required to attract and retain major clients over the long term. "Although some financial officers may be impressed by this flashy new concept, they'll see the deficiencies soon enough, and in the final analysis, that will be the deciding factor."

Although Main Hurdman's clients are generally reluctant to discuss their audit relationships, those willing to talk appear to be pleased with KMG's federated structure. Avon's chief financial officer, Jules Zimmerman, gives the firm high marks for what he calls "a balanced audit approach worldwide. With KMG we gain the services of the best firms in many of the countries in which we do business. This is of enormous help with our audit, tax, and borrowing activities. Although some observers may be confused because KMG goes under different names around the world, I think this expresses a fundamental strength rather than a weakness."

But it also makes for an image problem.

The multilingual collection of firm names linked to the KMG logo is downright confusing. Hickok is the first to admit it.

"You have to be with us when we're proposing to a client, informing them that Main Hurdman will do the work in the U.S.; Deutsche Treuhand-Gesellschaft will do the work in Germany; Klynveld Kraayenhof will do the work in Holland—well, my God, their eyes start to glaze over. And who can blame

Main Hurdman + KMG = The Big Nine

them? They can't even spell some of these names. Some of our competitors spoof the problem by calling us the KBG."

Art Bowman, editor of *Public Accounting Report,* notes that KMG's public image had produced a paradox of sorts. "On one hand, the merger has been successful in changing the business community's perception of the dominant accounting firms from the old 'Big Eight' to the new 'Big Nine.' But the public doesn't know who the ninth firm is."

Just how poorly KMG scores in recognition tests is evidenced by a conversation between the author and a New York–based Kidder Peabody vice president active in public financing.

MARK STEVENS (MS): Assume one of your proposed deals poses some thorny tax issue. Where do you turn for professional advice?

INVESTMENT BANKER (IB): We have close working relationships with all of the big accounting firms.

MS: The Big Eight?

IB: And some of the smaller firms.

MS: Ever work with Main Hurdman?

IB: Who?

MS: Main Hurdman.

IB: I've never heard of them. Are they an accounting firm?

MS: How about KMG?

IB: What's that?

MS: Klynveld Main Goerdeler. They're one of the largest CPA firms in the world.

IB: You're putting me on.

Although KMG senior partners are acutely aware of the firm's identity crisis (the *Chicago Tribune* has called KMG "the quiet giant" because of its poor name recognition) and are working to solve it, an easy solution is not likely to materialize. KMG's greatest asset—the member firms' strong domestic practices—

The Accounting Wars

is also the greatest impediment to developing a single audit signature. Fiercely proud of their individual identities, the members are reluctant to trade their venerable names for a concocted moniker that carries no weight with local clients. The U.S. firm, for example, would only further confuse the American business community by dropping Main Hurdman in favor of Klynveld Main Goerdeler.*

Says Hickok: "It wouldn't play in Peoria."

KMG's sensitivity to the name issue is evidenced by its overreaction to a routine press query. When word leaked out that *Fortune* magazine was interested in doing a story on the firm, the KMG's central management committee armed the partnership with a list of probable questions and suggested answers in the event they were called on by *Fortune* reporters. An internal KMG document on the subject listed these likely queries:

The professional press often mentions the name of KMG, but are there any major engagements conducted in the name of KMG?

Is this an obstacle to KMG's name recognition?
Why have few audit opinions been signed KMG?
What does "practicing internationally under a common name" really mean?
Why do KMG member firms not use a single name?

Suggested answers:
We have deliberately chosen not to practice as only one name. What is in a name after all? We are all KMG.

By continuing to practice in each country as a well-established, highly regarded national name we are putting our prestige and reputation on the line. What better assurance for our clients?

We respond to our clients' wishes. If they want our reports signed in the KMG name, that is done.

---

* In a ludicrous attempt to solve the problem, the firm made the earth-shattering announcement in September 1984 that it was reversing names, now putting KMG before Main Hurdman (KMG Main Hurdman).

Main Hurdman + KMG = The Big Nine

Using the same name everywhere does not do anything to improve the client services provided.

Name recognition has not been a problem for KMG.

Not been a problem! Clearly, this comes under the heading of wishful thinking. Hickok's candor about client proposals and playing in Peoria speaks to that. More important, however, is the assertion that "using the same name everywhere does not do anything to improve the client services provided."

Indications are that this is truer than the old-line Big Eighters would like to admit. The claim that working together over the years creates a bond unattainable by newly minted organizations is more fiction than fact. True, Peat, Marwick–Germany has been part of the PMM family since the late 1930s, but over the years partners, staffers, clients, and practice standards have come and gone in the kaleidoscope of change that typifies public accounting. The relationship between the independent PMM firms, to each other and to the central Peat, Marwick identity, is always in flux, changing to reflect developments in the profession, in the business community, and in the firms' internal politics. KMG's primary challenge—to help its member firms adjust to the demands of an affiliated practice—is closer to the same challenges the Big Eight face than they would like to admit.

In an era when clients are purchasing accounting services more on the basis of cost and efficiency than tradition and loyalty, just how long a firm's international network has been stitched together is not as important as how well it performs or how aggressively it prices its services. PM's O'Connor recognized this in his report to the firm's partnership:

"Perhaps a development at this point unique to the United States, but certainly a trend which is expanding worldwide, is the lessening 'brand loyalty' of a company to its accounting firm. It is not unusual today to find that the company's auditors are not the only accounting firm providing tax and consulting services to a client. The message here is that the companies are looking for the firm that can give it the best job and not necessarily the one with which it has had the longest relationship. This trend will very likely continue as the situation in our profession becomes more competitive, and it is something which we at PMM have to pay close attention to if we are to provide an expanding range of services to our existing client base."

Hard as this is to accept by those who've invested more time, talent, and money in creating and maintaining a long-standing international practice, a newcomer—in the name of KMG—has every chance of maintaining and even improving on its position in the Big Nine.

"KMG has drastically changed the complexion of European accounting," says *International Accounting Bulletin* publisher Michael Lafferty, hands down the most knowledgeable, objective observer on the Continent. "In the process, it has scared the hell out of the Big Eight. What just a few years ago was only a dream is now one of the largest firms in the world. That qualifies as a phenomenon.

"Perhaps the best indication of KMG's success is the impact it has had on that rather noxious term 'the Big Eight.' Some say KMG has caused it to be revised to 'the Big Nine.' But that doesn't go far enough. It has made 'the Big Eight' an obsolete, ancient, silly, and meaningless term that serves only to perpetuate a myth. KMG has proven that accounting skills, power, and marketing clout can emanate from Europe as well as from Chicago and New York. The era of the American oligarchy is dead.

"Amen."

3
Passage to China

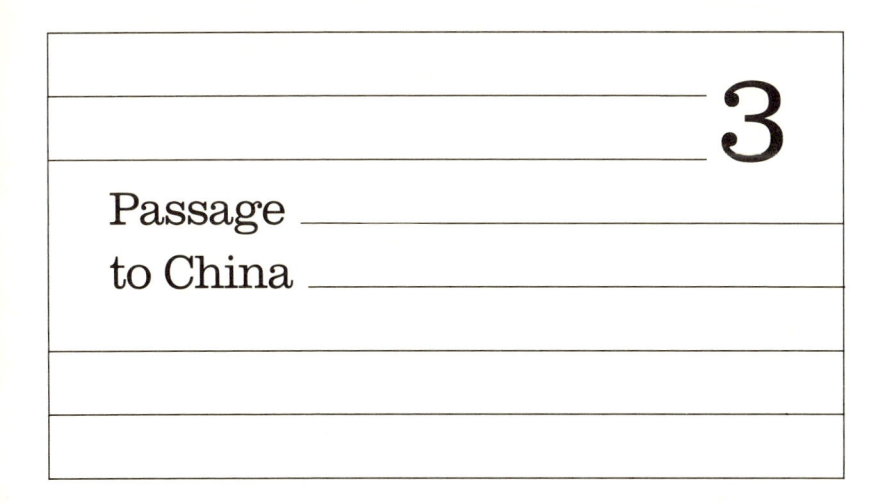

Dick Hammer would never make a good diplomat. A tough-minded Brooklyn-born tax man, he finds nothing wrong with the term Big Eight, with the firms that make up its practice, or with U.S.-based CPAs venturing far afield of their domestic markets. Perceptive, plainspoken, impatient with petty chitchat, he has a Trumanesque flair for reducing complex issues to simple declarative sentences. So when asked why he finds himself on a shuttle to Beijing, why old white-shoes Price Waterhouse is intimately involved in the People's Republic of China, he is characteristically candid.

Gazing across the dining room of his favorite watering hole, New York's Princeton Club, the class of '51 alumnus shrugs his shoulders as if the answer is so obvious it hardly warrants a formal response.

"Because we think there is opportunity there. An opportunity to expand our practice, to make money. Hell, we like to make money just as much as the next guy."

The Accounting Wars

No doubt this is true, but Hammer's straightforward response belies the multiple objectives Price Waterhouse hopes to achieve in Beijing and the ramifications its foray behind the bamboo curtain will have for its worldwide practice.

Beyond the obvious appeal of tapping a virgin market unprecedented in size and scope, PW's China campaign seeks to accomplish a checklist of strategic objectives shared by all of the accounting giants: to spread the firm's sphere of influence on a global basis, thus fostering ever-wider reliance on its partners' professional skills; to develop a multinational grid capable of servicing clients' interests worldwide; to perpetuate growth in staff and fees; and to diversify away from America's declining industrial base. In the process, the firms are positioning themselves for a more stable (earnings-wise) future but are also facing anew the festering issues of practice scope, quality control, and erosion of professional standards.

Let's explore the opportunities and the problems inherent in PW's China connection. In the thirty-five years since the Communists seized power in China, Beijing's public accounting profession, once a dynamic and influential group, has shriveled up to a clan of aged former practitioners. Banished to the countryside as agents of Western culture and capitalist interests, many of the CPAs practicing in 1949 were forced to endure the next three decades as agrarian laborers tied to the harsh climates and stubborn soil of the People's Republic.

"Public accounting was considered decadent—a materialistic, bourgeois occupation," says Margaret Jack, Price Waterhouse's partner in charge of the firm's China office. "Because of this thinking, the accountants were sent to the farms for 'reeducation.'

"This negative attitude toward accounting heightened during the Cultural Revolution, when Mao's followers cracked down on all forms of education considered scientific, capitalistic, or Western-oriented. As a result, the Chinese failed to educate an entire generation of CPAs. Those who'd been educated before the Communists took over grew old and completely out of date with modern practice."

As long as China remained a commercial recluse, the lack of accounting expertise hardly impacted on the national mission. But when Beijing launched its mid-1970s drive toward modernization, China parted the bamboo curtain just wide enough to encourage joint business ventures with foreign corporations capable of bringing the mainland two desperately needed assets: currency and technology. Faced for the first time in a generation with the prospect of capitalist entities—predominantly multinational oil companies—profiting within its borders, China recognized the need for tax laws designed to keep a fair share of the revenues inside the People's Republic while simultaneously encouraging foreign investment. Because the last generation of China's public accountants were dead, senile, or unfamiliar with modern tax theories, Beijing invited foreign CPAs and attorneys to consult in the formation of its tax laws and to help reeducate its accounting profession. The Big Eight rushed in to fill the void. Today, Big Eight firms have offices in four Chinese cities and are seeking to spread their influence throughout the People's Republic. Price Waterhouse, blessed with a strategic plum—the right to practice in Beijing—reaches out from its base in the Peking Hotel to the highest councils of the Chinese government, its fifty-four-year-old tax director, Dick Hammer, one of the principal consultants in the drafting of China's Foreign Enterprise Tax Law.

PW's China odyssey actually traces back to President Richard Nixon's televised eight-day trip (February 1972) to Beijing, Hangchow, and Shanghai, culminating in a joint communiqué with Premier Chou En-lai, announcing agreements to begin the normalization of trade and cultural relations between China and the United States.

"Sometime after Nixon's trip and the subsequent opening of

full diplomatic relationships with China, the partners in our international firm decided there would be a commercial future in China," recalls John Biegler, PW's chairman from 1969 to 1978, now retired. A jowl-faced gentleman with an uncanny resemblance to a well-groomed basset hound, Biegler evokes the courtly demeanor of the old-style managing partner that prevailed before the days of open competition. He would seek new business, yes, but would look askance at soliciting competitors' clients. "We realized that China's resources, most notably oil and its enormous labor pool, would attract energy and high-technology companies. The former would want to explore for oil, the latter to produce and assemble products on the mainland. Because our clients were among the companies most likely to do business in China, we believed that we should be on the scene to service them.

"So I dispatched one of my former partners, Tom Ganner, to explore the China market for the firm. Tom had been the number-two man under me until illness forced his early retirement. When he expressed an interest in returning to work to take on special projects, I offered him the China assignment.

"His unique blend of accounting skills and international experience made him ideal for the job and he accepted it eagerly, taking off on his first trip there in 1978. Working through our Hong Kong office, which then served as our window to China, he made some promising contacts on the mainland.

"Based on his highly optimistic reports, I believed there were four major reasons for opening an office in China. First, I saw it as a vital link for properly servicing our multinational engagements. As an international accounting firm, we must always be in a position to service our clients—our French, British, American clients, all of them—wherever in the world they do business.

"Second, because China's clock had stopped in the late forties, the nation was terribly backward in management techniques and accounting practices. I thought this presented an enormous opportunity. The Chinese would need help coming up to speed in the fiscal disciplines necessary for their commercial revitalization. We could provide that help.

"Third, if the West was going to make an investment in China—an idea the Chinese were actively encouraging—a rational system for taxing the earnings from these investments would be an absolute prerequisite. With our expertise in international taxation, we could be of assistance to the Chinese.

"Finally, there appeared to be long-term opportunities for auditing Chinese enterprises and for providing them with broad consulting services. Adding all of this together made for a promising picture. So I decided to apply for permission to practice in China. But no sooner had I given the go-ahead than Tom Ganner took ill again and died. That left us in the lurch. The rudimentary groundwork for our China office had been done, but we needed someone to carry the torch, to turn informal links with the Chinese into formalized agreements."

It was at this point that PW benefited from a fortunate coincidence. Margaret Jack (wife of PW's Hong Kong partner Graeme Jack)—an Australian-educated chartered accountant (CA) born and raised in Hong Kong—was planning to return to work after a hiatus following the birth of their child. A former tax professional with Touche Ross, Margaret was the ideal emissary to resume PW's China mission where Ganner left off.

At this stage, PW needed a go-between blessed with a working knowledge of both the local culture and international taxation who was capable of moving beyond the bowing and toasting stage of corporate diplomacy to the establishment of contacts with key decision makers in China's Ministry of Finance.

Margaret Jack's résumé came closer to the ideal than Biegler could have allowed himself to dream. Although thoroughly Western in her business outlook and a practitioner of Big Eight–style accounting, she spoke fluent English, Cantonese, and

The Accounting Wars

Mandarin—the official language of the Beijing government. Her parents, entrepreneurs who'd fled Shanghai when the Communists came to power, had relocated in Hong Kong but maintained contacts in China. Jack's background and her professional skills were just what PW needed to effectively play its China card.

Watching the woman in action, one is taken by her ability to personify two widely contrasting worlds. Visiting New York to report on her China progress to PW's headquarters staff, she glides through a Manhattan restaurant like a native-born executive powering her way up the ladder at CBS or Merrill Lynch. But there is another dimension. The Oriental birthright, as colorful and intriguing as the hand-painted pattern on her silk dress, reveals the influence of another culture that tempers the raw ambition, giving it a wiser and deeper perspective.

Precisely because she can operate knowledgeably within New York's and Beijing's power circles, and because she can command the confidence of its leaders, she is the pluperfect intermediary for an Anglo-Saxon capitalist institution seeking to penetrate a generation of mistrust and several thousand years of social and cultural tradition. When China's tax commissioner, Liu Zhi-cheng, visiting New York in July 1982 to address American business executives, met with the press, the *Wall Street Journal* noted that "he spoke through one of Price Waterhouse's Hong Kong partners, Margaret Jack, who acted as an interpreter."

"Trust," Jack says, pointing a finger in the air. "That must be your starting point. Without trust, without respect, you cannot hope to do business in Beijing. Their way of thinking is so entirely different from an American's. In the States, you can greet a stranger and get down to work with a few minutes of pleasantries. But in China, the getting-acquainted process can take many months. You must prove your capabilities, indicate an understanding of your clients' needs and concerns, and allow them to acquire that all-important trust and respect in you."

An effervescent personality and an indefatigable worker who commutes between Hong Kong and Beijing weekly, makes side trips to London and New York, and raises a child in the interim, Jack established herself as a known quantity in the finance ministry and Beijing's Accounting Society by knocking on doors, using one reference to gain access to another, and slowly cultivating a network of contacts in Beijing's commercial establishment.

"Because the Chinese government is such an intricate bureaucracy, you have to reach the leaders of each ministry by first working your way through a complex web of subordinates," Jack explains. "Everyone along the chain of command must be treated with the respect *they* demand or they'll thwart your efforts to deal effectively with those at the top. Were you to as much as irritate a junior translator—for whatever reason—he'll likely block your efforts to conclude a deal with the senior officials.

"I try to prevent this kind of bureaucratic interference by developing personal ties with all levels of government officials. For example, the Chinese customarily take a long business lunch, generally from eleven-thirty to two, working right through the meal. But I often turn the talk away from business, focusing instead on family matters—light conversation. Without fail, the Chinese respond favorably. I believe this breaks down the impersonal walls that can make the bureaucracy so frustrating."

Hammer, who occasionally accompanies Jack on her rounds, agrees. "To see Margaret at work in China, you'd think, at first blush, that she has nothing in common with her hosts. She's Western from her clothing to her attitudes. She's feminine, stylish, smartly dressed. The people she deals with, they're

The Accounting Wars

all in Mao jackets—even the women. I mean plain, somber, intentionally lackluster.

"But there's a common thread that seems to transcend the cosmetics. The Chinese know they share something with Margaret—be it their heritage or a way of relating to one another. In opening China's doors for us, she has succeeded where a Westerner would have failed."

PW's strategy, from the very beginning of its China connection, has been to tout the firm's prestigious reputation, to establish its partners as readily accessible sources of information, and, most important, to communicate PW's willingness to make its talents and services available to the Chinese government on a pro bono basis. Any talk of fees at this juncture would arouse Chinese suspicions about the capitalist interlopers and would interfere with the delicate process of making the Beijing government reliant on its Big Eight consultants. PW's master plan calls for far more ambitious objectives than simply collecting engagement fees for the creation of China's tax laws. Reading between the lines, it is apparent that the firm's long-term goal is no less ambitious than to make its work and its counsel indispensable to China's public and commercial sectors, for the effect this will have both within China and at the centers of corporate power worldwide.

To date, much of PW's strategy has gone according to plan. Since his first trip to Beijing in August 1981, Dick Hammer has emerged as the computer-age Thomas Jefferson of China's tax laws.

"I'll never forget the day our vice chairman of tax left word that he wanted to see me in his office," Hammer recalls. "That usually means he wants to raise a tax issue or complain about my expense account vouchers. But this time he hit me with a thunderbolt: How'd I like to go to China? I thought about it for just a moment, was thrilled by the prospect, and said yes. That night I took my wife to Chinatown to celebrate. Within weeks, I was in Beijing eating the real thing.

"Quickly, I learned that the Chinese are highly intelligent and extremely eager to learn all they can from those they regard as experts. The first time I reviewed their foreign-enterprise income tax law, which they put into place in December 1981, I really had to chuckle to myself because it was so obviously a collage of the tax systems of other countries. Bits and pieces were borrowed from the Americans, the Japanese, the British, and maybe a half dozen others.

"For example, they have a limitation on entertainment expenses that is geared to net income. Well, this is right out of the Japanese statutes. The premise here is that a business can deduct expenses for travel and entertainment, but only to a percentage of its total earnings. This notion of placing a ceiling on travel and entertainment clearly appealed to Beijing's policymakers."

Chinese tax proposals, whether original or "borrowed" from other nations, become law through a series of steps designed to simulate democratic processes: First, the tax bureau prepares a draft of the legislation, which is submitted for discussion and approval to the state council, where ministers of the various state agencies debate and amend the bill's provisions.

Upon approval by the state council, the legislation is considered for passage by the National People's Congress, which is authorized to vote it into law.

At the time of Hammer's first trip to Beijing, the Income Tax Law of the People's Republic of China Concerning Foreign Enterprises was in the draft stage. Much like their counterparts in other nations, China's tax authorities hoped to use the law as a mechanism claiming a fair share of the profits multinational businesses generated within the PRC. In an age of multinational commerce, nations participating in the widespread cross-pollination of goods and services must adopt recognized tax principles as the basis for reciprocal treaties. Those seeking to inflict severe terms on their trading partners find it discourages foreign investment and invites retaliation from the trade community.

Unlike their counterparts in Washington, Paris, and London, Chinese tax officials could not look to domestic precedent for guidance in developing treaty provisions. Owing primarily to Margaret Jack's skillful advance work, China's tax authorities came to see Hammer—a ranking tax partner for what they viewed as a prestigious accounting firm—as a creditable authority (one of several CPAs and lawyers invited for this purpose) to review their tax bill before it was passed into law.

"Because they saw me as some sort of tax guru, they may have given me more credit than I deserved," Hammer says. "They asked me detailed questions about the most obscure tax regulations in any number of countries and expected me to have encyclopedic knowledge of each and every provision. I must admit that I had to fudge my answers every now and then to protect my image. I couldn't tell them that you need a computer to keep track of tax regulations in the United States alone."

Certainly, data processing capabilities were not a requirement for reviewing China's draft law. For a practitioner accustomed to a tax system based on a veritable library of rules, regulations, codes, and court decisions, China's simplistic approach to international tax legislation was startling. The PRC's tax authorities hoped to address an almost infinite number of complex tax issues on the strength of a *two-page* tax document.

Foreign Enterprises—Income Tax Law, 1981

ARTICLE I
Income tax shall be levied in accordance with this law on the income derived from production, business, and other sources by any foreign enterprise operating in the People's Republic of China.

Passage to China

"Foreign enterprises" mentioned in this law refer, with the exception of those for whom separate provisions are stipulated in Article 11, to foreign companies, enterprises, and other economic organizations which have establishments in the People's Republic of China engaged in independent business operation or cooperative production or joint business operation with Chinese enterprises.

ARTICLE 2

The taxable income of a foreign enterprise shall be the net income in a tax year after deduction of costs, expenses, and losses in that year.

ARTICLE 3

Income tax on foreign enterprises shall be assessed at progressive rates for the parts in excess of a specific amount of taxable income. The tax rates are as follows:

Range of Income	Tax Rate
Annual income below 250,000 yuan	20%
That part of annual income from 250,000 to 500,000 yuan	25%
That part of annual income from 500,000 to 750,000 yuan	30%
That part of annual income from 750,000 to 1,000,000 yuan	35%
That part of annual income above 1,000,000 yuan	40%

ARTICLE 4

In addition to the income tax levied on foreign enterprises in accordance with the provisions of the preceding article, a local income tax of 10 percent of the same taxable income shall be levied.

Where a foreign enterprise needs reduction in or exemption from local income tax on account of its small-scale production or business, or low profit rate, this shall be decided by the people's government of the province, municipality, or autonomous region in which that enterprise is located.

ARTICLE 5

A foreign enterprise scheduled to operate for a period of ten years or more in farming, forestry, animal husbandry, or other low-profit occupations may, upon approval by the tax authorities of an application filed by the enterprise, be exempted from income tax in the first profit-making year and allowed a 50 percent reduction in the second and third years.

With the approval of the Ministry of Finance, a 15–30 percent reduction in income tax may be allowed for a period of ten years following the expiration of the term for exemptions and reductions mentioned in the preceding paragraph.

ARTICLE 6

Losses incurred by a foreign enterprise in a tax year may be carried over to the next year and made up with a matching amount drawn from that year's income. Should the income in the subsequent tax year be insufficient to make up for the said losses, the balance may be made up with further deductions against income year by year over a period not exceeding five years.

ARTICLE 7

Income tax on foreign enterprises shall be levied on an annual basis and paid in quarterly installments. Such provisional payments shall be made within fifteen days after the end of each quarter. The final settlement shall be made within five months after the end of a tax year. Excess payments shall be refunded by the tax authorities or deficiencies made good by the taxpayer.

ARTICLE 8

Foreign enterprises shall file their provisional income tax returns with the local tax authorities within the period prescribed for provisional payments. The taxpayer shall file its final annual income tax return together with its final accounts within four months after the end of the tax year.

ARTICLE 9

The method of financial management and the system of accounting of foreign enterprises shall be submitted to local tax authorities for reference.

Where the method of financial management and the system of accounting of foreign enterprises is in contradiction with the provisions of the tax law, payments shall be assessed according to the provisions of the tax law.

ARTICLE 10

Foreign enterprises shall present relevant certificates to the local tax authorities for tax registration when they go into operation or close down in accordance with law.

ARTICLE 11

A 20 percent income tax shall be levied on the income obtained from dividends, interest, rentals, royalties, and other sources in China by foreign companies, enterprises, and other economic organizations which have no establishments in China. Such tax shall be withheld by the paying unit in each of its payments.

For the payment of income tax according to the provisions in the preceding paragraph, the foreign companies, enterprises, and other economic organizations which earn the income shall be the taxpayer, and the paying unit shall be the withholding agent. Taxes withheld on each payment by a withholding agent shall, within five days, be turned over to the state treasury and the income tax return submitted to the tax authorities.

Income from interest on loans given to the Chinese government or China's state banks by international finance organizations shall be exempted from income tax. Income from interest on loans given at a preferential interest rate by foreign banks to China's state banks shall also be exempted from income tax.

Income derived from interest on deposits of foreign banks to China's state banks and on loans given at a normal interest rate by foreign banks to China's state banks shall be taxed. However, exemption from income tax shall be granted to those foreign banks accordingly in whose countries income from interest on deposits and loans of China's state banks is exempted from income tax.

ARTICLE 12

The tax authorities have the right to investigate the financial affairs, account books, and tax situation of any foreign enterprise, and have the right to investigate the withholding situation of any withholding agent. Such foreign enterprise and withholding agent must make reports on facts and provide all relevant information and shall not refuse to cooperate or conceal any facts.

ARTICLE 13

Income tax levied on foreign enterprises shall be computed in terms of Renminbi (RMB). Income in foreign currency shall be assessed according to the exhange rate quoted by the State General Administration of Exchange Control of the People's Republic of China and taxed in Renminbi.

ARTICLE 14

Foreign enterprises and withholding agents must pay their tax within the prescribed time limit. In case of failure to pay within the prescribed time limit, the appropriate tax authorities, in addition to settling a new time limit for tax payment, shall surcharge overdue payments at one-half of one percent of the overdue tax for every day in arrears, starting from the first day of default.

ARTICLE 15

The tax authorities may, acting at their discretion, impose a penalty on any foreign enterprise which has violated the provisions of Articles 8, 9, 10, and 12 of this law.

In dealing with those withholding agents who have violated the provisions of Article 11 of this law, the tax authorities may, in addition to setting a new time limit for the payment of the part of tax that should have been withheld and at their discretion, impose a penalty of not more than the amount that should have been withheld.

In dealing with foreign enterprises which have evaded or refused to pay income tax, the tax authorities may, in addition to pursuing the tax, impose a fine of not more than five times the amount of tax underpaid or not paid, according to how serious the offense is. Cases of gross violation shall be handled by the local people's courts according to law.

ARTICLE 16

In case of disputes with tax authorities about tax payment, foreign enterprises must pay tax according to the relevant regulations first before applying to higher tax authorities for reconsideration. If they do not accept the decisions made after such reconsideration, they can bring the matter before the local people's courts.

ARTICLE 17
Where agreements on tax payment have been concluded between the government of the People's Republic of China and the government of another country, matters concerning tax payment shall be handled in accordance with the provisions of these agreements.

ARTICLE 18
Detailed rules and regulations for the implementation of this law shall be formulated by the Ministry of Finance of the People's Republic of China.

ARTICLE 19
This law shall come into force as of January 1, 1982.

"Two pages!" Hammer exclaims. "Here I am reviewing the tax law for a billion people and they show me two pages. The articles, nineteen in all, addressed enormously complex matters in the most simplistic terms. Article two, for example, says the taxable income for a foreign corporation shall be the net income in a tax year after deduction of costs, expenses, and losses in that year. Guidelines on determining where the income was generated, how it should be allocated between corporate affiliates, and what percentage of corporate expenses can be attributed to operations in the PRC were notably absent. These gaping holes in the law concerned me because I knew that they were issues that would soon arise and that foreign corporations would not invest in China until and unless they had a clearer picture of the tax implications of doing so. So I pressed the Chinese to fill in some of the most glaring omissions by adopting rules that would serve as incentives for foreign companies to do business in China. Some of my ideas were incorporated into the tax law regulations first issued in January 1982 and others, although not yet written into the regulations, are nevertheless part of China's tax policy."

中华人民共和国财政部税务总局
People's Republic of China
Ministry of Finance
General Taxation Bureau

外国企业季度所得税申报表
The Foreign Enterprise Quarterly Income Tax Return

表式，F—1
Form:

一九　　年第　　季度
For _____ Quarter of the Calendar Year 19 _____

申报日期：一九　　年　　月　　日
Date Filed: _____, 19 _____

金额单位：人民币元
Monetary Unit: RMB¥

企业名称 Name of the Enterprise		地 址 Address		电话号码 Tel. No.	
业 别 Kind of Business		开业日期 Date of Establishment		资本金额 Amount of Capital	工商登记证字号 License No.

总机构名称 Name of Head Office	地 址 Address	本企业从业人员人数 Number of Employees of the Enterprise							
		合 计 Total		工 人 Workers		职 员 Staff Members		其 它 Others	
		人数 Number	其中：外籍 Including Foreigners	人数 Number	其中：外籍 Including Foreigners	人数 Number	其中：外籍 Including Foreigners	人数 Number	其中：外籍 Including Foreigners

上年度应纳税所得额（亏损） Last Year's Taxable Income (Loss)	上年度全年缴纳所得税额 Income Tax Payment of Last Year	本年度计划利润额 Amount of Planned Profit for This Taxable Year	本季度实际利润额 Amount of Actual Profit for This Quarter	本季前已缴所得税额累计 Amount of Cumulative Income Tax Paid before This Quarter	本季预缴所得税额 Amount of Income Tax Prepaid for This Quarter
	金额 Amount / 其中：地方所得税 Including Local Income Tax		金额 Amount / 其中：地方所得税 Including Local Income Tax	金额 Amount / 其中：地方所得税 Including Local Income Tax	金额 Amount / 其中：地方所得税 Including Local Income Tax

（企业盖章）
(Enterprise)

负责人
（签字或盖章）
Responsible Officer
(Signature or Seal)

会计主管人
（签字或盖章）
Accountant General
(Signature or Seal)

以下由税务机关填写 (Hereunder to Be Filled by the Tax Authorities):

收到日期		审核日期	
审核记录			
完税证字号		纳税日期	

主管税务机关：　　　　　　　　主管税务官员：

Foreign enterprises—Income tax return

Hammer, in his role as adviser to the Chinese government, has focused on these major issues:

Consolidated Earnings: The original draft of the Foreign Enterprise Income Tax Law did not provide for companies to offset profits and losses from multiple operations within China.

"For example, if an oil and gas company drilled in two different parts of the South China Sea, earning a profit in one and washing out in another, they weren't going to permit that company to combine its results," Hammer notes. "Well, I informed the Chinese that this was out of step with recognized practice, that the U.S. would probably not give its corporations credit for the tax if the consolidation were not permitted. The Chinese were very sensitive to this position and ultimately agreed to allow for the consolidated statements. I think they believed my warnings that the major oil companies would not invest in China were they not certain of gaining credit for Chinese taxes."

Intracompany Charges and Allocations: China's skeletal tax law did not specifically permit corporations to allocate to affiliated companies a percentage of headquarters expenses (including R&D and general and administrative) incurred to benefit the affiliates. For example, if a Houston-based oil drilling equipment manufacturer develops a high-tech device used by its overseas divisions, it will want to allocate to those divisions a portion of the cost of developing the technology.

The Chinese recognized the fairness of this provision as well as its wide application in international tax standards but, exhibiting a paranoia that complicates the PRC's tax policies, resisted it for fear that foreign companies would use inflated allocations to deprive them of taxes due.

Hammer's solution was to suggest that the allocation be allowed, subject to an audit by a public accounting firm. The tax authorities agreed—first adding the provision that the accounting firm must be registered in China.

The Accounting Wars

"I tried to assure them," Hammer says, "that the multinationals of the world are not crooks. They just want to make a fair profit and of course they want to take advantage of legitimate ways of reducing taxes—which is part of the game and is fair. I said, Why don't you require some kind of audited statement to support the charging of head-office expenses? It might involve research and development, it might involve general and administrative, it might involve some interest costs—the type of stuff that the head office would incur that benefits an entire group of companies. And they accepted that."

Taxability: Chinese tax authorities wanted to subject U.S. affiliates in the PRC to PRC income taxes whether or not the affiliates played a role in generating the income.

For example, if company A, headquartered in Chicago and with a branch office in Beijing, concluded a sale within China, PRC officials sought to tax the branch office even if it did not contribute to the sale.

Hammer pressed the Chinese to change their view on this, asking that they look not to the place of sale but instead to the economic activity responsible for it. "I tried to make them see that if the negotiations were conducted by a representative of the head office and the contracts were signed in Chicago rather than Beijing, there should be no tax on the income."

According to PW, recognized tax standards hold as a determinative factor whether there is authority, in the hands of a locally based employee or agent, to negotiate and conclude transactions (contracts) within the taxing jurisdiction in question. For example, an agent with the authority to enter into a binding contract in the PRC would be considered to be acting on behalf of the principal, and thus the principal would be engaged in taxable business activities in the PRC. The local agent would have the responsibility for filing income tax returns on behalf of the principal reporting the income derived from agreements concluded in the PRC.

Passage to China

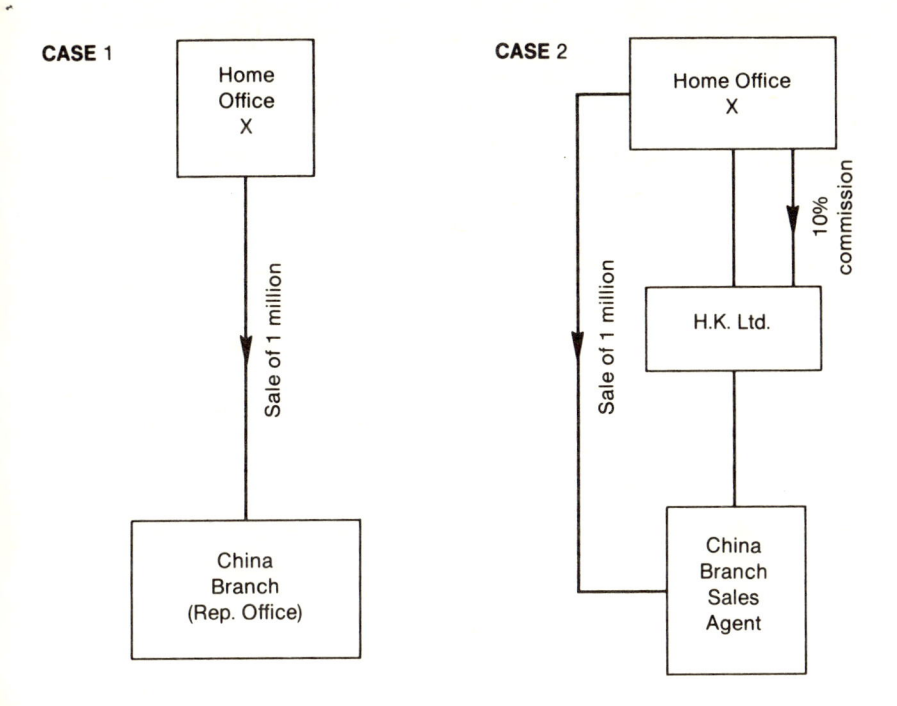

CASE 1

```
Home Office X
       |
       | Sale of 1 million
       ▼
China Branch
(Rep. Office)
```

CASE 2

```
Home Office X ─────────────┐
   |                        │ 10% commission
   |                        ▼
   |                    H.K. Ltd.
   | Sale of 1 million      |
   |                        |
   ▼                        |
China Branch ◄──────────────┘
Sales Agent
```

PW offers the following examples:

Case 1: Power to negotiate and conclude the sales contract by the China-based branch personnel of foreign corporation X would subject corporation X to PRC income tax on the profit on the sale of $1 million, because the contract was entered into on behalf of X *in China*.

Case 2: The sale is negotiated and concluded on behalf of foreign corporation X by the China-based branch personnel of a Hong Kong corporation, a 100-percent-owned subsidiary of X. This sale will also be subject to PRC income tax to X, albeit with a deduction for the commission paid to its Hong Kong subsidiary. Although the quantum of PRC taxable income will theoretically be the same, the aggregate tax liability will differ under a graduated rate table, since the income will be spread between two taxpayers rather than taxed to one.

"In determining the source of income resulting from sales transactions," Hammer notes, "the most significant criterion should be the situs in which the solicitation and negotiation processes take place."

Although the Chinese seem to be moving in this direction, the principle is not yet written into their tax regulations. As with scores of other questions, authorities have indicated a predilection to view transactions based on one or another concept of taxability, but there are no guarantees. Hammer, for his part, continues to apply pressure, using his leverage as a prominent consultant to get things done the Price Waterhouse way.

But persuasive as his arguments may be, Hammer's proposals do not always pass muster with the Chinese.

"I know Dick, and I'm somewhat familiar with his China activities," says a specialist in China deals for the investment banking firm of Lehman Brothers Kuhn Loeb. "Although the Chinese turn to him for ideas and opinions, he's only one of many. They talk to attorneys, to other Big Eight partners—I know Touche Ross and Peat, Marwick have been active there—and they factor all of this into the overall decision-making process. Sometimes ideas are passed over, ignored, or simply surface in a different form than originally suggested. The Chinese are independent thinkers."

From time to time, Hammer's proposals are flatly rejected.

One telling defeat, indicative of China's ingrained fear of being cheated, came in response to Hammer's suggestion to reduce the foreign corporate income tax from the 30-to-40-percent progression to a flat 30 percent.

In a letter to Lin Rong-sheng, China's vice commissioner of tax, following his August 1981 trip to the PRC, Hammer reiterated his thoughts on the subject: "With regard to the appropriate tax rate to be included in the law, which you personally seemed to be most concerned about, I believe that use of a flat rate would be the simplest approach. Graduated rates can be more complex and do not readily permit the foreign investor to forecast his China tax burden without having a relatively good prediction of the annual net income to be produced. Furthermore, I think the rate should be in the 30 percent neighborhood (with the 10 percent local tax bringing the overall rate up to 33 percent), comparable to the rate under the existing joint venture tax law, with no additional tax."

Hammer explains his position this way: "Because the Chinese did not have tax treaties with most of their trading partners, there was no mechanism for reducing the maximum tax on the major corporations doing business there. That's why I suggested the flat-thirty rate as one acceptable to foreign investors and still equitable to China. But they didn't see it my way and declined to go along with the reduction."

Hammer the adviser, Hammer the consultant to the Chinese government, is different from Hammer the New York–based tax director. In Beijing, surrounded by a contingent of attentive, Mao-suited, upper-echelon bureaucrats, he deals with the fundamentals of tax law as well as its most sophisticated theories. The state of Chinese accounting—rudimentary but maturing rapidly—demands a top-to-bottom restructuring, updating what remains of a badly disrupted past while fusing together the new patchwork of multinational tax provisions into a cohesive framework. In presenting his ideas, honed from twenty-five years of experience in international tax, Hammer finds himself learning to read his Oriental "clients" not only by what they say—few speak English—but by their body language, their facial expressions.

"Not that the way they cock their heads or fold their arms always signals a specific thought or idea," Hammer explains. "Reading body language is more of an art than a science, but when you have no other form of response, when people don't

The Accounting Wars

always volunteer their opinions across the conference table as they do in the United States, you improvise. I'm the kind of guy who needs feedback from my clients.

"This can get pretty surreal. For example, the Chinese often pretend to understand my English—they shake their heads as if they're following my thoughts—even when they speak only Mandarin. I know they're pretending because they stand there grinning at me when I'm not saying anything even slightly humorous."

Clearly, Hammer and the Chinese make strange bedfellows. As an American in Beijing, he rejects the "do as the Romans do" school of corporate diplomacy, clinging instead to a New York mindset and to an American way of conducting business. Certainly he finds little glamor in the Chinese capital.

"In China, there's really no first-class accommodations—not the hotels, the restaurants, or for that matter the national airline that jets you there. China Airlines flies direct from New York to Beijing, but I avoid that route by taking an American carrier to Hong Kong, then going from there to Beijing. It's indirect but far superior. One of my partners made the mistake of flying China Airlines, only to find that all three meals served on the flight were identical. The rice that he saw for breakfast he saw again at lunch and then once more at dinner.

"Hotel accommodations are equally spartan. The Peking Hotel, which is where I usually stay and where our offices are located, is a collage of three wings built in 1910, 1925, and 1955. During my first trip, I was put in the 1910 wing, and that was one of the worst nights I've ever had. The bed was about half my size; footboard at the bottom; bars for a headboard. They called it a double bed, but it was such a small double that I couldn't even angle across it to get comfortable. Jeez, what a night.

"Then I got moved to the 1955 wing, which was like a palace in comparison. But by American standards it's very modest—

very plain—with nondescript furnishings and air-conditioning that may or may not work when you turn it on. You have to hope luck is with you.

"At night, there's not a blessed thing to do. The Peking Hotel doesn't have a bar, so if you want to drink you have to buy a bottle of whiskey, take it up to your room, and drink alone. As for dining out, the best Chinese restaurants in Beijing don't compare to the mediocre restaurants in New York's Chinatown. It's obvious that all of the best cooks left China for more financially rewarding jobs primarily in New York and Hong Kong.

"Even when you find a restaurant that's fairly good—like a very nice Peking duck house I visited with one of my partners and his wife—the physical setting leaves much to be desired. In most of China's public buildings, it's either terribly cold in the winter or unbearably hot in summer. Throughout that meal in the duck house, the lady at our table had to wear her fur coat to keep warm."

Hammer's trials with local culture shock extend from the hotel room to the conference room, prompting him, in some cases, to adapt Chinese business practices to reflect his own Yankee standards.

"What the Chinese call a conference room bears no resemblance to the kind of conference room an American businessman is accustomed to," Hammer continues. "During my first visit to the Ministry of Finance, I was told, through an interpreter, that we would be attending a meeting in one of the building's conference rooms. Immediately I envisioned a modest-sized room, just large enough for a good-sized round or rectangular table surrounded by a dozen or so office chairs. Well, that's not quite the Chinese version of a conference room. Picture this: We enter a room roughly fifty feet long—somewhat equivalent to this (he points to one of the Princeton Club's rear dining alcoves). Lined up in rows of twenty are padded easy chairs—the kind you find in the old railroad club cars or the lobby of a rather dated hotel—in which are seated a contingent of bureaucrats. Margaret and I are led down a narrow aisle to a big sofa at the far end of the room. We're instructed to sit on one end, our host and his interpreter take the other, and the middle is reserved as a sort of neutral zone.

"I'm about to take my seat when one of the bureaucrats steps forward from his club chair to shake my hand. As I greet him, another hand goes out and then another and another. I'm not certain if I'm supposed to shake hands with all of those in attendance—some of whom are young underlings brought in to take notes—but I figure what the hell, better to cover my bases than to risk insulting someone. What I know about Chinese protocol you could put on the head of a pin.

"Well, anyway, the Chinese finally completed the greeting process and I got started on what I'd come there for in the first place: to talk about international tax. But something was out of whack. The environment was too damn stuffy, too formal, not at all the way I like it. So I decided to lecture in Beijing the way I do in New York or Atlanta—with a blackboard and a piece of chalk."

To break through the language and the cultural barriers, Hammer drew diagrams to illustrate his ideas. This loosened things up. The Chinese—prolific note takers all—scribbled down every mark, every symbol. Soon, some in the audience were getting out of their seats, assembling around the blackboard, whispering among themselves. From that point on, the sessions turned from lectures to discussions—with the aid of interpreters—and Hammer could sense a genuine rapport building between the Chinese and himself. He believed they started to accept him on a personal as well as professional basis, somewhat like colleagues trying to solve a problem together.

Just the outcome PW has jockeyed for ever since Ganner extended the initial feelers to the PRC back in 1978. Behind the commitment to actively explore the Chinese market; behind Hammer, Biegler, Ganner, and Jack's shuttles to Hong Kong and Beijing; behind the thousands of hours of tax research and pro bono consultations; behind the decision to open an office in the Peking Hotel and to make the woman in charge a partner; behind the PW-sponsored seminars introducing Chinese officials to American executives—behind all of this hand-holding and positioning and advising is a carefully calculated plan to establish Price Waterhouse as China's preeminent accounting firm, one with a direct line to Beijing's power circles.

Interestingly, Deloitte Haskins & Sells, another Big Eighter with grand designs for its China practice, has taken a different tack, aligning itself with the PRC's industrial technocrats rather than its political leaders. Although Price Waterhouse's partners claim that all of the Big Eight now active in the PRC worked behind the scenes for permission to set up shop in Beijing, Jim McGregor, DH&S's partner in charge of international operations, scoffs at this as "a severe case of competitive nonsense."

"We had an office in Shanghai for many years, so our first choice, once the Chinese reopened their doors to the West, was to reestablish our presence in that city. Not for sentimental value, mind you, but in recognition of Shanghai's position as the center of Chinese industry. As far as we're concerned, that's the place to be."

DH&S's marketing thrust—to establish itself as a well-connected presence in South China's industrial base—reflects McGregor's belief that the most substantial engagements will develop in the MAS area, with the plum assignments going to those accounting firms perceived by the multinationals to be most fluent in Chinese business practices and most intimate with industrial leaders. From one standpoint at least DH&S's strategy has paid off. The firm has completed one of the initial fee-basis engagements in the PRC, a $25,000* audit of an AMC Jeep manufacturing joint venture.

"Before taking on my current assignment, as partner in charge of our Hong Kong and China offices, I worked in Korea, where I had responsibility for a similar AMC joint venture," says DH&S's partner George Betts. "When AMC became active in the PRC, I was hired to audit the value of China's contribution —a manufacturing plant—to the Jeep production deal."

DH&S's fee for the engagement, although important symbolically as evidence of China's potential, falls far short of the firm's investment in the PRC. Much like its Avenue of the Americas neighbor Price Waterhouse, Deloitte has performed extensive pro bono consulting work for the Chinese government.

"We're helping with the reeducation of the accounting profession," Betts explains. "When the surviving professionals were called back into service in the 1970s, most of them were sixty to eighty years old and terribly out-of-date with modern techniques. You can include some of our former partners in this group. Interestingly, we've bumped into a number of them—elderly gents all—in the streets of Shanghai. What would have been the best years of their careers were taken from them.

"We've been directing our efforts at updating the skills of practicing professionals and, even more important, at training a new generation of CPAs. To achieve these objectives, we've consulted with professional and academic groups, have held seminars, and have even written books on modern accounting procedures.

"Why do we do this? I think it's safe to say that we have to.

---

* Touche Ross has since been engaged to do accounting and consulting work for the joint venture, called the Beijing Jeep Corp. Although Touche opened a PRC office in March 1984, the engagement is coordinated through the firm's Detroit office, which handles the AMC account domestically.

There's an unwritten rule in China that you must prove your good faith, your genuine interest in helping the government achieve its goals. When you apply for a license to practice there, you're told, in so many words, the kind of gratis consulting you're expected to do. Practicing in this market demands an investment that is unlikely to be paid back for years."

Just how long the Big Eight are willing to wait to cash in on their China investment is astonishing.

"Twenty-five years—I thought it would take twenty-five years to be well established and earning substantial fees in China," says PW's Biegler. "I made that projection based on my initial impression of the country and its leaders. Subsequent experiences, however, have given me reason to be somewhat more optimistic.

"At the time of my first visit, China had just opened her doors to the West and government officials, even those in senior positions, weren't quite certain just which way the political winds would blow next. When they met with you it was always in large groups—officials apparently wanted the protection of numbers—and they seemed genuinely concerned that whatever statements they made, regardless of how innocuous, might come back to haunt them should China do an about-face on U.S. relations.

"But when I made my second trip in July 1981, remarkable changes had already occurred. In a televised interview between myself and Vice Premier Gu Mu, a highly intelligent, extremely impressive young leader, he made no bones about the PRC's intention to get down to business, and he was quite candid, admitting on camera that the government made serious mistakes in the first stage of modernization—mistakes that would not be repeated. Steel mills, for example, built without adequate planning simply did not work. With disasters of this sort very much on his mind, he declared his intention to commission feasibility studies for all future projects and to ask Price Waterhouse and other major accounting firms to take on the engagements.

"I considered this public embrace of sophisticated management techniques, coupled with an admission of past errors, as a very promising sign. Oh, I'm still convinced that it will be some time before we're generating substantial fees in China, but we're willing to make the investment because the market holds exceptional promise."

That may be an understatement. The promise of China is in its size, its virginity, and its strategic location. Let's take one at a time.

First, with government leaders eager to bring financial sophistication to China's domestic and international affairs, and with a concerted drive to educate a new class of financial professionals, the public sector will experience an enormous demand for tax, MAS, and accounting services. Add to this the fiscal requirements of a now infinitesimal but rapidly awakening private sector.

Writing in the *New York Times*, Jude Wanniski described this budding entrepreneurship. "In my first visit to China, last month [September 1983], to look at the economy, two things astonished me. I found an economic boom unfolding whose implications are exciting for the world and never once during nine days in Beijing or Shanghai did I feel I was in a Communist country. China is running, not walking, down the capitalist road. . . .

"The *China Daily*, a government-published English-language newspaper with an upbeat, free-enterprise flavor and Wall Street market news, reports that 70,000 private enterprises were registered in Shanghai alone last year—an individual is now permitted to hire up to eleven people.

"The boom is evident in the cities and the countryside. It's seen in the markets, with good produce plentiful, and in shops, bulging with consumer goods and apparel that put Moscow's finest department stores to shame. It's seen in the housing and building construction all about. Mostly, it's seen in the briskness of the people, freed from the ideological penitentiary that the Soviet people still occupy, free to exploit their own energies and abilities in exchange for commensurate rewards."*

"Most of China's purely domestic businesses will be serviced by indigenous public accounting firms," says George Betts. "The government is now encouraging the establishment of one substantial-sized Chinese public accounting firm in each major city. Although the rules say that the local Chinese businesses are to use these firms, foreign CPAs will not be excluded from participating in the work. We are now negotiating relationships for joint projects, for client referrals, and for other mutual opportunities."

Second, with only a handful of foreign accounting firms now active in China—all in the start-up phases—the market for multinational clients doing business in the PRC is enormous. Those CPA firms now sinking their roots into the Asian soil, wisely ingratiating themselves with the key ministries, are in a position to inherit the bulk of the work that will flow from the thousands of joint ventures likely to develop in the eighties and beyond. Once the transition is made from pro bono to fee-basis engagements, the same Big Eighters that are being bludgeoned by some domestic industries may find they can practice in a distant market free of cannibalistic lowballing and amenable to fair if not generous fees.

"We've structured quite a few joint ventures between U.S. corporations and Chinese entities," says the Lehman Brothers executive. "In each case, the U.S. corporation has had a Big Eight accounting firm audit the Chinese component. If not for legal reasons, this is mandatory for sound business manage-

---

* *New York Times,* October 25, 1983, page A35.

ment. Touche Ross and Peat, Marwick have done this work for deals we've been involved in.

"This market will be growing—and growing substantially. That's because the climate for doing business in China has improved substantially. That's due to both the formalizing of the foreign company tax laws and President Reagan's trip there. Look for a flurry of activity in China-U.S. trade."

Third, with Western-based multinationals eyeing China as a vast untapped market for oil and gas exploration, and for selling a broad range of products and services, thousands of corporations will join the relative handful currently doing business in the PRC.

"By year end 1983, more than thirty oil companies had signed exploration contracts with China's National Offshore Oil Corporation," McGregor notes. "And historically, where big oil goes, big finance and big industry follow suit. I'm talking about the major banks, the petroleum services outfits, and on and on in natural progression."

Because a growing number of multinationals now demand that accounting firms service their far-flung interests worldwide, those CPAs with offices in the PRC will hold an important edge in winning global engagements. Big Eighters lacking representation in this strategic market may, at some future date, be vulnerable to client switches.

Of more immediate importance—and promising a faster payback—is that corporate pioneers exploring the Chinese market will want to consult with the established experts (i.e., those CPA firms practicing in the PRC) before committing to joint ventures, and they'll need substantial tax and MAS services should they proceed. With this in mind, PW has showcased its position as an intermediary wired into Beijing's Ministry of Finance by hosting a series of high-level seminars introducing its domestic clients to ranking Chinese officials.

Referring to a June 1982 Houston seminar featuring China's

minister of finance, John Biegler advised clients frustrated by the Chinese bureaucracy to use PW as a hot line to Beijing.

"After the tax law was promulgated, a number of foreign companies with offices in Beijing submitted questions to the finance ministry through the American embassy. However, no replies have been received so far.

"Those companies can come to the seminar. If the commissioner of taxation doesn't have the answers, I don't know where you're going to get them." *

The subliminal message: The shortest distance between the United States and China is through Price Waterhouse. "We've made an investment there and we intend to make it pay off." †

PW has already started to cash in on its China connection, doing fee work for companies exploring the PRC market. But this trickle of dollars is likely to turn into a windfall as its major clients—Exxon, Shell, Chevron, and Schlumberger—become fully operational in the PRC.**

Although PW partners prefer to sidestep questions about Exxon, the firm's largest client, ‡ "granddaddy," as the oil behemoth is referred to at Price Waterhouse, never seems to be far from Connor's or, for that matter, Hammer's mind. One gets the feeling that were there no other reason than to satisfy Exxon, PW would open a China office. Considering that Exxon is widely viewed as among the most prestigious engagements in the audit world, PW, operating at a time when other long-standing client relationships have come unglued, is clearly not of a mind to alienate granddaddy.

* Frank Ching, *Asian Wall Street Journal,* June 4, 1982.

† Interestingly, PW has some answers Uncle Sam apparently wants to know. "One of those attending the seminar had a name tag reading only 'U.S. Government.' He said he was from the CIA." (*Houston Business Journal,* July 12, 1982.)

** In July 1984, PW opened its second China office in Guangzhou (Canton), local headquarters for many of the multinational oil companies.

‡ PW's executive offices are housed in the Exxon Building at 1251 Avenue of the Americas.

The Accounting Wars

The commitment to properly serve a major client, while commendable as a management policy, poses delicate questions when viewed in terms of PW's role as a consultant to China's tax ministry. The question is, Where do the firm's loyalties lie? Although Hammer's integrity is unquestioned—the man is a thorough professional with a genuine commitment to accounting's code of ethics—can any PW partners engaged in the PRC freely make recommendations that run counter to Exxon's interests? Can they be truly objective and independent sources of information in light of their interest in accommodating an industry group—oil and gas—that accounts for a substantial chunk of PW's fees? In consulting on tax issues, will they recommend provisions to benefit the PRC or the multinational corporations (PW clients) doing business there? Are the Chinese bureaucrats, intelligent as they may be, savvy to the unwritten demands of client/CPA relationships?*

PW's petroleum clients, which rank among the major catalysts in China's commercial revival, are party to a thicket of transactions that will test and define China's formative tax laws. Consider the following: On the issue of "consolidated earnings," will PW recommend a tax policy that prevents oil companies from using losses incurred at dry holes to offset the income from successful wells? Will it suggest a tax provision that jeopardizes Exxon's foreign tax credit in the U.S.?

Referring to the issue of offsetting income, Hammer says: "I banged hard on that one. I said, 'Look, this is obviously for the benefit of the American oil companies. But if you want them to come, it's as simple as that, you're going to have to make this a creditable tax for them. Or they're just not going to come. If you don't care, they'll go elsewhere.'

"Well, you know, of the thirty-odd companies that did get

---

*Exxon declines to comment on the financial implications of its China operations and refuses to discuss its relationship with Price Waterhouse.

offshore tracts, sixteen are American. So they obviously did want the American oil companies. They changed that law. It took them a while, took me two visits more to find out they changed it, but they changed it. They said, 'Okay, we'll let them offset, we think it's fair.' "

In a letter (dated August 19, 1981) to the vice commissioner of tax, Lin Rong-sheng, Hammer advised the Chinese: "If your intentions are to attract U.S. oil companies in addition to those from other countries, as I believe you indicated to be the case, the law and regulations should carefully avoid imposing any rule or restriction which would result in having the U.S. IRS challenge the creditability of the tax under the U.S. foreign tax credit provisions. In particular, I refer to the present thinking in the General Taxation Bureau to require separate taxability of oil and gas operations in each territory of the PRC, rather than a consolidation of all PRC oil and gas results. This would mean that losses in one operation could not offset profits from other operations, and would almost certainly result in an IRS challenge to the tax as a credit for oil companies (and perhaps, as a result, for all companies irrespective of the type of business activity). Accordingly, I would suggest that, in the final regulations, the consolidation approach be adopted."

In regard to "intracompany charges and expenses," is it always in China's best interest to allow a multinational to allocate part of its general and administrative expenses to the tiny PRC branch office, which may be little more than a room in the Peking Hotel? Certainly, arguing in favor of this allocation favors the multinationals.

Asked about the potential for conflicts of interest, Hammer, typically candid, swats the air as if a gnat were circling his face. "When I went up there the first time, I said, 'Look, I'm with Price Waterhouse. We're a profit-making firm. We represent a lot of industrial concerns, oil companies, among others. But I'm up here without an axe to grind for my clients. I wasn't sent by them, I'm not being paid by them. I'm here to help you get what I think is a sound tax law. It just so happens that many of the things I might say to you might seem to some degree of benefit to foreign companies.' "

Reluctant as some are to admit it, Big Eight chairmen relish international engagements not only for the fees and the prestige they bring, but also for the belief that they will distance their firms from the class action lawsuits, the front-page controversies, and the on-again, off-again threat of regulatory intervention that plagues the market in the United States. Certainly, the spectre of regulation is not taken lightly. Asked about his concerns for Arthur Andersen, managing partner Duane Kullberg said this in an interview with *International Accounting Bulletin:* "The regulatory atmosphere is our primary concern—particularly in the U.S. The oversight of the accounting profession rises and falls from time to time. Ten years ago there was a congressional investigation of the profession: it might come again. . . ."

To think, as some may, that foreign practice diminishes this threat is an illusion. Global expansion compounds the perils of high-visibility public practice by complicating the efforts to establish and implement uniform quality controls. The broader an accounting firm's sweep of practice, both in scope and geography, the greater the challenge to ensure that the Price Waterhouse, the Ernst & Whinney, or the Peat, Marwick signature meets the same standards wherever it is applied. The risk of disaster—or simply of performing inferior work—multiplies as the firm transgresses a wider multitude of national borders, cultures, currencies, languages, and local perceptions of what profit, tax, and accountability really mean. This is most graphically demonstrated in the mystical, mysterious world of the People's Republic of China, but the very fact that the major firms have identified multinational expansion as a strategic objective raises the potential for grave problems—as well as seductive opportunities—in as many nations as there are members of the U.N.

4
Bulls, Bears, and CPAs

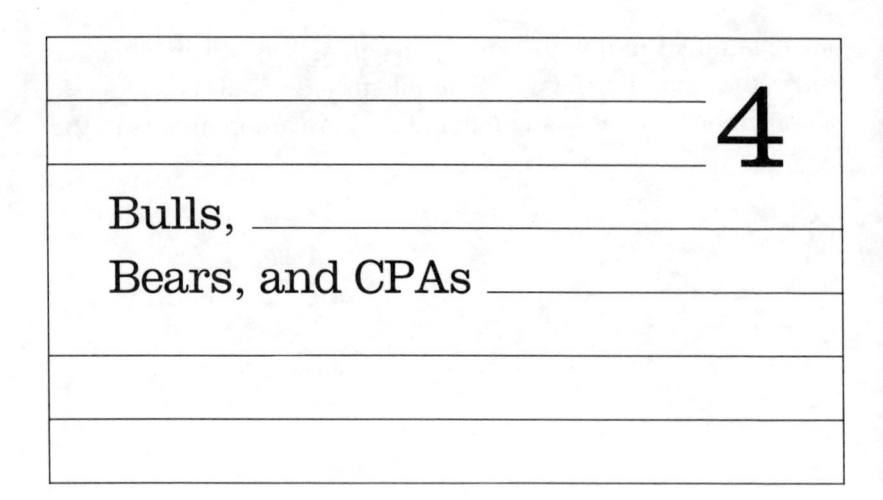

Tom Presby, Touche Ross's New York regional partner, squints against the brilliant sunshine that angles through the big picture windows of his nearly airborne office ninety-three floors above Manhattan's financial community in the World Trade Center. Fidgeting with a blue silk tie that lies slightly off-center on his crisply starched white shirt, the former London-based executive director of Touche Ross International reflects on his latest assignment—one with more parochial but perhaps more profitable horizons.

"Someone once said that people the world over think of two things when they think of the United States: Disneyland and Wall Street. While that may be an exaggeration, there's no denying that both are highly visible components of our culture. Although the former has little relevance for CPA firms, the latter, as a symbol of the financial community, is directly related to our profession. It is also a unique and particularly promising chunk of geography for accountants. It's here that we plan to accomplish something no other CPA firm has ever attempted."

The "something" is Touche Ross's gamble to establish itself as the premier *financial consulting firm* at the epicenter of capitalism. While many of TR's competitors have turned their attention overseas,* the firm that has been TKO'd from the worldwide Big Eight (still number eight domestically) has launched its most aggressive assault on a market less than three miles from its executive offices.

This contrarian strategy, typical of major league accounting's least predictable player, is based on nothing more exotic than traditional market research. When Touche's senior partners set out to uncover new practice opportunities and to position the firm for accelerated growth, Wall Street suddenly loomed as a tempting market within a market.

The fiscal twilight zone at the southern tip of Manhattan Island, now widely recognized as the world financial center and in some ways every bit as surreal as Disneyland, is home to a solid-gold menagerie of brokerage firms, banks, insurance carriers, investment banking houses, and stock exchanges that conduct—through securities sales, swaps, private placements, venture financings, leveraged buyouts, loans, and syndications—a lopsided percentage of the nation's major financial transactions. The venerable names on the oak-paneled boardrooms—Lehman Brothers, Morgan Stanley, Goldman Sachs—are, by way of their position as capital conduits, extraordinarily profitable. While observers now rank the United States as second, third, or worse in a growing string of industries it once dominated, the U.S., more specifically Wall Street, has emerged as the undisputed center of international finance.

But Wall Street's appeal for accounting firms knee-deep in stagnant industries extends beyond its income statement to a

---

* Not that Touche is without wanderlust. It too has opened an office in the People's Republic of China.

refreshing business psychology free of the petty fee-chiseling that sours CPA-client relationships throughout the *Fortune* 1,000.

"Wall Street," says Presby, his eyes scanning the downtown skyline partially shrouded by a dense, midafternoon haze, "is the world's greatest meritocracy. Perform well here and you get paid well. Nothing in business is supposed to be that simple, but in this case it is—I assure you it is.

"You have to understand, this little corner of the world has a singular preoccupation with making money, and they do it by the shovelful—the goddamn steamshovelful. Most important, they believe in using money to make money, and that philosophy extends to their relationships with accountants and other financial advisers. Succinctly stated, they demand superior work and they're accustomed to paying premium fees to get it.

"On Wall Street, accountants are judged by the same standards as bond traders: Are you contributing to the seven-day-a-week, twenty-four-hour-a-day crusade to make money? If you're judged to be meeting that acid test, no one blinks at your invoice. Our fees on the Street are higher than for any other Touche Ross office, but I've yet to hear the first client complain. Accountants think they're bottom line–oriented, and that may be true, but on Wall Street no one thinks of anything else. Ever."

Wall Street's appeal as an accounting market extends beyond its liberal view of professional fees to a fortuitous mix of service requirements geared primarily to consulting and taxes. At a time when the Big Eight are coming to view competitively bid audits as loss-leaders tolerated principally as entrées to more lucrative work, clients who share a preference for consultative services, who view the audit as little more than a by-product of a comprehensive professional relationship, are to be worshiped.

"Historically, new accounting offices opened their doors to do audit work and then glued on tax and consulting engagements as the practice expanded," Presby says. "But here on Wall Street we've flip-flopped that cycle, starting out in life as a full-service accounting firm that happens to do audits."

Just why Touche took this route, and how it came to its multimillion-dollar beachhead in lower Manhattan, can be attributed to the firm's timely inheritance, in 1982, of two major financial services clients—Dean Witter and Bache—and the election, in the same year, of TR's new management troika, managing partner David Moxley, chairman Grant Gregory, and the ghost of the man who ran the firm for ten years, Russell Palmer.

When Palmer was forced to step down in compliance with Touche's ten-year limit on the managing partner's term of office —a rule Palmer, then only age forty-seven, seriously considered challenging—the partnership felt rudderless after a decade of strong and dynamic leadership. A colorful and ebullient man whose Hollywood good looks and cocky salesmanship challenged the stereotype of the Bob Cratchit CPA, Palmer had led Touche to a 200 percent increase in annual fees. To replace him, TR's partners elected two of the firm's best and brightest: David Moxley, a fifty-two-year-old, twenty-five-year Touche Ross veteran would serve as chief administrative officer; Grant Gregory, age forty-three, with the firm twenty-one years, would focus on practice development. The awkward arrangement, described by TR's PR staff as a "balanced management team," is nothing more than an old-fashioned division of duties. Put simply, Gregory's job is to bring home the bacon, Moxley's is to fry it.

In many ways, Gregory is Palmer redux. Handsome, gregarious, he is just as much the dynamic charm 'em and disarm 'em business-getter as his illustrious predecessor. A former auditor,

The Accounting Wars

turned tax man, turned partner in charge (of the Omaha office), turned executive office marketing whiz, he plays the role of a Big Eight chairman to the hilt.

His office, big enough to house a small accounting firm or two, has to be among the most sumptuous digs in corporate America. Ankle-deep carpeting sweeps through what is essentially an oversized salon—richly appointed with cushy sofas and thickly padded club chairs—leading to a private dining room reserved for quiet lunches with distinguished guests (read: heavy-hitter clients). Clearly, these are offices designed for entertaining—the messy matters of cash-flow projections, LIFO elections, feasibility studies, and audit opinions to be conducted in less auspicious environs.

Comfortably ensconced in this regal setting as if he were born to it, Gregory greets a visitor with the graceful aplomb of the ambassador to the Court of St. James's. Resplendent in hand-pinned navy chalk-stripe suit, white shirt, red-and-blue silk tie, and sassy gold Rolex, he dominates the expansive office much as a Steinway grand dominates a concert hall. But his commanding presence, though it may work miracles with clients, does not always win popularity contests. It is a paradox of Big Eight accounting that a man's success can often be measured by the number and intensity of his detractors. In Gregory's case, the critics paint a decidedly unflattering portrait of a superficial pretty boy whose cosmetics carried him to the chairman's post. Says a former Touche Ross partner now with Main Hurdman: "Grant Gregory? Oh, you mean Robert Redford. I swear, I think he auditioned for the job."

But the portrait is inaccurate. Precisely because Gregory is handsome and fluent in the social graces many accountants sorely lack, some may write him off as a dumb blond in a business suit. The truth is that Gregory is a shrewd marketer and an innovative thinker. Although he may never qualify as a quoted authority on generally accepted accounting principles, it must be said that technical wizards are a dime a dozen. Some of the best minds in the Big Eight never make partner.

"It would be easy to take pot shots at Gregory, but that's a self-indulgence I'm not about to afford myself," says the vice chairman of a Touche Ross competitor. "I think it's more important and far more productive to spend my time defending against him. This guy knows precisely what he wants and exactly how he intends to get it. I'm not turning my back on Gregory, neither am I taking him lightly. That, I'm afraid, would be a mistake."

Adds a Touche Ross tax partner whose early skepticism of "Broadway Grant" has given way to grudging respect: "When Gregory first took his place at the top, the internal rumor mill pegged him as indecisive. It just seemed as if decisions weren't being made on any number of issues critical to the firm's operations. But the problem lasted for only a couple of months and the consensus now is that it had more to do with the dynamics of two co-equals settling into a working relationship than with timidity on anyone's part. Be that the case or not, Gregory doesn't seem to have trouble making decisions anymore."

The truth is that Gregory's theories and projections—all of which are developed from a marketer's perspective—figure prominently in Touche Ross's strategic plan and are interesting from the wider perspective as a view of where the accounting profession may be headed. Central to this is a conviction that American business is undergoing fundamental change— change that will shake the multinationals to their vortices, creating a flurry of disruption, and, as a by-product, opportunity for the accounting profession.

"I'm convinced that the business community is now experiencing conditions that are as dramatic, or traumatic, if you will, as those it faced in 1929," Gregory says. "Why? Because so many of the variables management used to be able to predict with some semblance of accuracy are now relatively unpredict-

The Accounting Wars

able. Take interest rates, economic cycles, and technology. While these factors were always subject to change, the changes occurred gradually, in most cases over the space of many years. But now interest rates can turn 180 degrees in less than a year and high-tech products can become obsolete soon after they hit the market.

"For example, a heavy industrial product typical of the prewar era, the Jeep, was introduced in 1939, and though it's undergone some changes and improvements since, the darn thing still looks and acts basically the same as the first one that rolled off the assembly line nearly a half century ago. Compare this to microcomputer life cycles. Units heralded as state-of-the-art wonders, that seem capable of capturing enormous market share, are knocked out of the box in a matter of months by a competitor's counterpunch.

"The fundamental question is, Why are some companies more successful than others at creating, and adjusting to, change? The answer demands a historical perspective: As it took shape in the late nineteenth and early twentieth centuries, America's industrial sector was organized in a hierarchical or pyramidal fashion, much like that of our churches and military. Translated to the corporate form, this setup provided for a large mass of employees, at the base of the pyramid, assigned to menial, repetitive tasks like welding fenders on Chevies. One every six minutes. The worker had absolutely no customer contact, no comprehension of the marketplace.

"In this type of capital-intensive smokestack industry, management expanded the company by obtaining more money for physical and human resources. The premise was simple: Shovel more capital into the furnace and more products will come out the other end. Management believed, and often correctly so, that if it could raise twice as much money it could generate twice as much sales.

"But with the emergence of the high-tech era, the rules

changed dramatically. The market was driven by creative people, who, rather than being buried in the bowels of a business, were given access to the marketplace. In a microcomputer company, or for that matter a financial services firm like Touche Ross, growth and profitability are a function of the employees' understanding of the market and of their ability to design successful products for it. The formula for success is no longer as simple as turning twice as much money into twice as much sales. Capital alone won't do it. Instead, enlightened management recognizes that it needs twice as many talented, creative people. Blessed with this resource it can expand the business not twice but fourfold."

It is in this restructuring—this urgent drive to meet the demands of a changing marketplace and a changing society—that Gregory sees the most promising market for accounting services.

"Where government rules and regulations, primarily in the form of audits and evolving tax obligations, once produced most of the CPA's work, spontaneous factors now generate a growing percentage of our engagements. In thousands of companies, from the *Fortune* 500 to small privately held ventures, management is repositioning itself, redefining its mission, revising its market strategies. It is asking questions: In light of increasing competition, should we abandon brick-and-mortar operations and turn to services? How can we prepare for unpredictable yet substantial changes in the cost of money, in technology, in competition? And in many cases that same management is asking accounting firms to provide the answers.

"Well, to reflect these concerns, to respond to them, I believe that accounting firms must also evolve from predominantly hierarchical pyramidal organizations defining themselves in terms of the audit function to increasingly market-responsive organizations active primarily in consultative work. Specifically, we need more creative, talented people capable of joining forces with the client to determine his needs and to design services to fulfill them. Essentially, the most significant opportunity for accounting as a profession is in our ability to work with clients advising them on prospective transactions rather than simply attesting to the accurate presentation of historical transactions. In a nutshell, we'll be lighting the future rather than just analyzing the past. That fundamental change, that enormous opportunity, will benefit only those accounting firms willing to make substantive changes in their practices."

Gregory's view of the future led Touche to turn a lucky run of client gains into one of the major commitments in the firm's history. When two megamergers of the early eighties—Prudential Insurance Company's acquisition of Bache Halsey Stuart Shields and Sears Roebuck's ingestion of Dean Witter Reynolds —added the Wall Street giants to its client list, Touche found itself an overnight factor in the securities industry audit market.

"Mergers and acquisitions can be disastrous for accounting firms," Tom Presby says. "You go to sleep one night with a profitable and professionally rewarding client relationship only to find that a deal struck by someone, somewhere, in the wee hours has snatched that client out from under you and into the clutches of another parent company, another auditor.

"But with the Bache and Witter acquisitions the dice rolled in our favor. Not only because our clients—Sears and Prudential—did the acquiring, but because they insisted that the brokerage firms retain Touche Ross as their auditors."

Says Milan Johnson, Prudential's chief internal auditor: "We wanted Touche to expand its responsibilities to Bache for several reasons. First, Touche had been auditing Prudential since 1969, when it acquired a local Newark-based CPA firm, Puder & Puder, that had been our auditor previously. We were pleased with the calibre of Touche's services and had every reason to believe we could expect this on the Bache engagement as well. Second, we believe that having a single auditor responsible for all of our operations facilitates reporting to top management, as well as to the board of directors, and fosters a better working relationship with the internal auditors."

Another factor figured into Prudential's decision. Because TR did not have a vested interest in Bache's financial reporting mechanism or its system of internal controls, Pru's management believed it could deliver a fresh and objective appraisal of the newly acquired subsidiary.

"Add it all together and we believed that replacing Arthur Andersen, Bache's former auditors, with Touche Ross would, and this is no reflection on Andersen, provide for a greater comfort level," Johnson adds.

For Touche, the quest for a uniform audit was particularly sweet because it delivered two deeply entrenched clients from Big Eight competitors, Deloitte Haskins & Sells (Witter) and Arthur Andersen (Bache), and because it gave Touche access to a burgeoning market—the securities industry—that was on the plus side of the economy's manufacturing-to-services transition. In terms of fees, the engagements were both in the million-dollar class for the audits alone—sums that could double or triple over the years with ancillary services.

But there were strings attached. Because Touche was new to Wall Street, the engagement would be closely monitored both by the accounting profession and by the securities industry. To complicate life in the fishbowl, the work would have to be performed under somewhat hostile conditions.

Bache and Witter were happily married to their existing auditors and had to be taken, by Prudential and Sears, kicking and screaming into the Touche camp. Precisely because an effective audit requires the client's cooperation, experienced audit partners are wary of accepting engagements where they find themselves persona non grata. In this case, the client's message, communicated without anyone having to write a memo on the subject, went like this: "Okay, Touche Ross, we're forced to work with you because that's the way headquarters wants it. But to be quite candid, we don't think you're up to the task. We'll let you proceed—we have no other choice—but we'll be scrutinizing your work like it's never been scrutinized before. Make just one major mistake, or confirm in some other way what we believe is your inexperience in the securities business, and we'll swarm all over you like a team of IRS agents descending on an abusive tax shelter."

The Wall Street community at large—probably the most hard-nosed in American business—was no more receptive to the newcomers than the lead skeptics, Bache and Witter. Before its timely inheritance, Touche's brokerage clients were limited to a collection of jerkwater (by Wall Street standards) firms, scattered throughout the Midwest. To the Street, which regards anything west of downtown Manhattan as bush league, Touche had yet to prove itself by the standards of Broad and Wall. Presby recognized this in a speech (April 26, 1984) to the Wall Street Planning Group, a local industry organization. "With few exceptions, we had no New York client base among the major banks or securities firms. We were certainly 'Mr. Outsider' in terms of the New York financial services industries."

The paradox of New York's financial community is that it is both competitive and fraternal. In an environment of secret deals and proprietary data, idle gossip on winners and losers travels quickly through the industry grapevine. Certainly, the CFOs at E. F. Hutton, Merrill Lynch, and Kidder Peabody would be sharing cocktail-hour opinions on TR's Wall Street performance.

Moxley and Gregory recognized that there was more to gain here than pleasing and retaining two prestigious and potentially profitable new clients. Were these the only objectives, the work could be farmed out of TR's New York practice office at 1633 Broadway. But because Touche's senior partners viewed the

Bache and Witter audits as beachheads to the financial community and ultimately as harbingers of a new era of consultative services, they were willing to make a financial commitment wildly out of proportion to the dual audits' projected return.

"There'd been talk around the firm for years about opening a Wall Street office and becoming a major presence there," Presby recalls. "After all, Touche, like most of the Big Eight, had started out downtown, only to join the wider corporate immigration to midtown years later. Still, like any business that has dozens of strategic objectives, I think this one would have stayed on the back burner for some time had the Bache and Witter engagements not come along; they served as the pinions on which to lever our entry into the market. Soon after the new clients were on board, Gregory and Moxley made the decision to launch a full-scale Wall Street office. By October of '82, the staff was in place, practicing from our new address."

But TR did more than open its eighty-fifth domestic office. It created the equivalent of a moderate-sized accounting firm specializing in services to the financial community. From the moment senior management flashed the green light, Touche embarked on a massive, firmwide effort to establish its newly created Financial Services Center as a model of the eighties consultative practice, as a blueprint for the CPA firm of the future, and as a power on Wall Street.

The first step was the appointment of a partner in charge, and on this account there are different versions of how Touche proceeded. The official version, as told by TR's managing partners, is that Presby was the unanimous choice, the only candidate considered for the job. His marketing skills, his high profile in the firm, and his dominating personality, they imply, made him ideal for the post.

But Touche's neighbor in the World Trade Center, Ed Lill, partner in charge of Deloitte Haskins & Sells's Wall Street practice, laughs that off as "just so much hogwash. Actually, Touche's people fell all over themselves trying to recruit one of our partners to run their office down here. The guy they wanted interviewed with all of the Touche honchos, up to and including Russ Palmer, who offered him what amounted to a blank check. Still he turned them down. Only then did Touche appoint one of its own to run the practice."

Regardless of his rank on the list of candidates, Presby does seem suited for the job.

A former marketing director and operating chief of Touche Ross International—responsible, in the latter post, primarily for overseas mergers and acquisitions—Presby seems to have the rare ability, in the manner of an Edwin Muskie or a George Shultz, to effectively balance his intense drive and ambition with a calm, almost fatherly countenance. This quality makes him instantly trusted and somehow as familiar as an old friend. An invaluable asset for an administrator bringing change to an established organization subdivided by personal fiefdoms, petty jealousies, and dotted lines of power and authority. To make the Financial Services Center a reality, Presby had to step all over the internal patchwork of egos and protectorates that run through big accounting firms without so antagonizing the partnership that it would work to sabotage the new offspring.

"He's the kind of guy who can get you to agree to do something that if anyone else asked you'd reject out of hand," says a Touche Ross partner who has watched, with considerable envy, Presby's rise up the management ladder. "I don't really know how he does it."

To bring his firm-within-a-firm up to speed, Presby was authorized to violate three policies previously considered sacrosanct at Touche Ross. First, he raided the firm's internal talent pool, recruiting some of the most valued managers and partners. Tax and MAS professionals experienced in brokerage and banking—suddenly hot properties at Touche—were offered promotions, bonuses, and salary increases to relocate to New York. Everyone, apparently, had their price. Presby, who for nearly half a year performed more like a corporate headhunter than an executive partner, successfully lured away personnel from TR's offices in Chicago, Minneapolis, Seattle, St. Louis, London, Montreal, Paris, as well as from Peat, Marwick, Andersen, and the Securities and Exchange Commission. His prized recruits must have felt like star centerfielders at the winter baseball meetings. To convince a thirty-year-old tax manager to give up the security and the unwritten promise of partnership at a Big Eight competitor, Presby arranged a breakfast meeting around a series of time-released perks he knew would bag the prospect before the croissants arrived. No sooner had the waitress brought the coffee than Presby went into action, placing a $15,000 check on the prospect's plate.

"Consider this a sign-up bonus," he said. "Commit to me now and it's yours,"

Struggling to keep his poker face, the CPA ran his finger across the zeroes. "Well, you know, I have to consider my long-term position with . . ."

Presby moved in for the kill.

"The $15,000's only a down payment. I'll also raise your salary by $20,000. And, although I can't promise it, I'll throw in a good likelihood of partnership within two years." That, as Presby would say, was "the clincher." The future TR staffer gently folded the check, slipped it into his wallet, and ordered more coffee.

The very success of the Wall Street practice hinged on these hardball recruiting tactics. Behind the scenes, Touche had assured Prudential's senior management that new faces would be brought in to shore up the firm's securities industry practice.

"Any concern we had about their lack of experience in the field was mitigated by the pledge to go out and hire people to fill out the ranks," says Milan Johnson. "The understanding was that they would go out and get the best—whatever that took."

Presby's second violation of the Touche rulebook came with the opening of a distinct and separate practice within the jurisdiction of a previously established office.

The firm's unwritten law held that new clients located within a clearly defined market area came under the auspices of the local partner in charge (PIC). This respect for territorial integrity minimized internal politics while simultaneously enhancing practice efficiency. Because Big Eight practice offices have always been run as semiautonomous entities, it was widely believed that the PIC had to retain responsibility for client opportunities in his market. This decentralization vested decision-making authority with those most familiar with the local market and gave the PIC the entrepreneurial stake that is essential to running an aggressive and profitable office.

But Presby insisted on violating territorial integrity, on opening a separate office a few subway stops from the New York headquarters. In part, this was to convince the financial community that the Financial Services Center was more than a satellite of a standard accounting practice. A clear show of autonomy, Presby believed, would add credibility to Touche's claim that it was introducing a truly innovative service to the Wall Street market. But another factor was likely at work here. At this stage of his career, after having served with distinction in national and international posts, Presby could not have relished the prospect of being second or third in command in a practice subdivision or of losing his straight-line access to the managing partners.

A measure of the esteem he carries in TR's boardroom is evidenced by his emergence as regional partner responsible for the entire New York, New Jersey, and Connecticut practice, including the Financial Services Center. Evidently, nothing would be allowed to compromise Presby's mission.

Referring to the establishment of the Financial Services Center, Presby told the Wall Street Planning Group that "it was clearly a 'slam-dunk' kind of approach and I am convinced that no consensus of partners could have ever been reached that would have given us the support and power to implement in the dramatic way we did. Too many oxen were gored. Too many feelings were hurt. Too much change was packed into a short period of time and in a short space to have ever been agreed upon by all the people affected. I believe that the slam-dunk approach is the only one that could have worked. . . ."

In shaping the Wall Street office, Presby violated yet another Touche Ross rule—common to the Big Eight—of creating generalist practices geared to serving the widest possible range of clients.

Under the traditional pattern, when TR opened an office to serve a major retail client's geographic expansion, it would seek to diversify from the retailing base by attracting clients in services, manufacturing, high technology, and the public sector, the theory being that a diversified client list reduces dependence on a single industry group, smoothes out cyclical patterns, and compounds practice opportunities. So, should a manufacturer come calling at a TR practice office dominated by retailers, the response goes something like this: "Welcome, manufacturers, you've come to the right place. We are accountants to some of the nation's leading manufacturing companies, including Chrysler. We would be pleased to provide you with audits, tax advice, and consulting."

Were Touche Ross successful in landing the client—providing it was a big enough chunk of business to warrant such an investment—management would make staff and partners experienced in manufacturing industries available to the practice office. But on Wall Street, the only acceptable clients are those capable of being serviced directly by the Financial Services Center. This "less is more" approach, specifically designed to reflect the brokers' and investment bankers' myopic view of the world, demands extraordinary discipline and forces Presby to adopt a policy that in any other part of the firm would be grounds for dismissal.

"Because our mission is both narrow and deep, we have to be prepared to do something that accounting firms generally don't do: reject new business," Presby says, sounding slightly uncomfortable with the impact of his own words. "That's right. If a manufacturer comes through the door we have to tell him that we can't service him here. Certainly we'll try our best to point him uptown and keep him in the Touche family, but we will not handle the engagement from this office—unless he's seeking to raise money on Wall Street."

From a dollars-and-cents perspective, Touche's commitment to the Financial Services Center is considerable. Office space, the most expensive of the firm's operation, runs to nearly $40 per square foot,* for a total of $1.5 million annually. Add to this computers, general office equipment, furnishings, personnel relocation, hiring bonuses, and marketing brochures for a one-time start-up expense of more than $10 million. Even for the Big Eight, which have a habit of throwing dollars at promising practice opportunities, this is a major investment. A mitigating factor, which management hopes will speed the payback period, is the high concentration of partners and managers (50 percent of the hundred-person staff) assigned to Wall Street. This raises hourly fees to more than twice the firm's national average. The pyramidal structure that characterizes most of the Big Eight is replaced by a partner-to-staff ratio more similar to that of a midsized corporate law firm.

In scope of practice, Presby's operation is a collage of ser-

---

* Compare this to the $18 per square foot TR pays for its Broadway executive offices.

vices (some copied from other firms) channeled through the following practice units:

Audit Group: Provides auditing services to an unimpressive list of financial services corporations, mostly the U.S. units of European multinationals. Although TR has added to its charter audit engagements, Bache and Witter, Presby has thus far failed to snare any of the big trophies—major American banks or securities firms—many of which are locked into long-term relationships with Deloitte Haskins & Sells, a Wall Street competitor Presby derides as old-world, old-school, and old-fashioned in its audit approach.

"In staffing up the Financial Services Center, I must have interviewed people from dozens of CPA firms, including all of the Big Eight," Presby says, "but you know, not even one of the Deloitte people interested me enough to make an offer. To a man, I found them stodgy, dated, and so hung up on the old concept of the numbers-cruncher CPA that they were totally incompatible with the new kind of practice we've introduced on Wall Street."

Harsh words for the generally diplomatic Mr. Presby. But his indictment of Deloitte must be viewed more as a marketing tactic attack than an objective appraisal. As a consummate marketer, Presby is aware that for new products (in this case, TR's Financial Services Center) to succeed, they must undermine confidence in the market leaders. DH&S, Presby's favorite target, has retained a Wall Street office for ninety years, keeping a downtown address even after the northward migration saw its executive offices relocated to midtown. A well-entrenched competitor for TR's audit group, DH&S's client list is laden with Wall Street lights headed by Merrill Lynch, Kidder Peabody, and, until the Sears merger, Dean Witter. Presby appears to take pleasure in knocking Deloitte, but one suspects he would love to have a bit of DH&S's prestige rub off on Touche.

Although DH&S's Ed Lill hotly contests Presby's claims to

The Accounting Wars

have rejected Deloitte staffers—"He nearly begged two of our managers to go with him,* promising them they'd make partner within a year"—there is no denying that the two Wall Street practices are built on widely divergent philosophies and operating styles. While Touche entered the market on the shoulders of two substantial audits, it has since focused primarily on tax and MAS, while Deloitte, with deep roots in Wall Street, remains heavily weighted toward audits (which account for 80 percent of its fees there). But forces shaping both the financial services community and the economy in general are moving the two competitors closer toward each other than either would like to admit. Deloitte, eager to shed its matronly image, is updating its securities industry practice, tying tax and MAS to the audit function in order to develop an integrated approach to client needs. The objective—established by an internal task force assigned to reposition the firm in the securities industry—is to bring the audit component down to 50 percent.

At the same time, Touche, eager to follow up on its inheritance of Bache and Witter, would clearly love to score direct hits on the DH&S audit clients. This bolstering of its audit group would enhance TR's reputation on the Street and would expand the base on which to build its consultative services.

Tax Consulting Group: Advises clients on the tax implications of mergers, acquisitions, securities sales, and financings and consults in the design of financial instruments and transactions. This is a fertile field. Because Wall Street is forever concocting creative strategies for raising money, financing ventures, and selling investments, its deals are often trial balloons, untested by either the courts or the IRS. To many clients, this is unacceptable. They want a professional review of the tax implications before proceeding. That's where the CPAs come in.

---

*Presby, who admits he subsequently hired the managers, says, "They were consultants, not auditors, and it's over audit styles that our firm and DH&S don't see eye to eye."

If multinational A seeks to dispose of subsidiary B through a leveraged buyout, with B using a sale/leaseback of offshore facilities to leverage the transaction, which entities will owe how much tax on what? Although the CPAs cannot speak for the IRS, they can provide informed opinions on the likely tax treatment. This allows the participants to cover their collective butts. It works this way: The CPAs sell their opinions to the investment bankers, who in turn pass them on to their corporate clients. Should anything go wrong, everyone has an out, including the accountants, who repeat that it was just "an opinion."

"If an investment banker comes up with a novel technique for off-balance sheet financing, he'll anticipate the corporate client's reluctance to adopt the technique until and unless he gets our opinion that it's a legitimate and viable procedure," says a Big Eight engagement partner for a major Wall Street brokerage firm. "I must admit that of those who read the opinion, few really understand the issues, or where we stand on them. Their only concern is to have something with our name on it to wave in front of their clients. Sometimes, it seems as if we're in the business of selling our letterhead. While that rubs me the wrong way, I've been at this game long enough, twenty-one years now, to recognize that it's a neat, clean, and quite lucrative billing opportunity. Because all of the work is done at the partner level, it's calculated at the highest hourly rate. And in one of the great paradoxes of the profession, these socko invoices are never questioned by clients. They'll dicker endlessly over a $40-per-hour charge for an audit junior, but never $250 for a senior tax partner.

"Yes, all things considered, I'll take as much of this deal/opinion business as I can get. Fortunately, there's always an abundance of it on the Street."

Management Consulting Group: The main vehicle for delivering Gregory's cherished consultative approach to the financial community, the MAS group offers general consulting with sub-

The Accounting Wars

disciplines in strategic planning, communications, and data processing. The mission is to orient brokerage and investment banking clients (traditionally seat-of-the-pants businesses focused primarily on breaking deals) to more formal management procedures, including long-range planning.

At first blush the opportunities appear to be enormous.

"Wall Street needs more help in managing its in-house communications and data processing systems than any other sector of American business," Presby gloats, delighted by the prospect of a zillion engagement hours. "Think about it. This is the only place where computers are no longer back-office support systems for selling and servicing products. Instead, they *are* the product.

"Take the cash-management accounts introduced by the brokerage houses. Boil these personal financial services down to their basic components and you find little more than computers and series of monthly printouts. Customers have virtually no contact with human staff—the success, or failure, of the services hinges on the performance of the computer systems. Wall Street's dependence on computers, already well documented, will grow over the years, and we intend to help our clients manage that growth.

"Related to this, we see extraordinary opportunities in strategic planning. For the first time, the financial services industry is starting to look beyond the next deal to a place somewhere down the road, be it five years, ten, or more. They're asking: Who am I, where am I going, what am I doing? Much of this introspection, this concern for the future, stems from the curtailment of government regulation. For years, Washington's regulatory efforts effectively exempted certain components of the financial community from Mother Nature. The banks, for example, had a nice little compartmentalized monopoly until deregulation came along, rewriting all the rules and allowing everyone to compete with everyone else. Now, with hungry competitors on their turf, the banks are forced to engage in what I call strategic planning with a capital S. The kind that says, Gee, it's possible I might not be here in five years. Because they're now governed by the rules of the jungle rather than the rules of Uncle Sam, they're taking capital S strategic planning very seriously."

This, Presby believes, will deliver clients to his door. But the blind spot in his scenario is that the financial services industry, like the stock market itself, is subject to wide cyclical swings that routinely turn the most cautious bears into aggressive bulls and then back to hibernation. These mercurial swings affect brokerage executives much as they do the investing public. When record trading volumes generate a tidal wave of commissions and an alarming increase in clerical, administrative, and accounting work, the firms, caught up in the euphoria of the moment, spend heavily on new computer systems, programs, and consultants. But the Street's on-again, off-again march toward sophisticated systems and procedures is routinely interrupted when the Dow drives southward, taking investor enthusiasm and trading volume with it.

"The crazy thing about this market is that when Wall Street gets into trouble, when it needs advisers most, it circles the wagons and tries to solve its problems from within," says the executive vice president of a small consulting firm now competing with the Big Eight for Wall Street engagements. "The egos here are so enormous, owing primarily to the fact that everyone makes so much money, they think they can wriggle out of any predicament by 'toughing it out' until the next big deal comes along. That's nonsense, but you can't tell them that. They have to learn it themselves—and believe me, many do. A goodly number of the enormous egos I've met on Wall Street, the tremendous earners who'd made a habit of $100-a-day Lutèce lunches, are now driving cabs. The problem is that once they learn their lesson it's too late. They're no longer in a position to hire you."

The Accounting Wars

Financial Advisory Services: Another component of Touche's Wall Street practice, this is a thinly disguised escort service. The premise is to use TR's strategic position in the financial community as leverage for representing clients seeking access to the capital markets.

The program has Presby's name written all over it. Similar to a program, introduced during his stint as U.S. marketing director, whereby multinational corporations making acquisitions in the United States were fed into a grid of TR's domestic services, financial advisory reflects the marketer's concern for creating an integrated practice and for treating all of the firm's assets as profit centers. TR includes among its financial advisory services: locating merger and acquisition partners; preparing business and financing plans; providing balance-sheet advice; conducting business valuations; and supplying introductions to the financial community.

Reorganization Advisory Services: Essentially a bankruptcy unit, RAS differs from the balance of TR's financial services practice in that it seeks to profit from the decline of heavy industry rather than the rise of the service sector. Reorganization advisory fits into the Wall Street scheme of things because of its proximity to the money-center banks, the Chase Manhattans and the Chemicals, that as major creditors can prop up or pull the plug on troubled companies. Services include:

Turnaround strategies for bankruptcy candidates,
Structuring of Chapter XI bankruptcies to give troubled companies a second life,
Representing parties at interest in bankrupt companies.

Clearly, this multidiscipline practice, a burgeoning service throughout the Big Eight, is a conscious attempt to play both sides of the street. Rather than bemoaning the decline of the Eisenhowers, the firms expand their practice webs not only to trap the fast-track service and high-tech industries but also to profit from the decline of the smokestacks. By helping to structure the former and disassemble the latter, they profit from success and failure.

Regulatory Consulting: Another offshoot of TR's financial services practice, regulatory consulting focuses not on clients' primary business activities but instead on the legal framework in which they operate. Even in a period of deregulation, banks, brokers, and insurers are subject to a changing patchwork of rules and guidelines established by national, state, and local regulatory agencies. The service includes:

Dealings with regulators and exchanges,
Interpretations of rules and regulations,
Determining the impact of regulations on new activities,
Tracking new regulatory activities,
Designing new regulatory systems for exchanges and regulators.

The latter—reminiscent of Price Waterhouse's China venture—illustrates just how effectively the Big Eight, with a bit of ingenuity, can create work for themselves. By first designing a complex system (be it for a foreign tax ministry or a domestic stock exchange) and then offering themselves as experts on it, they are in position to collect fees from those who govern the system and those who must use it. In the process, they become viewed as well-connected professionals whose advice and counsel are invaluable.

This kind of thinking led Touche to build its regulatory practice around two prized captives of the World Trade Center talent raids. Presby's recounting of how the men came on board is illustrative of his quick-strike tactics and his wide-angle view of the accounting profession.

"When I was recruiting personnel for the Financial Services Center, people I knew and trusted on Wall Street kept telling me that above all else I had to appoint partners who could deal with John Manley and Nelson Kibler, then senior officials with the Commodity Futures Trading Commission (CFTC) and the Securities and Exchange Commission respectively. The consensus was that these men were among the best informed and most influential regulators at the CFTC and the SEC and that we could benefit by having good relations with them.

"But I took it a step further. If they're so damned good, I thought, why don't we go out and get Manley and Kibler themselves? And that's exactly what I set out to do. Although they had routinely declined recruitment pitches by a host of private firms, my solicitation, coming at a time when the Reagan administration's policies were demoralizing many regulators, hit pay dirt. Both men agreed to join Touche Ross as partners. I was delighted because this assured our clients of incomparable counsel on regulatory matters."

Perhaps. But the practice, widespread throughout the Big Eight, of hiring well-placed government officials, doubling their salaries, and making them instant partners is flawed. Once the insider makes the transition from the public to private sector, he is a *former* insider, removed from his official position, its power and influence. The claim that the instant partner has something equally precious—direct access to a network of old school ties—is arguable. In many cases, these friendships cease the moment the former bureaucrat "sells out." Those still on the government payroll are often resentful and, gripped with self-righteousness, eager to build barriers of independence between themselves and their former colleagues. Whether the once-powerful officials are thwarted by these barriers, or can deftly surmount them, may not be as important to the Big Eight marketers as the fact that their presence on staff bolsters the firm's image with clients.

Bulls, Bears, and CPAs

In establishing its Wall Street practice, Touche Ross tried simultaneously to flaunt and conceal its accounting credentials. Yes, it is a CPA firm, but no, it does not want to appear as the stereotypical guys with the green eyeshades. Determined as they are to secure a place in the financial services industry, Gregory, Moxley, Presby, and company are making every effort to blend into the woodwork by imitating their clients' traditions and work habits. This extends from the construction of a private dining room in the World Trade Center office ("On Wall Street," Presby says, "you need a luncheon setting where deals can be discussed in confidence") to the creation of a telephone hot-line service that makes a coterie of senior Touche partners available for client calls seven days a week, twenty-four hours a day.

"In a sense, Wall Street never sleeps," explains hot-line partner Bob Kaye, Touche's technical guru and chairman of the firm's Professional Standards Committee. "Hostile takeovers, acquisitions, or major financing agreements can be structured anywhere in the world at any time of day or night. As such, our investment banking clients may need answers to tax or accounting issues on a Sunday afternoon or a Tuesday at three A.M. Because they are available around the clock, so must we. That's why clients have my home telephone number and the green light to call without regard to normal business hours."

Kaye is the kind of technical wizard CPA firms love to have on staff as walking, talking data banks but who are generally shielded from client contact because their interpersonal skills are not likely to win sales contests. The hot line is ideal because it allows the firm to market his considerable wisdom without revealing his rather lackluster appearance to image-conscious clients.

Hot-line issues—which focus on leveraged buyouts, mergers, acquisitions, and instrument design—tend to be complex, heavily weighted toward the consultative orientation Gregory is pushing for.

The Accounting Wars

"A typical case," Kaye explains, "involved a privately held company—represented by one of our investment banking clients—that was interested in acquiring another business through a pooling of interests rather than an outright purchase. According to the client's plan, this would be followed immediately by a public offering of the newly consolidated entity, thus allowing the principals of both firms to sell their shares.

"To make all of this possible, the acquiring company would have to comply with certain timing rules. SEC regulations, for example, require thirty days' combined published results before the stock can be sold. This is done to keep the acquired company's shareholders at risk for some period of time, otherwise the SEC views the transaction as a cash deal rather than a pooling of interests.

"The client question, posed to us through the investment bankers, was how soon they could go public without jeopardizing the desired pooling treatment. They wanted to know when they should file with the SEC for a public offering and when the offering would be declared effective.

"Based on their projected September 1 acquisition date, and knowing that their fiscal quarter ended September 30, we advised that they could file in September for an October effective date, providing they submitted a registration amendment reporting the thirty-day combined results.

"In another hot-line case, the client wanted to set up a preferred dividend strip in a separate publicly held vehicle for corporate investments. The amount of the dividend that would be declared and received on the preferred shares would go into a trust for the corporate investors. Obviously, they were looking to get the 85 percent dividends-received deduction, which is available when one domestic corporation invests in another.

"The question pertained to the projected balance-sheet impact on the corporation whose preferred stock was used to create the strip. How would the deal affect the treatment of the preferred stock? Would its value be reduced?

"The corporation would have to part with the stock as collateral for a period of five years, during which time it would be placed with a trustee. There was a hope, on the client's part, that Touche Ross would look at the preferred dividend strip as having no cost basis to the seller. In other words, all those dividends would come in—they'd get $50 million or whatever the figure was—and this would go straight into income.

"But we nixed that. Even though preferred dividends aren't an asset until declared, the preferred stock trades on the basis of anticipated dividends, so you've diminished the value of your principal, if nothing else. Based on this, we advised that they would have to apply a cost against this. Clearly, this threw a wrench in the works. The numbers just didn't add up and so the deal never saw the light of day. Bad news, yes, but more important is that the client learned what it could and could not do before committing to a major transaction."

Fees for the hot-line counsel are steep, ranging up to $350 per hour, but Presby claims it's a bargain. "Bob Kaye's the number-one accountant at Touche Ross and our other hot-line guys are also very senior people. When you're doing a deal, you can't put a price tag on the kind of advice they can provide."

To protect against unauthorized use of the hot line, clients provide Kaye and company with a list of approved "askers." When a Lehman Brothers partner (Touche advises Lehman on instrument design) taps into the hot line, for example, his name is first checked against the approved list to determine eligibility. If this checks out, Kaye starts his meter running, and billable time is charged to the caller's name or I.D. number. At close to $6 a minute, fees mount quickly, but clients, while they may contest Presby's notion that the service is "a bargain," rarely, if ever, nickel-and-dime hot-line invoices. Further evidence that partner-weighted consultative work, as opposed to audits top-heavy with junior staffers, is less vulnerable to loss-leader treatment.

"I know that a number of our corporate finance people use the hot line," says Al Hogan, Bache's chief administrative officer. "They'll dial up one of the Touche guys when a client needs a fast answer to an accounting-type issue. It appears to work pretty well."

For all the fanfare attending its introduction, Touche's hot line is actually a knock-off of similar services first launched by its Big Eight competitors. While Presby concedes this, he insists that it's a knock-off with a difference.

"We may have borrowed the basic concept, but that's where the similarity ends. We've made a substantive change in how the hot line functions and how it services clients. Most important, we provide 'answers that stick.' Instead of having junior managers at the phone, as did our competition, we've built our service around our top people. Every Big Eight firm has a Bob Kaye, but the all-important distinction is that theirs are locked away in the executive offices, buried up to their eyeballs in technical reports and committee meetings. Our Bob Kaye is on the hot line, fielding questions, making himself valuable in the real world. This is of enormous benefit to our clients. When an investment banker calls for a reading on a tax or accounting issue, our hot-line partners can offer an opinion: that binds Touche Ross to it. They can, as we say, 'commit the firm.' That's what's meant by answers that stick. A junior can't do that—not without checking with a dozen superiors. Once you introduce an elaborate approval process, you void the benefits a quick response hot line is designed to produce."

Presby omits an important caveat: The hot line is quick to respond only if the answer is readily available, and while the information may "stick," it is not guaranteed. Some claim that in trying to respond quickly, Touche has made some major errors.

"There've been a number of blunders with the hot line," says a partner with the midsize CPA firm of Oppenheim, Appel, Dixon. "You can't make snap decisions on the complex transactions they're reviewing. They've been embarrassed for it on several occasions."

A Wall Street force since the 1950s, Oppenheim includes among its clients Bear Stearns, Gruntal, and Drexel, Burnham. That's why the OAD partner's assessment of Touche as a major competitor—in spite of the alleged hot-line lapses—may be the best indication of Touche's early success on Wall Street.

"Andersen, Coopers, and Touche are our biggest competitors on the Street," he says. "Touche is making inroads because they are very aggressive—cold calling prospective clients and the like. Those are things we don't do, and I hope that never changes."

The thinly disguised potshot reveals a lingering insecurity at OAD resulting from the agonizing loss of its premier audit client, Salomon Brothers, in the early 1970s. Although Salomon was reportedly content with OAD, many of its European clients were unfamiliar with Oppenheim and preferred that financial statements carry a Big Eight name. Struggle as they did to keep the audit, the engagement went to Andersen.

"They probably won't admit it but the Oppenheim boys worry about Big Eight presence on the Street, especially because of the strength they can offer clients internationally," says one Wall Street attorney active in corporate financings. "Oppenheim is recognized as being very street smart—probably more so than any other firm down here—but competition is competition and they're keeping an eye out."

The Accounting Wars

Touche Ross is not the only Big Eighter masquerading in Wall Street garb. Price Waterhouse's lust for China has not blinded the firm to opportunities west of the bamboo curtain. At the same time that Dick Hammer is hosting working lunches in Peking duck joints, some of his newest partners are setting up shop in the financial nerve centers of New York, London, Zurich, Paris, Hong Kong, and Toronto. Operating under the auspices of a newly created entity, Price Waterhouse & Partners, four former bankers are taking PW further from accounting and closer to investment banking than Presby's shop takes Touche Ross. Although the PW venture functions on a smaller scale than TR's—it has a staff of twelve and a capital commitment estimated at $1 million—it represents a more radical departure from the accounting firm's traditional services.

What then is Price Waterhouse & Partners? What services does it provide? What position does it occupy in the financial services spectrum?

Technically, PW & Partners is a joint venture between Price Waterhouse, the accounting firm, and the four bankers—Claude Hankes-Drielsma, Eugen Roesle, Alexander Vagliano, André George—that serve as its operating principals. While PW's publicity mill refers to the firm as an "international financial consultancy," it is closer to a quasi-investment banking house, one imbued with the CPA's brand of independence.

The brainchild of Claude Hankes-Drielsma—an elegantly attired Briton given to classic banker's pinstripes—Price Waterhouse & Partners was launched to fill what he perceived as a void in international capital markets:

"As a former investment banker, I recognized for some time that investment bankers and their clients are often at cross purposes. When the client seeks to raise capital, the plan the banker presents to him may be most profitable to the banker but not necessarily most effective for the company.

"Precisely because the investment banker is compensated

for his efforts on the basis of commissions, and because different capital-raising strategies produce commissions of varying magnitude, the banker is not an objective source of advice on how the client should best approach the capital markets."

Alexander Vagliano, former executive vice president of Morgan Guaranty's international banking division, now a partner in the PW joint venture, embellishes the point.

"Typically, the borrower stands alone in the capital markets. The system makes no provision for his needs or for objectively defining how to best fulfill his capital requirements. While a mechanism of this sort would always have been welcome, it is now a necessity. With the world banking system in a precarious position—owing primarily to financial crises in much of the Third World—the need for a source that can bring greater intelligence and sophistication to major borrowers is indisputable."

Convinced that he'd hit on a winning concept, Hankes-Drielsma broached the prospect of a joint venture with his friend and business associate Michael Coates, chairman of PW's London-based international unit. As outlined in the proposal, the plan called for assembling a group of leading bankers in key financial centers and joining them in 50-50 partnership with Price Waterhouse. The concept—clearly an idea whose time had come—meshed nicely with PW's strategic plan for limited diversification into a broader range of financial services. About a year after Hankes-Drielsma first proposed the idea in early 1982, PW & Partners was on-stream, operating from the accounting firm's offices in financial centers around the world.

PW's swift decision to underwrite the effort is further indication that once-tradition-minded CPA firms are now taking a loose constructionist view of the accountant's scope of services. For example, as a quasi-investment banking house, PW & Partners duplicates the services of a Lehman Brothers or a

The Accounting Wars

Goldman Sachs, minus the securities-marketing arm that Hankes-Drielsma claims is the source of client conflicts.

PW & Partners performs the following types of engagements:

> Evaluation of financial requirements for long- and short-term debt,
> Borrowing strategies,
> Pricing and timing of issues in the international capital markets,
> Development of financing alternatives,
> Overall debt management,
> Consulting on currency exposure,
> Monitoring short-term debt,
> Feasibility studies for major projects and their financing.

"Our role is purely advisory," Hankes-Drielsma says, his clipped British accent underlining the "purely." "For example, assume Exxon approaches us saying it wishes to borrow $1 billion. We will act as an independent and objective adviser both on the most effective method of financing and on the institution in the best position to conduct the transaction. Our engagement would commence not with an examination of the most profitable course of action for Price Waterhouse & Partners—which, I hasten to add, is standard procedure in the merchant banking community—but instead with a probing analysis of the client's needs and objectives. We would inquire of Exxon: What is the purpose of the financing? When are the funds needed? For how long are they needed? Are currencies a consideration? Should the financing be in U.S. dollars only? Do you have a yen exposure?

"With this information firmly in hand," the Briton continues, "we would develop a financing plan for presentation to investment bankers and capital sources in various nations, soliciting from them proposals for implementing the plans including fees, other cost factors, and their opinions on the appropriate instruments, maturities, and market conditions. These findings, consolidated in a master report including all available options and strategies, would be presented to Exxon's senior management, who, should they decide to proceed with the financing, would then hire an investment banking firm to implement it."

Clearly, PW & Partners seeks to thrust itself into the investment banking relationship, replacing the time-honored emphasis on trust and confidence in the banker's capabilities with a coldly analytical approach that is the CPA's trademark. The big question is whether corporate clients, many of whom have enduring relationships with their investment bankers, will buy the claim that the banker's capital-raising function creates a conflict of interest.

To succeed on a long-term basis, PW & Partners must convince the business community that there is indeed an inherent conflict in the investment banker's dual roles of adviser and marketer. But this is, at the very least, hypocritical. The accounting profession has always contended that a firm's integrity rather than its client relationships is the determining factor in conflict of interest issues. When Price Waterhouse is accused of jeopardizing its independence by performing lucrative tax and management-consulting engagements for audit clients, Chairman Connor et al. correctly retort that a reputable professional firm retains its integrity regardless of fee considerations.

Apparently, PW & Partners does not believe that the investment banking community can live by this same standard. But the truth is that the conflict issue is actually more germane as it applies to PW & Partners than to the investment bankers.

Consider this scenario: PW & Partners is hired to assist the government of Brazil in obtaining additional financing. If an examination of the available options points to a restructuring of Brazil's debt, would PW & Partners recommend actions contrary to the interests of Brazil's lead banks, even if these banks were among Price Waterhouse's audit clients? Or, considering the hypothetical Exxon financing engagement, is Price Waterhouse not at cross purposes with its audit and capital markets arms? Can it be truly objective when its audit includes a financing structure it helped to design and implement?

Tom Macy, a Price Waterhouse partner representing the accounting firm's interests in the investment banking joint venture, is acutely aware of the risk to PW's professional bearing.

"Perhaps Exxon is not a good example of the kind of client Price Waterhouse & Partners might serve. Because we do their audit work, we might be reluctant to take them on for capital-markets consulting."

A sincere man with an understated manner very much in the classic PW mold, Macy appears to be typical of the great body of conscientious, tradition-minded accountants now struggling to adapt to a changing profession. Clearly uncomfortable with Hankes-Drielsma's more aggressive plans for the fledgling joint venture—especially as they relate to servicing Price Waterhouse audit clients—he appears nevertheless to be keenly aware of the growing pressures to expand beyond the CPA's traditional scope of services.

Questioned further on the ethics of an Exxon, PW & Partners relationship, Macy fudges. "Are you saying that Exxon's status as a Price Waterhouse audit client necessarily disqualifies it from being a client of Price Waterhouse & Partners?" Macy is asked.

"Well . . . ah . . . not necessarily. We would have to evaluate the nature of proposed services. I cannot say with any certainty that we would accept the engagement, nor can I say we would decline it."

Why Price Waterhouse has chosen to wade through this sticky wicket of professional issues for a venture that appears incapable of contributing materially to the accounting firm's revenues is a bit of a puzzle. Little more than a consulting

Bulls, Bears, and CPAs

boutique, PW & Partners performed only five engagements in its first year of operations* and would be hard-pressed to generate fee income of more than a few million dollars a year. Although the participants are all tight-lipped about the firm's capitalization (Hankes-Drielsma responds to questions by saying "I'll be happy to answer that" and then sidesteps the query entirely), one gets the impression that PW bankrolled the operation and assumed all of its start-up costs. Price's willingness to make this commitment must be viewed more as an image-making exercise and a marketing tactic than as an attempt to create a significant profit center. The underlying premise is that financial consulting, much like the firm's international practice, can draw new clients into the PW web ("if you like our capital-markets expertise you'll love our tax services") and can offer existing clients a smorgasbord of financial services within the Price Waterhouse family. To underline this, the PW & Partners marketing brochure notes that the accounting firm offers "a wide range of services" complementary to those available from the joint venture, including:

Review of management controls and performance,
Business valuations,
Taxation planning and advice both nationally and internationally,
Structuring of new business ventures,
Financial planning and control,
Litigation support.

Precisely because the financial community is viewed as prime turf for practice expansion, the big CPA firms have decided to establish a presence there. Not as outsiders but as members of the family.

* Begun in May 1983.

The Accounting Wars

But try as they do to position themselves in this way, Touche, Price, et al. recognize the fundamental difference between CPAs and their banking/brokerage clients. While the former are compensated on an hourly basis, the latter earn transactional commissions based on a percentage of the business deals they structure. For this reason, there is often an enormous earnings gulf between the CPAs and the investment bankers. For example, should First Boston find a worthy merger partner for one of big oil's Seven Sisters, it may earn $25 million for its role as corporate marriage broker. This for a few months' work by a partner and a half-dozen associates. But the CPA firm hired to audit the consolidated entity resulting from the merger —a year-long engagement demanding the services of up to a thousand staffers—will earn $5 million for its efforts. Similarly, Price Waterhouse & Partners, whose fee schedule is similar to that of accounting firms, might earn $50,000 for recommending a financing strategy while the merchant bank marketing the instruments earns $5 million.

The disparity filters down to personal earnings, pitting a heavy-hitter engagement partner's $250,000 a year against a similarly placed investment banking partner's $1 million-plus. CPAs familiar with this earnings curve find it hard to accept that the investment banker's year-end bonuses can be triple their own annual compensation. Quickly they learn the difference between hourly and transactional businesses and quickly they learn to resent it. But while this disparity in their respective earnings irritates the CPAs, especially because many believe themselves to be smarter and better-educated than their banking/brokerage clients, they are unwilling to cross the DMZ that separates the professions from the laissez-faire marketplace. Much as they may covet Wall Street's handsome paychecks, they are inclined to retain the professional designation that provides virtual assurance of a steady and respectable income through recessions, depressions, black Thursdays, and assorted economic crises. The bent of personality that leads one to a career in public accounting generally keeps the same cautious individual from engaging in dicier pursuits.

"Yes, the boys on the Street make big money, enough to fill Bekins trucks, but that's this year and next," says one Big Eight partner active with Wall Street clients. "What they can't tell you is how they'll do in 1986, and they don't have an inkling of what tidings 1990 will bring. If the deals don't come together, if the stocks don't sell, they don't make money.

"Well, as much as I'd like to triple my earnings—who wouldn't?—I'm more interested in knowing I can cover my mortgage for as long as I want a roof over my head. Life has imponderables galore. I don't want to add to the list of unknowns by playing Russian roulette with my income.

"Accounting, though it may not produce millionaires, is a nice, clean, lucrative profession. They say you can't have your cake and eat it too, but I don't think that's true. Accounting gives you both—you just can't be a pig about it."

5

The Great American Tax Shelter: Where "the Name" Is the Name of the Game

But just where does aggressive professionalism end and plain old gluttony begin? At what point can it be said that the CPA is looking not only to eat his cake, but the plate and silverware too? Tax shelter engagements may qualify for this dubious distinction. Another hotly contested frontier for partner-weighted, consultative engagements, the tax shelter market is, in a sense, a professional minefield that tests the accountant's discipline, ethics, morality, reliability, and honesty.

In a sense, the CPA in tax shelter practice shares the unhappy fate of his clients: Even the most ingenious shelters are, at best, deferrals, destined to haunt the taxpayer, and in many cases his accountant, years after the fees have been collected, the money spent.

Robert Holody,* a middle-aged, jut-jawed New Yorker, a partner with a Second Eight CPA firm, can attest to that. Alone

---
* The CPA, Robert Holody, and his client, Len Donner, are composite characters who bear no relationship to specific individuals. The names are fictitious.

The Great American Tax Shelter

in the master bedroom of his Westchester, New York, center-hall colonial—dressing for a formal country club dinner dance on a sticky August evening—he answers the telephone that serves as a domestic hot line for client calls.

"Bob Holody here."

"Bob!"

"Yes."

"Bob!"

"Yes, this is Bob Holody."

"Bob! Bob! It's Len Donner. Jesus Christ, Bob. Jesus, Jesus, Jesus, Jesus. You really fucked up."

Holody pulls the string on the black bow tie that only moments before he'd carefully tied and centered in the formal shirt's crisply starched wing collar.

"Get ahold of yourself, Len. Calm down. Tell me what's wrong."

"Everything. Jesus Christ. Everything."

"That isn't telling me anything, Len. Start from the beginning."

"Middle, beginning, end—it's all the same damn thing. It's all gone bad."

Holody scanned his memory for details of Donner's financial affairs, assembling bits and pieces of data into a sketchy profile. Owner of a multistore retail chain, he drew down an annual salary of $350,000. Investments, mostly blue chip stocks, were worth about $1.5 million. Considering that his client was a twenty-hour-a-day workaholic, consumed by his business, Holody surmised that his anxiety attack had something to do with the stores. Had there been a fire? Had Sears decided to enter his market? Were sales, for some inexplicable reason, off by 50 percent?

"Len, please, tell me what's gone bad."

"The coal mine! The goddamn coal mine."

"The what?"

The Accounting Wars

"Bob, think back three years ago. Remember that coal mine tax shelter deal I brought to you? I've heard from my cousin, who as you know also invested in the shelter, that the deal is being audited, that the IRS is disallowing most of the deductions, and that all the investors, yours truly included, are going to have to give back the $467,000 we wrote off plus penalties and interest. Do you realize how much money that is, how much goddamn money that is!"

"Look, Len, all you have so far is hearsay and—"

"How could you let this happen to me, Bob?"

"Len, with all due respect, you've got this wrong. Although I must admit I don't recall the specifics of that particular shelter, I do know that the decision to invest was yours."

"Correction, Bob, you told me to do it."

"Can't be, Len, I'd never do that. Never."

"Then you told me it was a sure thing. A guaranteed write-off."

"Impossible, Len. I'd never do that either."

"Bob, excuse me, but you're just covering your ass on this one. You say yourself that you don't recall the deal. How can you be so holy-water sure that you didn't tell me it was guaranteed?"

"Because, Len, there's no such animal as a guaranteed shelter—not with a multiple write-off. What I probably told you, as I've said to many clients over the years, is that the deal seemed to be legitimate, seemed to comply with existing tax laws, and although every shelter implies some risk, it seemed to be within reasonable limits."

"Bob, do you realize how much this is going to cost me? Shit, I would have been far better off paying the tax in the first place. Now, with the penalties and God knows what else, it could cost me twice as much—probably more. I hold you responsible, Bob, if not you personally then your damn firm."

"My firm?"

The Great American Tax Shelter

"I see, Bob, that you don't remember this deal at all. I have the offering statement right here. Your firm did the accountant's opinion. Your firm signed off on it."

"What does it say, Len? Read it to me. On second thought, don't bother. I can probably tell you what it says. And if you look closely, you'll see that even the firm's opinion doesn't guarantee anything. It can't. Guarantees and tax shelters are like oil and water. The fact is, Len, you made the investment and you'll have to live with it. But I'll call you first thing Monday morning and we'll see if we can't salvage something here."

Holody's sticky wicket illustrates the peculiar dynamics of tax shelter engagements. Whether the client is an investor in, or syndicator of, tax shelter deals, the CPA knowingly commits to an engagement that he cannot perform according to his usual standards of reliability. Although this may be abundantly clear to the professional, the same cannot be said of his client.

But let's start at the beginning. What are tax shelters, and why are they tolerated in a system ostensibly structured to provide for an equitable sharing of the tax burden? Even the term "shelter" appears to fly in the face of this underlying principle.

Theoretically, personal income is subject to a graduated tax established by Congress and collected by the Internal Revenue Service. By offsetting income dollar for dollar, standard deductions for medical expenses, interest payments, and casualty losses reduce the individual's tax liability.

Because it is generally financed with a long-term mortgage (the interest on which is tax deductible) the purchase of a house qualifies as the most basic and widely used of all tax-advantaged investments. For the 50 percent bracket taxpayer, the net after-tax cost of a $2,000 monthly mortgage payment is slightly less than $1,000. In effect, Uncle Sam eases the financial burden of home ownership. The interest deduction is clearly a legislative attempt to create and maintain a strong housing industry. Although critics claim that this discriminates against renters and deprives the treasury of much-needed revenues, the mortgage-interest deduction has a ring of fairness to it. It conforms to the classic American ideals of hard work and thrift and the notion that those with the gumption to develop their own homesteads deserve to be rewarded for their efforts. Much as the original land grant programs awarded property to pioneer settlers, today's tax system upholds the tradition of individual home ownership. It is a tool for achieving broad social and political objectives.

"The tax system is complex and ever changing because legislators and administrators alike have found it the most responsive and efficient way of fine-tuning the American economy and of meeting the volatile needs of the American taxpayer/voter," says Bill Raby, PIC of Touche Ross's Phoenix office and former chairman of the AICPA's federal tax division.

In effect, the tax system creates government-supported subsidy programs. Proponents of this approach view it as a coolly effective way to manipulate the economy without adding to the already bloated bureaucracy.

"Let us use the example of a subsidy program that the government sets up to stimulate the purchase of energy-conserving devices. Setting up such a subsidy program would be a time-consuming and administratively expensive task. First, enabling legislation would have to be passed. Then an appropriation would be required. Either an existing agency would have to staff up to meet the demands of this new program or a new agency would have to be brought into existence. Regulations would have to be printed and application forms and procedures adopted. The first requests for the subsidy money might take quite some time to process. Perhaps two years after the legislation was proposed, an actual program might be in operation, by which time the emerging problem would have passed beyond the point where that program would be of any help.

"Contrast this with using the tax system to provide this subsidy through either a deduction or a credit. The minute a program was proposed, tax people would start monitoring on behalf of their clients. The enactment of the proposal would result in almost instantaneous communications to affected clients about how they could take advantage of it. Clients in manufacturing or selling—of solar panels, let's say—would quickly advertise the new subsidy. Marketing programs would be operational based upon the tax practitioner's interpretation of the new statute—and the first installation actually generated would be almost concurrent with legislative enactment."*

Rational, sensible—few can argue with the logic of this approach. But Raby's example omits two key factors. First, the tax system's built-in incentives are not always put to socially responsible objectives (i.e., energy conservation). "Tax shelters are not a new form of investment, nor were they created by any particular group for any particular purpose," says IRS Commissioner and former Price Waterhouse partner Roscoe L. Egger, Jr. "They began as a reflection of certain provisions of the Internal Revenue Code designed to foster positive capital investments. Congress intended these provisions as incentives for useful economic purposes, recognizing that legitimate investments in sound business activities should be encouraged. In fact, existing tax laws in many cases are structured for this very purpose, so obviously there are legitimate (nonabusive) tax shelters. However, we are now seeing a perversion of these provisions into *abusive* mechanisms to intensify improper tax avoidance or deferral."

In many cases, enormous deductions are claimed for transactions providing little or no benefit to the general economy. Tax-advantaged investments in motion pictures, for example, which were all the rage in the mid-1970s, did little to improve the state of the union or for that matter the quality of Hollywood

---

* William Raby, *Tempo,* Touche Ross, November 1983.

films. And yet, once it became apparent that certain provisions of the tax code allowed for substantial write-offs associated with film production, CPAs launched "almost instantaneous communication to affected clients about how they could take advantage of it."

Investments in high-multiple write-off deals—from motion pictures to coal mines—lured thousands of affluent investors because they offered the opportunity to shift capital from a guaranteed dead end (payments to Uncle Sam) to potentially lucrative deals (blockbuster movies). With write-offs of two to one or better, the 50 percent taxpayer investing in a film had no out-of-pocket expense.* Dollars otherwise directed to the federal treasury were redirected to a B-grade low-budget murder mystery that just might, with equal parts luck and good timing, be the sleeper of the year returning twenty times the investors' stake in the film. But even if the production flopped at the box office, even if it failed to earn back even a fraction of its budget, the backers considered themselves no worse off than if they'd paid their taxes. At the two-to-one multiple, they were protected by the tax system. At four to one (common for movie deals), they actually stood to earn money on the film's failure, saving cash that would have gone to taxes.

CPAs who made "instantaneous communications to affected clients about how they could take advantage of" the inherent tax benefits of movie deals were sanctioning, even if indirectly, investments that were vulnerable to attack by the IRS. And this is precisely what has happened. Many of the movie deals of the 1970s have come unglued, with the IRS disallowing, on a retroactive basis, the write-off schemes used to fund them.†

---

* However, deductions in excess of the amount of the actual cash investment would have been subject to recapture at a future date.

† As evidence of the IRS's crackdown on abusive shelters, the number of tax shelters under examination has increased from 400 in 1973 to more than 300,000 in 1983.

The Great American Tax Shelter

Just how a shelter scheme is closed off—in spite of the syndicators' efforts to circumvent government limitations—is revealed in this eulogy (prepared by Arthur Young's Richard Shebairo) of coal-mining deals.

Coal shelters sold prior to January 1, 1977, typically involved the deduction of substantial prepaid minimum annual royalties. In many cases, taxpayers received tax deductions in the initial year of the investment equal to 300 percent to 400 percent of the amount of cash invested.

In the typical transaction, a limited partnership would be formed to lease coal property from the mineral owner. In addition to paying the customary annual royalties on production, the syndicate would also agree to pay a substantial lump sum advanced minimum royalty, all or a large portion of which was paid through the issuance of nonrecourse notes. The shelters were sold on the basis that the lump sum advanced minimum royalty was currently deductible. Authority for this position was contained within the existing regulations under Internal Revenue Code Section 612, which allowed the payor the option of treating advanced royalties paid in connection with mineral property as deductions from gross income in the year they were paid or accrued. Additional support was found within Revenue Rulings 70–20 and 74–214; it should be noted, however, that neither of these Rulings involved payments through the issuance of nonrecourse promissory notes.

On October 29, 1976, the Internal Revenue Service issued a news release suspending the two rulings referred to above and announcing a proposed amendment to the Section 612 Regulations which, in effect, prospectively eliminated the current deduction for lump sum advanced royalty payments. The ruling provided that no deduction would be allowed currently for advanced minimum royalties if the deduction of such amount resulted in the distortion of income unless such payments were subject to a binding agreement dated prior to the date of the announcement. The effect of this amendment was to limit the amount of the currently deductible payments until such time as the partnership earned the income (i.e., actually sold the coal) against which the royalty related.

It was generally known that this announcement was imminent; consequently many promoters scrambled around to set up "preexisting" part-

The Accounting Wars

nerships which entered into binding advanced minimum royalty arrangements prior to having investors. While in theory these partnerships should have been grandfathered, it is unlikely that such an approach would pass muster.

A further and perhaps more significant limitation on the deductibility of coal shelter expenses became effective on January 1, 1977. As of that date, if the coal transaction was carried out in partnership form, the at-risk rules applied. Previously, investors could put up a small amount of cash and sign a large nonrecourse promissory note and take deductions equal to the sum of the cash invested plus the face amount of the note. Under the at-risk rules, the deductions were limited to cash invested and recourse notes. Since the rules at that time applied only to partnerships, promoters tried to circumvent the rules by selling interests, not as partnership units but rather as individual operating interests. Transactions were structured in such a way as to appear that the investor was the sole operator of a coal mining property. In fact, however, the deals were really indistinguishable from partnerships and such an approach should not have been effective in circumventing the at-risk rules.

On December 14, 1977, the proposed regulations under Section 612 were finalized, ending once and for all the question as to whether advanced minimum royalties could be deducted currently. In addition, the Internal Revenue Service issued Revenue Ruling 77–489, formally revoking the two prior rulings which allowed tax deductions for advanced minimum royalties paid.

The combination of the at-risk rules, the new Regulations, and Revenue Ruling 77–489, in effect, eliminated coal mining as a viable tax shelter.

This example indicates in a very rough way the relationships of investments to deductions which characterize the old coal shelters and pro forma results under the new rules.

Example

"OLD" DEAL

Year	Investment	Loss
1	$100,000 cash	$400,000
	400,000 nonrecourse note	
2		50,000
3		25,000
4		25,000

PRO FORMA RESULTS UNDER NEW RULES

Year	Investment	Loss
1	$100,000 cash	$75,000
	400,000 nonrecourse note	
2		25,000
3		0
4		0

Note that under the new law no loss may be deducted beyond the actual at-risk amount.

The Tax Equity and Fiscal Responsibility Act of 1982 widened the crackdown on abusive shelters.

"With the passage of TEFRA, the government has taken a harder line on exotic shelters designed primarily for tax avoidance," says Leonard Padolin, managing director of tax policy for Arthur Andersen. "These are deals that generally have little or no economic substance and would require nothing short of a miracle for the investors to earn a profit.

"TEFRA discourages these investments by requiring that all tax positions be based on 'substantial authority' and that the taxpayer have a 'reasonable belief that his tax treatment is more likely than not the proper treatment.' Failing this, the taxpayer may be liable for a 10 percent penalty as well as back taxes plus interest should the shelter be disallowed by the Internal Revenue Service. The problem is, the government rules raise more questions than they answer. What is 'substantial authority' or 'reasonable belief'? No one really knows. That makes it hard to tell when and where the penalty will be applied. What's more, the Deficit Reduction Act of 1984 further strengthened the government's ammunition against so-called abusive tax shelters. For example:

"Under TEFRA, interest on tax deficiencies was adjusted semiannually in relation to the prime interest rate. The Deficit Reduction Act increases the interest rate by 20 percent for deficiencies stemming from tax-motivated transactions. If the old rate was 12 percent, the new rate would be 14.4 percent.

"TEFRA held that those aiding and abetting the filing of false tax returns were subject to a $1,000 penalty per document or tax return. The Deficit Reduction Act added a new provision enabling the IRS to get an injunction against the individuals aiding or abetting in this way.

"Taken together, these changes have brought about an increased level of sensitivity among tax advisers and shelter promoters."

An Arthur Young tax shelter report underlines the dangers of investing in abusive shelters, warning that they "may result in a very unfavorable rate of return on investment when all the consequences are considered. In addition to the substantial fees generally charged by the promoters of such shelters, there is an increased possibility of an IRS audit examination of the return. If the return is examined and a tax deficiency is assessed, not only must the taxpayer pay the tax due and the interest on the underpayment, but significant nondeductible penalties may be imposed.

- If a property involved in the shelter is found to be overvalued by 150 percent or more, without a reasonable basis for the valuation, and an underpayment of tax in your return of at least $1,000 is deemed to result therefrom, a penalty would be imposed. The amount of the penalty ranges from 10 to 30 percent of the tax understatement depending upon how exaggerated the valuations.
- If it is determined that the amount of your tax understatement was substantial, a 10 percent nondeductible penalty is imposed. A substantial understatement is a reported tax liability that understates the correct amount of tax by the greater of 10 percent or $5,000 for individuals. Such understatement, however, does not include the additional tax resulting from overvaluation understatements noted above, where a penalty was imposed. With respect to tax shelters, the amount of the understatement to which the penalty applies can be reduced only if the taxpayer can establish that he/she believed that the tax benefits were more likely than not correct. We advise that taxpayers be certain they have a tax opinion to this effect with respect to the tax shelter in order to mitigate this potential penalty.
- In certain aggravated situations, the IRS may also try to assess penalties for negligence or civil fraud.

TEFRA also armed the IRS with an especially potent weapon in its crusade against abusive shelters: the ability to audit limited partnerships at the partnership level.

"Previously, audits could be performed only at the partner level. Since a large proportion of tax shelters are structured as partnerships, the legislation greatly increases the scope of IRS audit coverage. For example, if a shelter partnership has a hundred partners, the IRS must contend with only a single audit, administrative appeal, or judicial proceeding when challenging such a shelter arrangement."*

Most ominously for accountants, Congress aimed one of TEFRA's tax shelter torpedoes directly at CPAs, forcing them to share the responsibility for tax returns based on abusive shel-

---

* *Washington Tax Report*, Main Hurdman, November 1983.

The Accounting Wars

ters. A Main Hurdman memo, marked For Internal Use Only, alerted the firm's tax partners to this. Code Section 6701 imposed a penalty on "any person (1) who aids or assists in, procures, or advises with respect to the preparation or presentation of any portion of a return, affidavit, claim, or other document in connection with any matter arising under the Internal Revenue laws, (2) who knows that such portion will be used in connection with any material matter arising under the Internal Revenue laws, and (3) who knows that such portion (if so used) will result in an understatement of the liability of tax of another person."

The memo goes on to warn that "these provisions . . . could have a significant impact on our practice that could result in penalties to our clients and to ourselves which could be very costly."

Of the thousands of multiple write-off shelters that have been disallowed by the IRS, and that, like Holody's coal-mining partnership, have been forced to pay the piper with back taxes and penalties, few, if any, CPAs are known to have admitted wrongdoing, responsibility, or even a lapse in judgment for their role in the transactions. That's because when it comes to tax shelter engagements, accountants couch their advice in terms that appear to offer professional counsel while actually freeing them from liability should the deal fall through.

S.K.,* a self-employed businessman, recalls this conversation—typical of tax shelter powwows—with his CPA, a partner with an L.A.-based accounting firm.

SK: Did you look at that oil and gas deal I had Cindy send over to you last week?
CPA: Oh, yes. Cover to cover. [He stares at the client as if the conversation had run its course.]

* S.K. are fictitious initials that bear no resemblance to the name of any specific individual.

The Great American Tax Shelter

SK: And?

CPA: And? What exactly do you want to know?

SK: Come on, I want to know if I should invest in it. What else would I want to know?

CPA: Let me ask you a question. What do you hope to gain from this investment?

SK: What kind of question is that? I want to cut the hell out of the taxes you're telling me—telling me every day now—I have to pay.

CPA: Tax savings are only one part of a shelter. Have you given any thought to the economic aspects?

SK: I haven't given any thought to anything. I can't make any sense out of that damn offering. It's as thick as the telephone book. All I know is that the broker promises me a 2.2-to-1 write-off and that's all I think I need to know. It sounds very attractive to me.

CPA: You're not hearing me. The tax saving is only one consideration. You have to consider the economics as well.

SK: Okay, I'll consider them. How are the economics?

CPA: Not all that good. Although I'm no authority on deep drilling, I do know that a lot of these wells never produce a drop of anything and even if they do, some experts—did you catch yesterday's *Wall Street Journal?*—are now projecting excess reserves of oil and natural gas. Prices could plummet.

SK: But aren't you missing the point? Who the hell cares about wells and prices and all of that; the broker tells me that if they don't find anything more valuable than rock and red clay, I'm even because of the write-offs. I'm asking you one thing: Is *he* telling the truth? Can I bank on that?

CPA: The best approach is to look for a deal that combines tax savings with sound economics.

SK: It's December 18. I don't exactly have time to go shopping. Please, please answer my question. Is the broker correct?

Can I write off 2.2 times my investment? Will I get the tax savings he says I'll get?

CPA: The way I read this, if all goes according to plan, you should be able to deduct in excess of $125,000 on an investment of $57,000.

SK: So how can I lose?

CPA: Well . . .

SK: Will this hold up in an audit?

CPA: It should.

SK: What do you mean, "It should"? As much as I want this deduction, as much as I desperately need this deduction, I don't want to do something that's going to come back to haunt me later. I don't want to lose any sleep over this.

CPA: There's no reason for that. Let's not get paranoid now.

SK: I don't want to. I just want to make an investment. Look, let's cut out the ifs, ands, and buts. To repeat my question, if the IRS audits this deal, will it hold up?

CPA: I don't see why it wouldn't.

SK: Is it possible there's something here that you don't see?

CPA: That's not likely.

SK: Now we're getting somewhere. So the final question is, should I send them a check?

CPA: Given your stated objectives, I don't see any reason to tell you not to.

While it is true that the CPA has not pushed his client into this deal—and has, in fact, made him cognizant of potential hazards—he does appear, in the final analysis, to sanction the investment. Equally important, he has failed to inform his client of two significant caveats. First, the term "tax shelter" is, in itself, a misnomer concocted by syndicators to create the impression of an omnipotent shield protecting the investor's income from taxation. The very word *shelter* plays to the beat-the-system mystique that captivates affluent superachievers imbued with faith in the manipulative abilities of high-priced legal and financial counsel.

"There is a semantic problem at work here," says IRS commissioner Roscoe Egger. "We'd all be better off without the term 'tax shelter,' because it means different things to different people. When I think tax shelter, I think of the home mortgage deduction, IRAs, Keoghs, and so on. But when others talk of tax shelters, they have high-multiple write-offs in mind. In some cases, what they call tax shelters, I call fraud." Egger tells of a California-based company that was reportedly manufacturing and selling solar panels as tax shelters. Twelve hundred investors put up $8.3 million in cash and $33.4 million in promissory notes. They were then advised to claim a total of $27 million in tax credits and deductions.

"Incredibly, for the most part, the panels were never made. Investors filed for investment tax credits, unaware that the panels had in fact never been produced. In some cases, the investments were backdated so that false deductions would be claimed by the investors. . . .

"The facts are indeed sordid. Apparently, large amounts of company funds were diverted into the pockets of a Las Vegas dancer. She received $50,000 in cash and a new Cadillac."

What many investors fail to recognize is that high write-off deals, were they fully accepted by the IRS, would only defer rather than waive the taxpayer's obligation. Shelter deductions are only deferrals that must be taken as income at some time in the future.

The anticipated tax benefits of the tax shelter in a particular situation may not always be realized. Although initial tax benefits flowing from a shelter may lower a taxpayer's current tax burden, the actual tax benefits realized over the life of the investment depend on a taxpayer's present and future individual tax posture. For instance, the investment may be sheltering income from tax currently at rates that are lower than when the investment "turns around" and generates taxable income. This may mitigate or even eliminate the tax advantage of the shelter and reduce the overall rate of return. . . .*

Although the deferral of taxes is of significant value, akin to a tax-free loan from the government, it must be viewed in terms of the shelter's cumulative impact on income and taxes. Few CPAs make their clients fully aware of this. But the second, and perhaps more startling omission, has to do with the CPA's own limitations. His wishy-washy response to the critical question "Will this shelter hold up in an audit?" is based not on indifference but instead on his inability to make a definitive statement on the subject—a shortcoming most accountants refuse to admit to their clients.

"An occupational hazard of this profession is that the client/accountant relationship is often expected to live up to unrealistic standards," says B. Z. Lee. "In many cases, the client expects the CPA to be a source of unlimited knowledge and the CPA is not always willing to let on that he is not. The practitioner is wary of his client, for fear not so much of losing him as of shaking his faith in his professional capabilities."

There is truth to this. Clients expect more from their accountants than their lawyers, or even their doctors, because the CPA's practice is deemed to be an exact science—one with a clearly discernible bottom line for every current or projected transaction. This expectation of mathematical accuracy prompts the CPA to fudge his response to the question "Will the shelter survive an audit?" because the only honest answer is to admit that he doesn't know. Tax shelter practice is rife with too many gray areas to make definitive statements about what will survive an audit and what will fail.

To understand why this is so, we must remember that aggressive shelters do not emanate from the U.S. Treasury, but instead are structured and marketed as investment products by

* Arthur Young Tax Brief.

The Great American Tax Shelter

a highly aggressive, intensely competitive subdivision of the financial services industry.

"Most of what are commonly referred to as tax shelters were created not by Congress but by accountants and attorneys—acting for syndicators—who have distorted the tax laws," says House Ways and Means Committee member Byron L. Dorgan (D-N. Dakota), a former tax commissioner of his home state. "A group of paper entrepreneurs spend all of their time eating away at the tax code and we, in turn, on Ways and Means have spent too much of our time plugging the holes. It all started when people recognized that it was, indeed, easier to grant tax incentives to accomplish certain social objectives than to get appropriations for the same activity. Although this may have been justified in certain limited cases, it's been vastly overused today.

"For example, the city of Knoxville sold its sewer system to a group of investors—a limited partnership searching for tax subsidies—and then leased it back from the group. How absurd! A city should never be involved in providing fodder for the tax shelter industry. It should handle its own financing without involving those who want to use the city for very narrow personal gains.

"When you look at this thing realistically, you have to see that the tax code has become part of a game board for the rich. Because the paper entrepreneurs—those CPAs, lawyers, and syndicators—have a strong profit motive in creating and selling these shelters, they keep coming in a steady stream. It's like a feedlot for the financially obese."

When an individual invests in a shelter, a substantial part of his investment goes to the deal makers and salesmen who create and market it.

"The syndicators and brokers take a big bite (over 20 percent) out of the client's investment before it's put to work. That alone can make an otherwise good investment produce a mediocre return. . . .

The Accounting Wars

"Let's look at a relatively 'conservative' deal: How would you like to buy a piece of the five-star Boca Raton Hotel and Club, one of the choicest resort properties in the U.S.? Sound great? It's for sale by VMS Realty, Inc., at $200,000 a unit, using Prudential Bache Securities, Inc., as the middleman. . . . VMS recently paid $100 million for it to Arvida Corp. Investors from all over the country will have put up $50.6 million in cash and notes and will have $90 million worth of first and second mortgages on the property to go with it: total, just over $140 million.

"Now, think that one through. With a stroke of the pen, VMS and its friends ask investors to cover another $40 million in price—including transaction costs—on top of VMS's purchase price, which may not have been a bargain in the first place. Assume the true market value is what VMS paid for it. In that case, the public investors get some $10 million in equity for their $50.6 million. There's quite a deal!

"Where's the rest of their equity? Before a dime goes into the property itself, 15 percent of their investment is taken off in third-party front-end fees. This is fairly typical as these costs go. More shameless syndicators eat up even more. . . .

"A big chunk of the 15 percent goes to Pru-Bache and others for selling units to investors. They will earn $3.5 million in sales commissions, plus a $1-million 'Non-Accountable Expense Allowance.' . . .

"The biggest beneficiary of all: the sponsor, VMS Realty. In addition to an $8-million mark-up added on to the property for acquiring it, VMS will receive about $1.5 million in consulting and partnership monitoring fees over several years. VMS also expects to get supervisory management fees over the next fifteen years, totaling over $20 million, based on its own estimates. . . ."[*]

To collect these princely fees, the syndicators must first

[*] Howard Rudnitsky and John Heins, *Forbes*, December 19, 1983, pages 143–145.

structure marketable deals—i.e., those with the lure of attractive write-offs. This quest for "sexy shelters" creates much of the gray area in tax shelter law.

As the IRS continuously narrows and changes its definition of abusive shelters, the syndicators, forever resourceful and often downright brilliant, are pressed to find loopholes through, and detours around, the new restrictions.

"Even while Congress is working on proposals to take the steam out of tax shelters, real estate syndicators are plotting ways to adjust to them. The syndicators that buy properties and sell partnerships in them, often with substantial tax benefits, say they can restructure most deals—by adjusting appraisals and interest rates, and perhaps even fees—so that future investors will make out about as well as investors do now."*

"The syndicator thinks in terms of sales," says William Spiro, partner in charge of Seidman & Seidman's New York tax practice. "And he knows that the better the write-off he can offer, the more sales he'll make. Well, those substantial write-offs don't come by playing it safe. You get them by structuring investments that are at the cutting edge of tax avoidance or tax deferral strategies. This puts the deals squarely in the gray areas. How the Service will react to this or that depreciation formula, this or that valuation, isn't known until and if they decide to review it. As tax practitioners, all we can do is to inform our clients as to whether or not the deal appears to conform to the tax code. We can't say that it definitely does because every deal is different and even a slight variance here or there may cause the Service to disallow all or part of the shelter."

Spiro's colleague, Seidman tax partner Roxanne Cody, adds: "Take the rule that you are allowed to deduct real property over fifteen years.† That's a black-and-white issue. But the gray area

---

* Joanne Lipman, *Wall Street Journal,* March 7, 1984, page 33.
† Subsequently changed to eighteen years.

is in how much you are entitled to depreciate. The Service may claim that you're including items in the depreciable base that should be considered syndication costs. This distinction is important because syndication costs are capitalizable, but unlike real estate they are not amortizable or depreciable. Another sticky issue concerns the valuation of the property. The IRS may contend that the market value is far less than the partnership claims it to be, thus significantly reducing the amount of acceptable depreciation.

"Valuation is a very sensitive issue with the IRS. Assume a syndicator buys property and sells it to a limited partnership. Naturally, the syndicator is interested in marking up the property on the resale in order to maximize his profits. But there's also a perceived benefit here for the tax shelter because the higher price translates into a bigger tax deduction for the limited partners. If the purchase price is deemed to be far in excess of market value, the IRS is likely to disallow depreciation based on that sum. Even if the property's value is established by an independent appraiser, the deal may still be vulnerable in an audit. How did the appraiser project the property's future value? What assumptions did he make concerning inflation and rent increases? The point is that there are few hard and fast rules. It is impossible to predict exactly how the IRS will respond to any approach. Again, more gray areas."

Not surprisingly, Roscoe Egger blames the syndicators, not the IRS, for tax shelter insecurity. "Much of the confusion concerning tax shelters stems from the syndicators' efforts to outsell their competitors," Egger claims. "There are tax-advantaged investments that syndicators could structure with virtual certainty of IRS approval. But they aren't satisfied with that. They keep stretching the limits in order to make their deals more attractive. That's why there are always gray areas in this field and why everyone involved in it has to keep up with changing issues."

The Great American Tax Shelter

Clearly, tax shelter engagements force the CPA to shoot at a moving target. For much of his practice, the answers to his clients' "what ifs" are only as far away as the nearest Hewlett-Packard calculator. How much will ABC Company's monthly debt service increase if the prime tacks on two points? Punch it out on the old HP. What's the maximum annual contribution for a sixty-one-year-old entrepreneur's defined-benefit retirement plan? Check the actuarial tables.

Not all of the CPA's functions are reducible to published charts or to lines on computer screens, but for most engagements the CPA can base his actions, as well as his answers to client queries, on a body of recognized principles or mathematical formulas. Tax shelters are an exception. In part, the CPA is a victim of his environment. Sound as tax shelter theory is in principle—as in Bill Raby's incentive-subsidy-capital-allocation mechanism—there is reason to doubt that the IRS has ever really accepted the notion that taxpayers investing in designated industries are entitled to liberal deductions in return for their capital commitments.* Were this the case, the IRS could structure a limited number of prototype shelters—say one each for energy, assorted high-tech projects, oil and gas, and real estate—assuring taxpayers that investments in shelters identical to the prototype would be guaranteed the specified write-offs. This rational approach would provide a safe haven for prudent taxpayers seeking to make legitimate tax-advantaged investments; would enable CPAs to recommend government-sanctioned deals for which they could answer, positively and definitely, "this shelter will survive an audit"; † and would direct capital to worthy industries.

Instead, the Internal Revenue Service, in behavior typical of enforcement agencies, is driven by an "us-versus-them" syn-

---
* Section 8 public housing deals are a notable exception.
† Providing the economic aspects, such as property valuations in real estate deals, were legitimate.

The Accounting Wars

drome. The nation's tax system, based theoretically on voluntary compliance, looks to the Service to police the revenue collection process through fear, intimidation, and random audits. The IRS takes this mission very seriously, exceeding, in the opinion of many, its legislative mandate.

"They just don't like shelters, period," says Seidman & Seidman's Bill Spiro, a trace of anger piercing his normally calm, reflective demeanor. "The service intentionally creates a climate of uncertainty around tax shelters. By constantly changing the rules, by making negative rulings retroactive, they bring a chilling effect to the tax shelter business.

"Their action on the Rule of 78s is a good example. Explained in the simplest terms, the Rule of 78s is a method of accruing interest on a note so that heavier interest charges are applied at the earlier stages of the loan. Syndicators have long favored this approach because it allows for accelerated deductions to limited partners and thus bigger write-offs in the first years of a deal.

"With the Rule of 78s, you add the sum of the months outstanding on the loan and this becomes the denominator for figuring the interest allocation for the current year you are calculating the tax deduction for. On a one-year deal, the first-month denominator is 78—you get this by adding the sum total of the remaining months: 12, 11, 10, etc. So interest due in the first month is 12/78 or about 15 percent of the total. Without the Rule of 78s treatment, the interest due in the first month would be 8.5 percent.

"Let's see how this applies to a typical deal. Assume a $100,000 one-year loan at 10 percent interest starts December 1 and ends November 30 of the following year. With a standard treatment, the interest deduction in the first month of the first year of the shelter would be $850, but with the Rule of 78s that increases to $1,500."

Adds Cody: "For years, syndicators used the Rule of 78s to

structure their deals. All the while, the IRS made known its contention that this was inappropriate, but it never took formal action. Then, suddenly, without notice, it came out in March 1983 with revenue ruling 8384, which held that the Rule of 78s was not a proper method for computing interest deductions even if the note called for interest to be computed on this basis. This applied to long-term debts of five years or more.

"Suddenly, the deals already out there with Rule of 78s treatments had to be changed. Investors had to take back as income part of the accelerated deductions. When this came in the later years of a tax shelter investment—at a time when the cash flow in most deals is already positive—the additional income had a very damaging impact. It could reduce or totally eliminate the shelter's overall tax benefits."

If tax shelter investing, and the accounting practice related to it, are fraught with unknowns, blame for this must be placed, at least in part, on ambiguous language. By rigging the tax code with highly subjective terms—favorites include "reasonable," "substantial," and "likely"—the government makes it difficult for taxpayers and their CPAs to determine in advance which tax treatments will be acceptable and which will be disallowed and subject to penalties. The climate of uncertainty discourages many from investing.

"I have some very wealthy clients that never invest a dollar in shelters," says a Main Hurdman tax partner. "To them, not knowing how the deal will fare in an audit, should there ever be one, is like playing Russian roulette with the government holding the gun."

If the IRS doesn't hold the patent on vagueness it has certainly developed the practice into a fine art. Conversations with staff members, with press aides, and with senior officers are Kafkaesque affairs. Simple questions are bucked up and down the chain of command only to bounce back to the questioner in a rhetorical echo that casts little if any light on the subject. The

The Accounting Wars

operative theory, one assumes, is that if the rules are never clearly spelled out, the contestants will never know how to play the game.

Although this murky indecisiveness is typical of bureaucracies, many in the accounting profession are convinced that in the case of the IRS this is a carefully calculated policy rather than an inevitable by-product of government operations.

"When the average IRS examiner sits across the table from one of our experts on a tax shelter issue, that examiner is totally mismatched," says a partner at one of the Big Eight's Philadelphia practice offices. "The Service knows this and compensates by creating escape hatches—safety valves—call it what you will, to give their people a way out when they're up against an issue they can't defend. Ambiguity is intentional—they hide behind it.

"Let's call a spade a spade. There's an adversarial relationship between CPAs and the Internal Revenue Service. They feel inferior to us, which, professionally speaking, they are. They covet our earnings and our prestige. How do they get back? By trying to make us look bad to clients. By using every conceivable tactic to beat us at our own game. In tax shelter practice that means closing down the best tax deferral opportunities as quickly as CPAs and their clients can identify them.

"In one relatively new tactic, known as the 'prefiling notification,' the IRS scouts the market for what appears to be abusive shelters, warning prospective investors, before they commit to the deals, that deductions or credits taken on their personal returns will be audited and disallowed.

"The idea is to get to the investors before they commit to the shelters, thereby making it difficult for the promoters to market the deals. The letter-writing campaign is supposed to scare people—and it does just that. This is hardball the IRS way.

"You have to understand that the IRS has a paranoid vision of the world. Instead of an equator, it sees the globe divided by

Internal Revenue Service
District Director

Department of the Treasury

Date:

Tax Shelter Promotion:

Tax Year:

Person to Contact:

Contact Telephone Number:

    Our information indicates that you were a partner in the above partnership during the above tax year. Based upon our review of the partnership's tax shelter activities, we have apprised the Tax Matters Partner that we believe the purported tax shelter deductions and/or credits are not allowable and, if claimed, we plan to examine the return and disallow the deductions and/or credits. The Internal Revenue Code provides, in appropriate cases, for the application of a negligence penalty under section 6653(a), the overevaluation penalty under section 6659 and/or a substantial understatement of income tax penalty under section 6661 of the Internal Revenue Code with respect to the partners.

    If the Tax Matters Partner decides to claim such deductions and/or credits on the partnership return or the partnership return has already been filed claiming such deductions and/or credits, you may wish to file a request for administrative adjustment as provided by section 6227 of the Internal Revenue Code to amend partnership items. If you choose to file an administrative adjustment request, please file such with your service center at the following address:
Internal Revenue Service Center
Attention: Pre-filing Notification Coordinator

                                        Sincerely yours,

                                        District Director

Sample letter   **Letter 1842(DO) (9-83)** an imaginary line, pitting the CPA and his clients, who the IRS sees as overpaid and underworked, on one side and the agent and his colleagues on the other.

"Somehow, these guys, and I'm talking all the way up the IRS pecking order, think that every tax shelter investor is wealthy—which is absolutely untrue—and that every Big Eight partner is rolling in dough—which is even further from the truth—and their mission is to even the score. Well, this kind of vendetta introduces an irrational and emotional element into tax shelter practice. There's a powerful force out there trying to foil our work not because it's right or wrong but because it serves the interests of our clients.

"This puts CPAs like myself—those with individual as well as corporate clients—in an untenable position. We can't recommend that our clients simply abstain from shelters. They'll just turn to another accountant with a more aggressive outlook. As well they should. Most legitimate shelters either avoid audits or come through them relatively unscathed. On the other hand, we can't assure our clients of this, can't guarantee them that a specific shelter won't be disallowed somewhere down the road. Because it's hard to explain this convoluted system to clients, and because they really don't want to accept our limitations, we can only make them aware of the caveats and leave it to them to make the final decision. I think you'll find that most reputable CPAs won't try to stop their clients from investing in what appear to be safe shelters, but neither will they coax them into deals or vouch for them in any way."

Yes and no. As much as accountants, acting as individual practitioners, are, in a sense, hostages of the tax shelter game, CPA firms, especially those with the most prestigious names, are active players in a system that lures investors into risking their money on questionable and often disastrous shelter schemes. This role of tax shelter catalyst stems not from advising individuals on tax shelter investments, but instead from

The Great American Tax Shelter

selling the CPA firm's imprimatur—the tax shelter industry's version of the Good Housekeeping Seal of Approval—to shelter syndicators.

To understand how and why this works, we must return to the fact that tax shelter investments are financial products to be marketed, much like stocks and bonds, for substantial profits. The key selling point—the promise of significant write-offs and/or capital appreciation—is only as effective as the syndicator's creditability. Claims of investment performance, as even the most naive investors are aware, are often exaggerated by those selling the investments. With tax shelters, there is an additional threat: Projected write-offs may be more in the way of pie-in-the-sky than bankable deductions. The surgeon, the corporate V.P., the entrepreneur—poised, checkbook in hand, to make his initial payment of $30,000, $50,000, or $100,000 to a tax shelter deal—asks himself the now familiar question "Will this investment survive an audit?"

Anticipating this, the syndicator cleverly builds a security blanket, in the form of "the accountant's letter," into the offering memorandum. Prepared on the accounting firm's letterhead, the document is designed to assure prospective investors that a knowledgeable and reputable third party has blessed the deal, finding it thoroughly up to snuff. Framed in a separate section of the offering memo, conspicuously set off from the body of the text, the letter imitates the auditor's statement in a corporate annual report. To the untutored eye, it has the appearance of an objective confirmation of the syndicator's tax strategy. But it is nothing of the kind. Unlike the auditor's report, the tax shelter letter is not signed on the basis of a comprehensive review of the entity's financial position. The syndicator assumes, and he is most often correct, that investors will fail to make this distinction, viewing the accountant's name as ample insurance that independent CPAs have rigorously examined the deal and have found it to be in strict conformity with current tax regulations and fully capable of performing in accordance with the syndicator's claims.

That otherwise intelligent individuals will put blind faith in a CPA's signature was made evident by the Cohen Commission,* which found that stockholders view the Big Eight signature in a corporate annual report as a guarantee of financial well-being—to the extent that they don't bother reading the statement that precedes the Price Waterhouse or the Arthur Andersen name.

"If a user is generally unfamiliar with the limitations of financial information and the audit function, he may tend to view the auditor's report as a seal of approval and place unjustified reliance on it." †

Along the same lines, the Financial Forecasts and Projections Task Force of the AICPA recognized the prestige a CPA firm can bring to a document when it noted that "an accountant's association with a financial forecast tends to lend credibility to the forecast. . . ."**

In effect, the CPA firm's signature can be an influential—and in some ways misleading—symbol. This is doubly true for tax shelters, where the engagement that precedes the signature is far less comprehensive than corporate audits.

Consider this discussion between Seidman's Bill Spiro and the author:

MARK STEVENS (MS): When a tax shelter goes bad, when it is disallowed by the IRS, you don't have the same feeling of exposure as you do with an audit failure. Is that correct?
WILLIAM SPIRO (WS): That's true, because we have written a different kind of letter.
MS: You've really insulated yourself from all the responsibility.

* A study group established by the American Institute of Certified Public Accountants to report on auditors' responsibilities.
† Cohen Commission Report.
** September 20, 1983.

ws: That's true, because we don't start off with the same degree of certainty. When we audit something, we've examined it by generally accepted auditing standards. Here we're not saying that and therefore we have less responsibility. Also, the public can feel a lesser degree of security.

But unlike the accounting professional engaged in tax shelter practice, the typical investor is not aware of this distinction. To him, the CPA's signature is synonymous with security.

"When reviewing a private placement memorandum that carries an accountant's letter, the average investor thinks the CPA is implicitly or indirectly endorsing the investment," says Charles Wellerer, editor of *Real Estate Tax Shelter Review*, based in Concord, New Hampshire. "But the paradox is that while the CPA's involvement in a tax shelter is much less than for a corporate financial statement, the public's reliance on the accountant's opinion is probably greater with shelters than with corporate reports. That's because few syndicators are household names. In all likelihood, the investor probably never heard of the syndicator he's about to invest with—even active shelter investors know, at the most, a half dozen syndicators by name—so he wants to see a name that gives him some confidence in the deal. In most cases, that name turns out to be the CPA's.

"But were there ever a case of false security, this is it. The fact is, the investor is not learning anything of real value from the accountant's opinion because it doesn't refer to the tax issues at hand. We analyze five or six deals a month for our newsletter subscribers without ever paying the slightest attention to the accountant's report."

Just how important the accountant's letter can be to the syndicator's marketing efforts is revealed by this conversation between the author and a sales representative for a New York–based syndicator.

The Accounting Wars

SYNDICATOR (S): Mr. Stevens, did you receive the information we sent you on our most recent limited partnership?*

MARK STEVENS (MS): Yes, I've been reviewing it.

S: Can I answer any questions for you?

MS: Just one. I noticed that the offering does not include an accountant's letter. Is there a reason for that?

S: I'm pleased that you brought that up. It supports what a number of us in our marketing department are trying to accomplish.

MS: I don't understand.

S: Forgive me, I've gotten ahead of myself. It has not been our practice to include a CPA's letter in our offering documents, primarily because we've wanted to spare our limited partners the expense of an accountant's fee. But many investors, such as yourself, have been asking for a CPA's letter, so we're planning to include one in our upcoming proposals.

A week later, the sales representative called back.

S: Mr. Stevens, have you made a decision on our limited partnership?

MS: I'm currently reviewing it along with several others.

S: Well, I thought I'd let you know that we've decided not to limit the CPA's letter to future deals. We're having one prepared for our current deal. I know you're concerned about this so I'll get it out to you just as soon as it's ready.

Those investors who see the medium as the message, and who thus fail to read the text of the accountant's letter, may be surprised, if not shocked, by how little it says and how little comfort one can glean from it.

* Unaware of Stevens's journalistic interests, the syndicator's representative believed the author to be a prospective investor.

The Great American Tax Shelter

The paradox of shelter engagements is that name accounting firms affix their Good Housekeeping seals to the offering memorandums, only to issue convoluted statements freeing them from responsibility should the shelters collapse. The syndicators hope, and the accountants are apparently willing to go along with this, that few will read the fine print.

Some in the accounting profession have a rationale for this. Call it caveat emptor. "Why blame the accountants when investors fail to read the key documents that should form the basis of their investment decisions? Anyone who acts on the strength of a signature only, who assumes that because the accounting firm's name appears on the offering document that the firm endorses the investment, is making an unwarranted assumption. He's reading something into the signature."

Adds Bill Spiro: "I think we're entitled to assume that investors are willing to read the entire letter. Because otherwise you might as well forget the small print on everything. Don't put a warning on cigarette boxes. What's the difference?"

Support for this view comes from the highest councils of the IRS. "You can't hold accounting firms liable for investors' failure to accept their own investment responsibilities," says Roscoe Egger. "If they study the CPA's letter, they will understand exactly what it is and what it is not. And it is not intended to be a guarantee of anything. They are commenting on the projections and that's what the letter says they are doing. Those taxpayers investing in tax shelters must accept responsibility for reading the relevant documents pertaining to those investments."

But just how closely do the CPAs themselves read, and analyze, projections—including notes and assumptions—they are lending their name to?

Consider this conversation (paraphrased) between the author and a CPA firm's tax team concerning their letter for a tax shelter offering memorandum.

The Accounting Wars

MARK STEVENS (MS): There is a reference in the offering memorandum, under Notes and Assumptions to Projections, to a consulting fee of $15,000 and nonsolicitation fee of $38,700. Do you know who earned these fees and what they were for?

The CPAs glance at the memo, at each other, back to the memo, back at each other—each hoping the other will respond.

CPA: We know it as a firm, but we may not know it as individuals.

MS: Are they broker's fees?

CPA: No, they wouldn't be broker's fees.

MS: What would they be?

CPA: Ummm... it's hard to remember with each deal what every particular item is for.

MS: The footnote says, "These fees will be paid to the seller of the property at closing." Why would the seller of the property get a consultant's fee?

CPA: For some ongoing service that he's going to render. Maybe they have to have help in renting the building and this guy's an expert in local real estate.

MS: But look at the memorandum. There's also a nonsolicitation fee.

CPA: Well, you know what that could be—a fee not to compete for tenants.

MS: First you say he might be getting paid for soliciting your tenants. Now you're saying he might be paid for not soliciting your tenants—for not competing with you.

CPA: It could be that he's not going to solicit your tenants.... It's like a "covenant not to compete," which is common. If General Motors buys out the owner of a small business...

MS: I understand what "covenant not to compete" is. But I don't know what these fees are for, and although you reviewed these Notes and Assumptions and Projections, you don't seem to know, either.

The Great American Tax Shelter

CPA: We can't remember every detail of every deal, but it's all in the work papers. We could get you the answer in a moment by having the staff check the file. There are a lot of things we know institutionally that we don't know off the top of our heads. The accountant's letter doesn't say that we remember everything we review.

What does an accountant's letter actually say? Let's explore a Seidman & Seidman letter, dated April 4, 1983, to investors in a $1.25 million real estate partnership ($62,500 per investment unit) formed for the purchase and management of a 24,000-square-foot office building.*

To the Partners of [syndicator's name withheld]

We have [1] reviewed the Accompanying Financial Projections, including Notes and Assumptions ("Projections") of [syndicator], a limited partnership.

The Projections [2] were prepared by the General Partners of [syndicator] on the basis of information provided and assumptions made by them, which are described in the Notes and Assumptions to Projections. The Projections should be read in conjunction with the Confidential Offering Memorandum in connection with the offering of limited partnership interests in [syndicator]. Particular attention should be directed to the sections captioned "Risk Factors" and "Federal Tax Matters."

[3] Our review included tests of the computations and inquiries as to the methods of compiling the data set forth in the Projections.

The [4] Projections have been derived from assumptions as to future events inasmuch as the Partnership has no operating history. The Projections could be significantly affected if actual events and transactions vary significantly as to occurrence, time of occurrence or amount from the assumed events and transactions and by changes in Federal income tax law or regulations. [5] Further, the Projections could be significantly affected by adverse determinations by the Internal Revenue Service with respect to the deductibility of certain expenditures

---
* The client's name has been removed at Seidman's request.

The Accounting Wars

and the appropriate periods in which interest expense and other expenditures may be deductible for Federal income tax purposes. We understand that legal counsel, upon closing of the transactions contemplated in the Confidential Offering Memorandum and assuming no changes in the facts or Federal income tax law, will express an opinion to the effect that [name of partnership omitted here] should be classified as a partnership for Federal income tax purposes. We also understand that no income tax rulings have been obtained from the Internal Revenue Service and that none are being requested.

[6] Since the Projections are based on assumptions (the reliability of which is dependent on future events and transactions), as independent accountants, we do not express an opinion on the achievability of these Projections. However, our review indicates that the Projections were compiled on the basis of the assumptions set forth by the General Partners of [syndicator] in "Notes and Assumptions to Projections" and [7] that under current law the Partnership's tax returns can be prepared and filed reflecting the proposed tax treatments.

This report is intended for the information of the partners to whom addressed and the offerees of the limited partnership interests and is not to be included, referred to, or quoted by excerpts in any registration statement, prospectus, and loan or other document, without our consent.

[8] The terms of our engagement are such that we have no obligation to update this report or to revise the Projections subsequent to the date of this report.

[9] Seidman & Seidman
Certified Public Accountants

    The opening sentence (1) reveals the true extent of the engagement, noting that the CPAs "have reviewed the Accompanying Financial Projections,"* which, as the passage (2) reveals, were prepared by the general partners. The CPAs' engagement then is concerned with (3) "tests of the computation

---

* For private shelter deals only. CPAs engaged for public syndicators generally limit their services to the partnership's financial statements.

The Great American Tax Shelter

and inquiries as to the methods of compiling the data set forth in the projections."

Strip away the accounting jargon and the statement could be rephrased as "We've checked the syndicator's math—his addition, subtraction, and multiplication—and found it to be accurate."

That major CPA firms should be hired to confirm mathematical accuracy appears to be a clear case of overkill, except when you consider that the real purpose of the engagement is to affix the CPA's reassuring seal to the offering memorandum.

Even the blessing on the projections (4) is contingent upon the accuracy of the syndicator's assumption. Seidman notes that the projection could "be significantly affected if actual events and transactions vary significantly as to occurrence, time of occurrence, or amount from the assumed events and transactions and by changes in Federal income tax law or regulations." Translation: Everything hinges on the soundness of the projections developed not by the accountants but by the syndicators —who, it must be said, have a vested interest in presenting a highly attractive, marketable deal.

Even the AICPA's *Guide for Review of a Financial Forecast* holds that a "financial projection for an entity is an estimate of financial results based on assumptions that are *not* necessarily the most likely."*

A financial "forecast," which is deemed to have more substance than a "projection," is still based primarily on the assumptions of the company—or syndicator—issuing them. Let's review a CPA's tax shelter letter based on a financial forecast (note the italicized phrases).

The accompanying Financial Forecasts of _____ Limited Partnership for the period of February 29, 1984, to February 28, 1994, includ-

---
*Second Edition, page 2.

ing the notes and assumptions to Forecasts, present, *to the best of management's knowledge,* a summary of *expected* results of operations and cash flow for the Forecast period. Accordingly, the Financial Forecast reflects *management's judgment,* based on present circumstances, of the expected conditions and its expected course of action.

We have reviewed the Forecasts in accordance with guidelines for a review of a Financial Forecast established by the American Institute of Certified Public Accountants. Our review included those procedures we considered necessary to evaluate both the assumptions used by management and the preparation and presentation of the Forecast. We have no responsibility to update this report for events and circumstances occurring after the date of this report.

Based on our review, we believe the accompanying Forecasts are presented in conformity with guidelines for presentation of a Financial Forecast established by the American Institute of Certified Public Accountants. We believe that *the underlying assumptions* provide *a reasonable basis* for *management's Forecast.* However, *some assumptions inevitably will not materialize and unanticipated events and circumstances may occur; therefore, the actual results achieved during the Forecast period will vary from the Forecasts and the variations may be material.*

The one phrase that appears to give the investor some faith in the deal—"we believe that the underlying assumptions provide a reasonable basis for management's Forecast"—is hollower than it appears. The AICPA's *Guide for Review of a Financial Forecast,* which is the bible on handling such engagements, states that "most probable means that the assumptions have been evaluated by management and that the forecast is based on management's judgment of the most likely set of conditions and its most likely course of action. Although the accountant can reach a conclusion that the assumptions provide a reasonable basis for the forecast, he cannot conclude that any outcome is most probable because (a) realization of the forecast may vary, depending on management's intentions, which cannot be reviewed; (b) there is substantial inherent uncertainty in forecast assumptions; and (c) some of the information accumulated about an assumption may appear contradictory."*

That the CPAs are not attesting to the shelter's fundamental tax strategy, which is, undoubtedly, the pivotal factor in its ability to survive an audit, is evidenced by this caveat in the Seidman letter. (5): "Further, the projections could be significantly affected by adverse determinations by the Internal Revenue Service with respect to the deductibility of certain expenditures and the appropriate periods in which interest expense and other expenditures may be deductible for Federal income tax purposes." Translation: Of course, the IRS may disallow the deductions on which your write-offs are based. If that happens, remember, we told you so.

More qualifications. (6): "Since the projections are based on assumptions (the reliability of which is dependent on future events and transactions), as independent accountants, we do not express an opinion on the achievability of these projections." Translation: In case you didn't hear us the first time, we're not making any guarantees.

One of the more meaningful statements in the letter (7) is that "under current law the Partnership's tax returns can be prepared and filed reflecting the proposed tax treatments."

"Just how much comfort the prospective investor can take from this depends on the calibre of the accounting firm that signed the return," says a CPA and one-time Price Waterhouse staffer now with Robert A. Stanger & Company, publishers of a tax shelter newsletter and consultants to shelter investors. "Although the accountant's letter has little substance as it appears in the offering document, the better firms, including the Big and Second Eight, go through established procedures to satisfy themselves that the deal is legitimate. Before committing to sign

---

*Second Edition, page 9.

the return, they'll look for some assurance that they're not getting themselves into a deal that's likely to be quashed by the IRS.

"But then again, what constitutes 'assurance' to one firm may be balderdash to another. What really happens out there is that the syndicator, turned down by one CPA firm, just shops the market until he finds an accountant willing to play ball with him. This can take some amusing turns. I've seen instances where one office of a Big Eight firm refused to work with a syndicator, but another office—in another city—of the same firm agreed to take on the engagement. The second office just happened to be more aggressive.

"Even when all the top firms turn thumbs down, there's always an unscrupulous little-known outfit out there that's just tickled pink to give the syndicator what he wants—and to collect a banner fee for doing so. The proof is in the pudding: There are still some six-to-one deals out there, complete with accountant's letters. But anyone with any knowledge of the tax laws knows that six-to-ones aren't going to hold up today. Still, Schmuck, Schmuck & Schmuck will provide the letter, pocket the fees, and some investors will think this means the shelter's legit. That's life—in the tax shelter business anyway."

Finally (8): "The terms of our engagement are such that we have no obligation to update this report or to revise the Projections subsequent to the date of this report." Translation: We were paid to review these projections and report on them as of the date of this letter. Should subsequent developments affect the projections, we are not obligated to make that known.

The CPA signature (9), which carries a going price of about $50,000 for a standard shelter, is what the syndicator is really after. The symbol of objectivity will, if all goes according to plan, convince investors to write out their checks.

CPAs are not the only shelter participants given to ambiguous statements. In the "Notes and Assumptions to Projections"

The Great American Tax Shelter

—material included in Seidman's review—the general partners in the office-building deal note that the projections and assumptions are contingent upon the following: that the Partnership will be treated as a partnership, and not as an association taxable as a corporation, that the taxable income of the additional limited partners will continue for at least 10 years to be at a level sufficient to subject the partners to effective marginal tax rates of at least 50 percent, that no interpretation of or amendments to the Internal Revenue Code will change the projected tax benefits, and that losses as projected for tax purposes will not be adjusted on audit by the Internal Revenue Service.

Taken with the accountant's letter, these caveats make for a double sidestep. The sponsoring party—the syndicator—presents a proposal riddled with ifs, ands, and buts, and the independent CPAs back it up with another layer of equivocation. The investor has little to go on.

Questioned about the absence of a bankable opinion in the accountant's letter, Seidman's top shelter duo, Bill Spiro and Roxanne Cody—both capable and conscientious professionals —argue that much of their due diligence work goes on behind the scenes and is not revealed in the printed opinion.

"You have to recognize that the syndicator who engages us gets more than a few pieces of paper for his fee," says Cody, a pleasant, slimly built woman with a sharp grasp of tax issues. "There's a heck of a lot of tax experience in this firm and our clients benefit from that. Much of our discussions and negotiations with the syndicator may never find their way into the accountant's letter because they lead to actions or changes that are made before the final deal is hammered out, before the document is written. But we've played a role in shaping that deal, that document—in determining how they are structured."

Pausing momentarily to read Spiro's poker face for some sign of approval from the boss, she continues.

"Syndicators we work with on a regular basis will call us, as they're putting together deals, to ask our opinion, for example, on using certain depreciation techniques. Well, if we suggest that this or that approach is outside the letter or the spirit of the tax codes, they may drop the idea or find some other way to do it. Should the shelter emerge utilizing a different and more acceptable depreciation technique, we've played a role in that—a role in protecting investors—even though that fact doesn't show up in the accountant's letter."

But this check and balance on the syndicator's work doesn't always sit well with the client. Few general partners want their CPAs meddling in the mechanics of the investment. Were all the "what ifs" and "maybes" written between the lines of a shelter brought to attention and forced to a definitive conclusion, few deals would get off the ground. For the most part, the general partner hires the CPAs to check the math and to comfort investors. The handling of the offering memorandum within the CPA firm supports this. When the document is delivered by the syndicator, it is routed not to the firm's tax partners, whose expertise allegedly comes—like the prize in the Cracker Jacks box—with the opinion letter, but to the audit department, which is not qualified to render an informed opinion on tax issues.

"But that's only the first step," Spiro chimes in, apparently concerned that his colleague has downplayed the senior partners' role in the engagements. "Roxanne or I review, in full, every deal that comes into this firm, and we satisfy ourselves that it meets with our standards or we don't sign our name to it."

But what does the review, at any CPA firm, really entail? What comfort does it give the investor? The answer goes back to item one: not enough to ensure that the deal will survive an audit.

"Our responsibility is to the projections," Spiro says. "If our signature is on the letter, then we've checked those projections and we believe their underlying assumptions are sound. But as to the fundamental tax issues—as to how the IRS will treat the projected deductions and if, in fact, they will view the investment structure as a genuine partnership for tax purposes—for these determinations we rely on the attorney's opinion."

Now we're getting to the heart of the matter. Professionals lending their names and collective prestige to tax shelters typically hinge responsibility for the deals on each other's opinions or on a long list of caveats. The result is an interlocking set of nonassurances that can prop up shelters much like a house of cards. Treasury Department rules governing professional practice before the IRS on tax shelter opinions excuse CPAs from material responsibility for the accuracy of tax positions taken by shelter syndicators, providing the CPAs' opinions are limited to projections, and other professionals (generally lawyers) offer opinions on the tax issues.*

Financial forecasts or projections often include assumptions as to the tax return reporting positions to be taken with respect to material tax issues. Tax shelter forecasts or projections therefore could mislead investors by implicitly suggesting that the tax return positions they reflect are proper. For this reason, the final rule treats forecasts or projections involving any tax assumptions as "tax shelter" opinions. If the forecasts or projections themselves do not address all of the material tax issues in the required manner, all material tax issues that form the basis for such forecasts or projections must be fully addressed by the practitioner or some other practitioner in a tax opinion (or elsewhere in the offering materials) that meets the criteria set forth in the rules. . . .†

---

* Should the CPAs be found *negligent*, however, in providing opinions on *projections and forecasts* that turn out to be erroneous, they are subject to three types of action by the Treasury Practice Division: a reprimand; a disciplinary proceeding resulting in possible suspension from practice before the IRS; a proceeding resulting in possible disbarment from practice before the IRS. This applies to individuals only, not entire CPA firms.

† Rules and Regulations 6719, *Federal Register,* Vol. 49, No. 37, February 23, 1984.

The Accounting Wars

The same rules also give the attorneys a margin of comfort. Under the heading of Due Diligence as to Factual Matters, the rules state that "a practitioner generally need not conduct an independent verification of the facts unless he knows, or should know, that the facts provided to him by the promoter or another person are untrue."

Let's explore the attorney's opinion in one tax shelter deal.

The lawyers begin by noting that *their* opinion is based on the opinion of another law firm, which did the due diligence work. The legalese reads like this: "For the purposes of this opinion, we relied on the aforesaid opinion from (the other law firm) and have examined such documents and materials as we deemed relevant including, without limitation, original documents and records of the partnership and copies thereof certified to our satisfaction. In such examination, we assumed the authenticity of the documents, the accuracy of certified documents, the genuineness of tax signatures and the authority of all signatures signing in a fiduciary capacity."

Based on this, the attorneys state their opinion on three key facets of the deal:

(1) For the reasons set forth in the Partnership's Confidential Offering Memorandum (the "Memorandum"), under 'Federal Tax Matters'—'Classification as a Partnership,' the Partnership probably could not apply for a ruling from the Internal Revenue Service as to its status as a partnership for Federal income tax purposes. However, for the reasons set forth in the foregoing subsection of the Memorandum, we are of the opinion that, for Federal income tax purposes, the Partnership should be treated as a partnership and not as an association taxable as a corporation at the time Additional Limited Partners (as that term is defined in the Partnership Agreement) are admitted to the Partnership.

(2) Each investor acquiring a Limited Partnership Interest in the Partnership should be entitled to deductions on his Federal income tax returns for his share of the Partnership's losses from and after his acquisition of a Limited Partnership Interest in the Partnership, to the extent of the ad-

justed basis of his Interest in the Partnership. In determining the adjusted basis of his Interest in the Partnership, each Partner should be entitled to include in basis his proportionate share (based on his proportionate share of profits and limited for this purpose to the fair market value of the properties subject to such liabilities) of the Partnership's outstanding Wraparound Note liability.

(3) The discussion entitled 'Federal Tax Matters' relating to Federal income tax matters is accurate in all material respects, as of the date hereof. In our opinion, the aggregate tax benefits of significance to investors acquiring Limited Partnership Interests should be realized over the term of the Partnership.*

Certainly, this goes much further than the accountant's letter in providing some measure of comfort on the shelter's projected tax benefits. But immediately following the three-part opinion comes this statement, which, if carefully read, would likely leave the concerned investor as wary as ever.

However, the resolution of many of the issues discussed in the memorandum is essentially dependent on factual and legal determinations which will control both the availability and the timing of specific deductions. Accordingly, except as specifically set forth in paragraphs (1) and (2) above, we express no opinion as to the probable outcome on the merits of the particular tax issues discussed in the Memorandum if the Partnership's position on any such issues, as such positions are described in the Memorandum, were to be challenged by the Service.

Perhaps the most significant caveat—this one issued by the syndicator and buried deep in the text of the offering memorandum—carries this ominous warning under the heading Risk of Audit:

"It is the policy of the Service to audit tax returns filed by tax shelter–oriented limited partnerships such as the Partnership. In addition, since the Partnership will admit Limited Partners who have substantial net worth, individuals with respect

---

* From the attorney's letter.

to whom there is a high probability of audit, the likelihood that the Partnership's tax returns will receive close scrutiny by the Service is exceedingly high.

"The Service is paying increased attention to 'tax-shelter' partnerships, particularly those reporting annual losses in excess of $25,000. The Partnership anticipates losses substantially in excess of $25,000 in 1983 and for several years thereafter. See the Projections annexed hereto. Any audit of the Partnership's tax returns which lead to an audit of any Partner's tax return may result in an examination of all items contained in such return, including those not related to the Partnership. Accordingly, any such audit of a Partner's tax returns could result in adjustments of items relating to the Partnership's results of operations as well as items unrelated to the operations of the Partnership. Furthermore, as a result of the Tax Equity and Fiscal Responsibility Act of 1982 (the '1982 Act'), partners' distributive shares of items of partnership income, loss, deductions, and credits may be determined for all partners at the partnership level in a unified partnership proceeding rather than in separate proceedings with each partner as was the case under prior law.

"Under Code Section 6224 as enacted by the 1982 Act, the General Partner of the Partnership designated as the 'Tax Matters Partner' may in some circumstances bind the Limited Partners to settlement agreements for purposes of determining Federal income tax liability without the consent of such Limited Partners. Furthermore, under Code Section 6226, each person who was a partner in the Partnership at any time during the Partnership taxable year in question is made a party to any judicial determination of Federal income tax liability made with respect to such year. *The effect of these provisions operating in conjunction with the expanded audit coverage instituted by the Service in connection with tax shelter–oriented partnerships, may significantly increase the likelihood that a tax deficiency may be assessed in the event the service challenges any of the tax positions taken by the Partnership* [emphasis added]."

That such warnings do not send all but the most determined risk takers scurrying for safer investments may be a function of the fact that the caveats are not widely read.

"The offering memorandum is written in such a way as to discourage anyone from trying to read it in full," says a registered investment adviser and tax shelter salesman.

"When reviewing a deal for my clients, I focus on three things: the general partner's track record; the offering summary, which is basically a capsulization of the projected tax benefits; and the name of the CPA firm that signed off on the memo. The latter is among the most important indicators of a legitimate deal. If I see a Big Eight name connected with a real estate partnership, then I'm inclined to feel pretty good about the shelter. Those guys are the mavens on real estate deals."

Precisely the mindset that led Bob Holody's client to invest in the ill-fated coal-mining deal. Regardless of Holody's personal caveats on the investment, assuming he made them, the fact that his firm signed the accountant's letter had the effect, if only by appearance, of legitimizing the deal.

In the rush to cultivate promising practice opportunities for the eighties and beyond, CPA firms are embracing tax shelter engagements because they appear, at first blush, to be the best of both worlds: basically an audit function under the guise of consultative services. This sleight of hand turns a routine $5,000-to-$10,000 fee into a $25,000-to-$50,000 engagement. To sweeten the pot, clients rarely question the CPAs' shelter-related invoices. Unlike the traditional audit, which is often compulsory, tax shelter "audits" produce a tangible asset (the CPA's signature) that can aid the client's marketing mission and ultimately increase his profits. The fee is viewed not as an expense but as an investment.

The unwanted by-product, however, is that tax shelter work

prompts CPA firms to lend their names to transactions for which they can make no definitive statements, and to give investors a false sense of security in the syndicator's ability to deliver and sustain projected write-offs. The lesson here is that in searching for new practice opportunities, marketing directors may want to balance their aggressive salesmanship with the countervailing principle, borrowed from architecture but equally true in managing professional firms, that "less is more."

Perhaps they should bear in mind a message Mitchell Feinglass, an investment adviser with Asset Management Group, passes on to his more adventurous clients: "In spite of the IRS crackdown on abusive shelters, there are people out there selling five-to-one and six-to-one deals. Naturally my clients, who, as a group, are always on the prowl for maximum tax deductions, learn of this through the grapevine, the news media, what have you. Without fail, they call me up in a huff, demanding to know why I'm putting them into one-to-one or two-to-one deals when another guy out there is offering write-offs of double and triple that size.

"At that point, I have to calmly but forcefully remind them that the IRS is taking a dim view of 'abusive shelters,' that these high-multiple write-off deals are likely to be audited and are unlikely to hold up. After concluding my spiel on the tax reform laws and the like, I conclude with a truism that everyone in the tax shelter game, yours truly included, should live by: 'If something seems too good to be true, it probably is. Keep your distance.'"

6

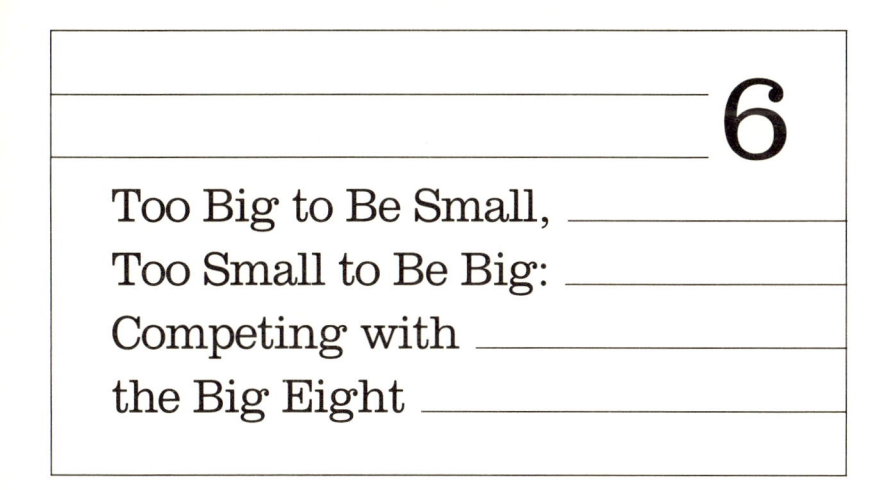

Too Big to Be Small, Too Small to Be Big: Competing with the Big Eight

Tax shelter practice illustrates the great dichotomy between major league accounting—the top fifteen to twenty firms—and the thousands of comparatively smaller practices that round out the profession. Syndicators out to reassure a wary public are well aware of the direct relationship between an accounting firm's rank in the CPA hierarchy and the level of confidence it instills in prospective investors. For this reason, the most prominent firms have a lock and key on the shelter-signature market. Syndicators are not about to pay $50,000 or more for the right (a dubious one indeed) to affix "Schmuck, Schmuck & Schmuck's" seal to an offering memorandum.

The few shelter engagements channeled to the less-celebrated firms generally fall outside the major firm's self-prescribed parameters of acceptability. Include in this category virtually any deal promising multiple write-offs of four to one or better. Regardless of the tax issues involved, the premier CPA firms prefer to steer clear. The spoils go to a handful of smaller firms that, with less riding on their prestige, are willing to risk the pitfalls of marginal shelters in return for the promise of substantial fees.

But competing with the biggest firms—outside of the tax shelter market, that is—can be far more rewarding than simply fighting for the leftovers. At a time when the Big Eight are revising their standard shotgun marketing strategy for a more selective approach that homes in on the most lucrative (consultative versus audit) and fast-growing (services versus Eisenhowers) engagements, they are finding, much to their consternation, that smaller firms have already established themselves as formidable competitors in some of the choicest markets. Here the tables reverse, with many of the plum engagements going not to the largest firms but instead to those with the strongest network of local connections or the greatest proficiency in specialized fields or industries. Here, "less is more" may be the operative principle.

Let's look closely at the accounting market from the standpoint of two firms that fit this mold: Israeloff Trattner and Laventhol & Horwath. Starting at the low end of the size spectrum, Israeloff Trattner makes for an interesting case study as much for the way the firm was started as for its current position in a strategic accounting market. Managing partner Bob Israeloff—a tough-minded practitioner who inherited the seeds of the firm from his father—has built what is today a thriving, $7-million-a-year practice on the basis of a shrewd business strategy best described as "bury 'em and buy 'em out." It all started when Israeloff, then a twenty-three-year-old junior on Arthur Young's New York audit staff, made an observation that influenced the course of his career and set in motion his efforts to build a substantial, midsized accounting firm.

"My dad was a sole practitioner who provided accounting and bookkeeping-type services to a ragtag collection of clients in Manhattan," recalls Israeloff, a pale, bespectacled man who looks older than his forty-six years but whose energy and enthusiasm are those of a youngster.

"He kept a mail drop at 76 William Street but actually worked out of the basement of our home in North Woodmere. When I graduated from the Wharton School in 1959, his practice had an annual gross of $18,990. Like most loving fathers, he wanted me to go into business with him, but with numbers like that, I wasn't even tempted. I had Big Eight on the brain."

Recruited by all of the Big Eight except Price Waterhouse, Israeloff accepted Young's bid and promptly went off to work on "glamor" audits like Sinclair Oil and American Airlines. Supervised by Sanford Burton, then Arthur Young's audit manager, who went on to become chief accountant of the Securities and Exchange Commission, Israeloff thoroughly enjoyed the job and gleaned from it some of the finer points of CPA-client relationships. Observations that would ultimately shape his own business career.

"Until I came on board at Young, my exposure to the accounting profession was pretty much limited to observing my dad at work. The contrast was remarkable. Always fearful of losing clients, Dad would always approach them with great intimidation and they responded in kind, often berating and abusing him. In one case he asked a client, for whom he'd been spilling his blood and guts for years, for a $5 fee increase—from $50 to $55. Well, the guy tore into him as if he'd asked for his house and firstborn child. Dad immediately retreated, agreeing to carry on at the old rate. He didn't dare challenge the client. I thought that was standard operating procedure until my first major client contact at Young changed my mind—changed it permanently.

"I was working on the audit of a big New York Stock Exchange company when I discovered that a $600,000 fixed-asset voucher hadn't been booked. Obviously, someone had made a mistake. Well, I was convinced I'd be a hero. Each person up the chain of command on the audit staff had me explain my discovery to the next higher level, and when this reached the partner in charge, he asked me to accompany him to a meeting with the client's chief financial officer. Heady stuff for a twenty-three-year-old, and the proceedings in the CFO's office turned out to be a real eye-opener. The Young partner presented our findings firmly. He was polite, mind you, but he operated from a position of strength. I learned on this occasion—and others to follow—that the accountant could bring strength to client negotiations.

"As it turned out, the $600,000 was not deemed to be material to the audit. My budding heroism was crushed, but I wound up gaining more from the experience than I could have anticipated at the time."

A year and a half after his debut at Young, Israeloff's father, stricken by an apparent heart ailment, asked his son to run the family practice until he was back on his feet. Moved partly by guilt, partly by loyalty, Israeloff asked for and received a leave of absence from his Big Eight employer.

"As it turned out, Dad's illness was misdiagnosed. Further tests revealed that his apparent heart disease was really only a hiatus hernia. Within two months, he underwent surgery, recuperated, and was back at work serving his clients. This was my cue to return to Arthur Young, but Dad wasn't letting go so easily. He pleaded that I stay with him, that we work together as father and son, and that I eventually take over the business. When I reminded him that his eighteen grand a year wasn't much to share, he swore there'd be much more if I came into the practice."

Too hardheaded to be swayed by his father's unbridled optimism, and with the lure of the Big Eight still very strong, Israeloff declined the paternal appeal.

"As I recall, my answer was 'Thanks, Dad, but no thanks.' My only concession was to stay with him for a while after he'd resumed his practice just to help with the driving and such. The surgery had weakened him and I didn't want to return to Young until he was 100 percent.

"It was during this period—what I thought would be my swan song days as a small-practice CPA—that one of my dad's old cronies, a retired postal clerk, died. He'd been a trained bookkeeper and as a sideline had built up a $6,000-a-year business doing tax write-ups for local stores.

"Soon after the funeral, his family approached my dad with a proposition: to take on the deceased's clients and to pay the widow some reasonable compensation in return. A part of each fee, a few dollars a month, whatever."

With the senior Israeloff eager to effect what amounted to a 30 percent expansion of his practice virtually overnight—a practice he'd built dollar by dollar, client by client, for over twenty-six years—father and son hatched a strategy for acquiring the postman/accountant's former practice.

"Armed with a sob story about our old friend's long illness, of his deathbed request that we take over his business and provide for his widow, we made the rounds to all of the clients," Israeloff recalls, "getting 100 percent of them to agree to the new arrangement. A real coup, to be sure, but this was more than simply a matter of gaining additional fees.

"From my perspective, the really important thing was that Dad and I had stumbled onto a fundamental law of the accounting marketplace: that an established practice could be transferred from one principal to another with no loss of business. I knew there was something to that, some way to profit from that lesson."

That "way" turned out to be a simple but brilliant strategy for building a substantial and highly profitable accounting practice on the "bury 'em and buy 'em out" formula.

Says Israeloff: "After the success with the postal clerk's business, I started looking for similar situations where we could take over practices from dead, dying, or retiring practitioners in exchange for a modest payout to either the principal or the widow. You see, buying out a guy's practice when he's forty to forty-five, and at the top of his stride, usually requires the payment of a hefty premium—that is if you can buy the practice at all. But by getting a practice without a principal, as in the case of a recent death, or where the principal has one foot in the retirement home, then it's a buyer's market. You gain the clients, the fee income, the goodwill—all for a song."

With his Big Eight ambitions gradually superseded by a growing conviction "that you can really expand a small practice into a substantial business," Israeloff spread the word to attorneys, bankers, and accounting colleagues that he was in the market for small practices, or, to put it another way, to take on the clients and take care of the widows. From 1961 to 1964, the budding merger king—as he would come to be known—brought his expanding firm's consolidated fees to $55,000. In 1964 he consummated his first substantial merger, combining his firm with Dick Trattner's ($22,000 in fees) to create Israeloff Trattner. The new entity then went on to purchase or merge with another practice in 1965, two in 1966, two in 1968, and one each in 1969, 1972, and 1975. All transactions, except the 1970 merger with Harvey Berkowitz (now an Israeloff Trattner partner), were based on deaths or retirements.

Over the years, Israeloff's deals have followed a fairly standard formula. Typically, he pays the principal or the heirs a multiple of one to two times gross fees, with 10 to 20 percent down and the balance over four to five years. The earliest deals, negotiated when there was less competition for small accounting practices, were especially sweet, with the purchase multiple rarely exceeding 1.5 (closer to 2.0 today) and with no interest due on the payout. In addition, Israeloff allocated only a small part (an average of 10 percent) of the purchase price to goodwill,

Too Big, Too Small: Competing with the Big Eight

thus enabling him to deduct virtually the full amount of the investment.

To protect himself against major client defections jeopardizing recently completed acquisitions, Israeloff built a provision into the purchase agreements providing for a debit of one and a half times* the client fee for all clients leaving Israeloff Trattner within two years of the acquisition.

Starting off as he does with a propitious purchase price, and then covering his risk from all directions, Israeloff is virtually assured of a successful acquisition. His twenty-three-year buying and merging spree has produced a string of thirty-seven deals that have nurtured his firm's bottom line and, even more important, have fulfilled the master plan he concocted as an ambitious young man.

"I always viewed the merger and acquisitions strategy as a means to an end," he says. "That being the establishment of a sufficient fee and client base to achieve considerable internal growth, to invest in staff and technology, and to compete with virtually any firm, of any size."

Although he is light years away from his biggest competitors (namely the Big Eight), Israeloff has succeeded remarkably on all counts, establishing his firm as a force in the Manhattan and Long Island markets.† While IT cannot even touch a world-class audit—the kind that for the Exxon engagement alone yields for Price Waterhouse a megafee that approaches the sum total of Israeloff Trattner's annual income—it is probably better off without these colossal engagements. As a firm of small business specialists, IT is deeply immersed in a generalist practice that is consultative in nature and weighted toward the high end of its hourly rate curve ($125 per hour for partners). Here, in the land

---

* The same multiple used to price the practice.
† Israeloff Trattner keeps offices in New York City and Valley Stream, New York.

183

of local retailers, seat-of-the-pants garment manufacturers, and small industrial plants, the CPA is an integral part of the client's management team as well as a valued personal adviser. This respect for, and reliance on, the practitioner—vastly different from the cold, contractual relationships between the Big Eight and their audit clients—insulate IT and other well-entrenched market niche firms in its class from the nickel-and-diming that has reached epidemic proportions throughout *Fortune* 500 land. Although Israeloff clients occasionally bitch about fees, as every accounting firm's clients are wont to do, in the final analysis most pay and pay well. Precisely because the firm's services are not viewed as a commodity, because they are seen as integral to the bottom line, IT's clients rarely ask their CPAs to compete with other accounting firms solely on the basis of fees.

"I refuse to be treated like a whore!" Israeloff snorts, waving a fist in the air. A normally calm and thoroughly civil man, he rages at the slightest mention of low fees. Clearly the vision of his elderly father receiving a tongue-lashing from an abusive client has been branded into his consciousness and has become an integral part of his management philosophy.

"I force my clients to respect me much as I respect them. For example, it's often taken for granted in this profession that clients pay late and that there's nothing you can do about it. I refuse to accept that. What do I do about it? Simple: just like any other businessman, I charge interest—one percent a month on payments delinquent sixty days or more. My objective isn't to grab for every dollar I can get—I'm not a pig—but instead to give clients reason to pay within a reasonable period of time. If they don't, I may have to borrow money. Which means, in effect, that I'm subsidizing their delinquency. Why should I do that?" Sitting in on a management meeting for a major client—where he was asked to present his views on strategic issues facing the firm—Israeloff found himself being harangued by the company's chief financial officer over an IT invoice for

Too Big, Too Small: Competing with the Big Eight

$13,000 in interest payments on unpaid fees. He seethed—not because of the size of the outstanding balance, but because he'd learned through the grapevine that the CFO made light of the invoices, cavalierly tossing the bills in the wastebasket.

"When I confronted him about this, he flatly admitted as much, saying, 'I don't pay interest charges.'

"No doubt, he thought I'd put my tail between my legs and slink away, happy to have the client—interest charges or not. But I wasn't about to do anything of the kind. The conversation went like this:

BOB ISRAELOFF (BI): Bullshit, you don't pay interest. I don't accept that. That's the price of paying late and that's our policy. Period.

CLIENT: Okay, okay, we'll settle. I'll give you $2,000.

BI: You're getting me angry. Don't insult me with an offer like that.

CLIENT: Bob, would I insult you? Okay, $3,500. That's my best offer.

Israeloff stormed off telling his client, "You can take your best offer and walk with it."

He recalls what happened next.

"One of my junior partners, who was by my side during this exchange, told me later that he'd wanted to slap his palm over my mouth. Naturally, he was afraid we'd lose one of our clients. But just the opposite: the incident actually strengthened the client relationship. Not only did he pay $9,000—the amount we eventually settled on—but he said, 'Bob, I always knew you were tough, but when you told me to walk, well, I must admit I really respected you for that.' "

Israeloff's lack of tact was probably less of a risk than it appeared to his young partner.

"When the principals of a business get together to chart their future and ask you to join them as the only outsider,

185

there's a message there about your value to the organization. That's what gives this practice strength. I'm not out to exploit the fact that my clients need me, it's just that respect factor I'm looking for. It has to be mutual. That's what leads to long-standing and profitable relationships. My responsibility is to perform for my clients and their responsibility is to pay me."

Where Israeloff Trattner is at a disadvantage vis-à-vis the Big Eight is in the ability to sustain unprofitable relationships for the sake of achieving long-term marketing objectives. The high tolerance for oozing red ink without bleeding to death gives the major firms enormous flexibility in cultivating new markets. Much as Price Waterhouse is willing to sustain two decades of losses to build a base in Red China, all of the Big Eight, in their rush to capture the entrepreneurial clients that are Israeloff's bread and butter, can accept initial engagements for lowball fees with the hope of turning the corner on profitability somewhere down the road. The first year or two of professional services becomes, in effect, a loss leader.

The vice president of a Long Island–based commercial bank sees this as a matter of course: "Quite often, small companies seeking loans will approach us with financial statements that we think are poorly prepared. At times, we can trace this to the CPA involved, who is either out of date, over his head, or just plain incompetent. In any event, we don't have the kind of assurance we need to proceed with the loan. So we may ask that the prospective borrower submit revised financials, using any of three or so CPA firms we'll recommend—firms we've worked with before and we know are up to our standards.

"Quite often, the minilist includes a Big Eight, a Second Eight, and a crackerjack local firm. When the would-be client asks each of them to propose, he generally gets a very broad spectrum of fees, with the big firms, interestingly enough, sometimes asking for as little as half as much as their smaller competitors. Many clients can't resist the low fee. Would you,

Too Big, Too Small: Competing with the Big Eight

after all, pay more for an unheard-of ten-man firm than for one with national prominence? The big firms use discounting as an effective marketing tool. Because of this very process, we bankers are accused of being in bed with the Big Eight."

Israeloff agrees: "The Big Eight is prone to lowballing. I've seen engagements where the reasonable fee would be $25,000 to $30,000. When a Big Eight firm proposing on the engagement wants the client badly enough it'll come in at $12,000 to $14,000. Not that they're in business to lose money, but they can afford to do so in order to pursue their primary objectives. That is, to establish a relationship with the client, to woo him into a state of trust and confidence in his CPA and then to sell him a laundry list of services including microcomputing consulting, estate planning, and the like.

"So yes, we lose clients to the Big Eight—and to the Second Eight, which is also given to lowballing, although not as aggressively. But do I care? Not when it's due to discounting. In the first place, I'm not about to give away services, I wouldn't do it if my firm was ten times the size of the Big Eight. That diminishes the profession. Second, I'm doing better than they are anyway. So why the hell should I care?"

There is some truth here. From a personal and professional standpoint, Israeloff has no one to apologize to. He earns more than half a million dollars a year, lives in a gracious home on Long Island complete with tennis court and swimming pool, and maintains a second residence in Longboat Key, Florida. He is sought after as a merger candidate by the big firms, whose advances he routinely rejects. "Bob's the kind of successful, local practitioner who thrives on running his own shop," says the executive partner of a top-fifteen firm that has made repeated passes at Israeloff Trattner. "For now, he's committed to remaining independent. You're talking about a big ego there—the kind that doesn't easily submerge itself into another firm."

Says Israeloff, "I never could have done this well at Arthur

The Accounting Wars

Young unless I went on to become the managing partner, and I don't know if he earns as much as I do. Also, I run my own business; he doesn't." But the "merger king" is also keenly aware that Israeloff Trattner is not Arthur Young by any stretch, and the man at the top, though he may be on an equal footing from the standpoint of personal earnings, is way down the ladder in terms of professional stature. Perhaps to compensate for this, Israeloff is highly active in his profession's organizational hierarchy, having served as president of the New York State Society of CPAs and president of the Foundation for Accounting Education, among other key positions. Clearly, he enjoys the limelight and the power that were he managing partner of a world-class firm would come with the turf.

Not that his extracurricular activities don't provide tangible benefits. The competition for clients in the New York/Long Island market pits Israeloff Trattner against a wide spectrum of CPA firms up to and including the Big Eight. Just who walks away with most of the business is a function, in part, of who is best known. In spite of the profession's growing dependence on a smorgasbord of hard-sell marketing tactics, old-fashioned work of mouth is still the most productive source of new clients.

"Bob's worked it out so that when some of the most influential people on the Island, those who are consistently asked to recommend accountants, think of a CPA firm, they think of Israeloff Trattner," says a veteran observer of the Long Island accounting scene who has observed Israeloff in action for more than a decade. "This doesn't happen overnight, nor can you trace it to a single newspaper write-up or any one of the leadership posts he's managed to get elected to. No, it comes as a result of consistent self-promotion. Of keeping his name up there in the spotlight, so that people keep hearing it and seeing it time and again. The cumulative effect of this long-term exposure is that people come to think of Israeloff as the ultimate authority in accounting—the best CPA you can hire."

Too Big, Too Small: Competing with the Big Eight

Israeloff freely admits that his pro bono activities produce cash dividends.

"Being well known in the business and professional community helps us to gain clients. I'm not bashful about that. Why should I be? The role of a managing partner in a firm of this size is not to do audits but instead to establish, through your own conduct, a high level of visibility and prestige for the firm. In many cases, clients see the managing partner and his firm as one and the same. Because my clients think I'm the best son-of-a-bitch accountant in the world, they think my firm is the best son-of-a-bitch accounting firm in the world. That's the benefit, and the responsibility, of my position."

If there is a secret to Israeloff's success, it is that he is every bit as much a businessman as a CPA. Those clients willing to concede to him the title of "best son-of-a-bitch accountant" might want to change the last word to "entrepreneur." His most creative thinking comes not in the form of tax planning or cash management, but instead in innovative acquisition strategies and marketing tactics. Typically, the local CPA seeking the same measure of Israeloff's success—that is, the creation of a highly lucrative midsized practice—believes that he can accomplish this simply on the basis of technical prowess. That is a pipe dream. It takes a talent for self-promotion, for salesmanship, and for original thinking. Consider Israeloff's integrated approach to winning new business:

"There's a line of thought, I assume you could call it a cliché now, that the best way to get new clients is to tap the referral network that runs through the legal, banking, and accounting professions. The theory goes like this: When your client, a small business, wants to form a corporate subsidiary for developing high-technology products, you can call in ABC law firm to do the legal work and XYZ bankers for the financing. The unwritten understanding is that ABC will return the favor when one of their clients needs a business valuation for an estate plan

The Accounting Wars

and XYZ will refer you to prospective borrowers in need of an audit.

"Now don't get me wrong. I'm a believer in this. I ask that each of my partners take a banker to lunch at least once every other week. That means, over the course of a year, each partner is seeing almost twenty-five bankers. Multiply that by eighteen partners and you come up with a nice little network of contacts. And on the legal flank, we've established a litigation support department to mesh our services with those of the legal community.

"But . . . but . . . when you look at the referral system alone —as I have on quite a number of occasions—you realize that there's less here than meets the eye. My analysis shows that we pick up 5, at the most 10 percent of our new clients through lawyer/banker referrals. Not bad, but by spending so much time milking this cow, we ignore a far more fertile source of business, that being our own client base. If we take the time to inform our clients of the full range of our services, and if we demonstrate how they can benefit from services they are not currently receiving, we can generate far more through internal growth than through the acquisition of new business.

"A recent encounter with a corporate client really drove this home to me, made me realize just how remiss we are in maximizing our client relationships. When I suggested to this particular client that he avail himself of our estate planning service, he said, 'I didn't think you guys could take on new business. You always seem too busy for that. And to tell you the truth, Bob, I didn't know you do estate planning.' "

To bring a tiny CPA firm (as IT was as recently as 1975) into competitive form, to enable it to compete occasionally with the Big and Second Eight, the managing partner must gradually move away from the lilliputian clients that account for the firm's initial fees to an ever-larger client base. This takes discipline. In today's fiercely competitive markets, a client spurned is not necessarily a client replaced. But only by graduating from the lowest common denominator can the small firm with ambitious designs hope to develop the staff, the technology, and the organizational strength to service substantial corporations.

Israeloff has managed this well. In a pattern now common throughout the profession, he has launched a paraprofessional division to service those clients—predominantly gas stations, pharmacies, and the like—too small to warrant the attention of staff accountants. By having the bulk of this work (basically bookkeeping functions coded into the firm's computers) performed by paraprofessionals, Israeloff can direct the professional staff's efforts to a higher plateau.

Today, the typical IT client—a closely held, family-owned manufacturer with $10 to $12 million in sales—pays $30,000 in annual accounting fees that cover tax returns for the corporation and the principals, a year-end audit, tax planning, and general hand-holding. It is a solid, profitable, entrepreneurial client—the kind dearly sought by all levels of the profession.

What Israeloff has recognized almost from the day he decided to go AWOL from Arthur Young was that the sole practitioner—and the very smallest multiple-practitioner firms—are an endangered species. Although his father fought for and kept a place in the profession, and actually maintained a rather comfortable life-style, this feat is increasingly hard to duplicate. To adequately service today's emerging corporations, even local CPA firms need specialists in audit, tax, estate planning, microcomputers, and pension plans. As small businesses become increasingly sophisticated, and as high-powered, national CPA firms compete more aggressively for their business, local practitioners are forced by the marketplace to make substantial investments in staff, practice offices, and computer facilities. Those unable or unwilling to do so will lose emerging clients just as they make the transition from start-ups to profitable companies.

The Accounting Wars

This is best illustrated by bank referrals. The same banks that routinely recommend Israeloff Trattner, along with the Big and Second Eight, have demanded that prospective borrowers sever ties with their old accountants as a requirement for obtaining a loan.

"I lost a client because Citibank insisted that the company switch from me," says Harvey Stein, formerly a sole practitioner in New York's Westchester County.* "Why? Ostensibly because they were dissatisfied with my financial report, which was a review.† The client didn't want to leave me, was satisfied with my service, and made his opinion known in no uncertain terms.

"But the bank was adamant. I mean, they even refused to discuss the matter. Although I just about pleaded for the chance to introduce myself, to demonstrate my capabilities, they wouldn't hear of it. The message I kept hearing was that they wanted a larger firm to do the work and they weren't going to hear any arguments to the contrary. The fact that I am a professor at Pace University** and that I teach all the kids who are recruited by the Big Eight made no difference.

"What really gets me is that you take on a new client, a start-up company, and you invest in it. By that I mean you keep your fees very modest to reflect the company's limited resources. The hope is that as the firm expands, so will your services and management's ability to compensate you adequately. But when you take a company to that position and you lose it through the bias of an influential third party rather than a fault of your own, well, that's not easy to take.

"Naturally, the Citibank client did switch to a bigger firm. Did I blame him? Absolutely not! In fact, when the principal apologized to me, which he had no obligation to do, I told him

---

* Now executive vice-president of a Boston-based corporation.

† A substitute for a formal audit, often prepared for small, privately held companies seeking bank or other financing.

** Now retired from the faculty.

that when it comes to survival, we each have to worry about our own."

The truth is, the smallest practitioners are on a treadmill. Their growth from zero revenues to $250,000, although difficult, is much easier than subsequent expansion. The initial challenge of making enough to pay the founder's salary is quickly superseded by an even greater challenge—that of supporting a growing staff, a network of offices, and a burgeoning overhead. Without Israeloff's merger strategy, which accomplishes significant growth in major chunks, the firm is unlikely to keep pace with its market and its fastest-growing clients. As such it is vulnerable to competition and is often relegated to the marginal businesses (in size and fees) that larger CPA firms have cast off or shifted to paraprofessionals.

Unfair as it may seem for the banks and the business establishment to discriminate against small practitioners, regardless of their professional capabilities, there's more at work here than the old bias that bigger is better. Once a firm passes the threshold of fifty professionals, once it develops a "critical mass," it must establish organizational checks and balances to help the executive partners manage the practice and ensure clients of minimum standards of quality control. While the sole practitioner's work is rarely subject to peer review, partners and staffers in more substantial firms find that their efforts are subject to checks and cross-checks.

At Israeloff Trattner, for example, financial statements prepared by any of the firm's offices must pass through the financial statement review department. This department, in turn, is under the direct supervision of IT's Accounting and Auditing Committee, whose function is to advise and instruct the professional staff on the most current accounting procedures for financial statements.

"There's a difference between a collection of partners, which you can get in a business that has gone through numerous mergers, and a unified professional firm," says a tax attorney practicing in IT's market. "Israeloff Trattner is very much the latter. That's because they've established uniform standards for professional practice, and everyone, Bob Israeloff included, must comply with those standards. I've seen it firsthand: one's work does not go out without first being scrutinized by the review committees. If it's not up to par or if it is contrary to their standards, it does not get to the clients. Sure, some things slip through the cracks, but the system seems to do a reasonably good job of screening out the errors and inconsistencies."

Put in perspective, Israeloff Trattner's greatest strength, and the same can be said for other well-managed firms its size, is its place at the midpoint of the accounting spectrum. Dwarfing the sole practitioners at the base of the profession, it can thumb its nose at the nickel-and-dime engagements, pawning off this business to its bookkeeping division. On the other hand, because Israeloff Trattner is still a gnat—albeit a pesky one at times—in the eyes of the Big Eight, and because it competes only occasionally with the giants, it is spared the prohibitive costs and the lowballing that is endemic at the high end of the spectrum. Within this DMZ it is at once protected and profitable.

In the yawning gulf between Israeloff Trattner and the Big Eight, an eclectic mix of firms are romancing the $10-to-$100-million-a-year closely held businesses that make up the most promising market, in terms of untapped potential, for accounting services.

One of the most interesting of this breed likes to call itself "the big accounting firm with a little firm inside." And it is an apt description. More than any of its competitors in the Big Eight—and more than some in the second tier—Laventhol &

Horwath* is ideally positioned to harvest the growth companies first emerging as voracious consumers of tax, audit, and financial consulting services.

Much like Israeloff Trattner, L&H traces its roots to humble beginnings, in this case to two small firms, Horwath & Horwath (1915) and Laventhol, Krekstein (1923). Both built successful, if marginal, practices servicing small, entrepreneurial clients primarily in Philadelphia (L&K's hometown) and New York. Pleased with their standard of practice and their steady, if undazzling, growth rate, both sailed into the 1960s—a decade of turmoil in the accounting profession—confident of their capabilities and certain of a prosperous future.

"But we found ourselves forced to examine our positions," says L&H's executive partner George Bernstein. A compact workaholic whose low-key style and penchant for nondescript clothing plays into the stereotype of the cautious CPA, Bernstein is nevertheless widely credited as a decisive decision maker with a sharp-focus view of accounting's future and his firm's place in it.

"A growing sophistication on the part of our clients and competitors forced us to explore ways of significantly expanding our professional capabilities. The choice, it appeared, was to merge with larger firms or to conduct a merger of our own. We chose the latter. In 1967, Horwath & Horwath and Laventhol, Krekstein merged, creating a combined entity with twenty-five offices, 108 partners, and $9 million in annual fees."

What Bernstein fails to mention is that by remaining small, basically local operations, the merger partners feared that they were vulnerable to major client defections. Because many of the founding firms' longtime clients—Horwath & Horwath's in the hotel field; Laventhol, Krekstein's in manufacturing and retail-

---

* Ranked tenth or eleventh largest in the nation, depending on who's counting.

The Accounting Wars

ing—were moving, inexorably, toward national operations, it was becoming clear to the accountants and clients alike that their businesses would need the services of national CPA firms. This was the primary motive behind the merger, and one for which the two firms were ideally suited. Much as the Grant-Hurdman union was nixed on the grounds of geographic overlap (both were basically strong in the same places), the Horwath and Laventhol deal was born on the basis of geographic integration. With Laventhol well established in Philadelphia and New York and Horwath boasting a network of offices in twenty cities, the merger promised to create a combined entity that met the acid test of a sound merger: one greater than the sum of its parts.

With a single stroke, the players could claim to be national firms. But this was somewhat of an exaggeration. Yes, Horwath & Horwath's branch network stretched from coast to coast, but the vast bulk of the offices were hand-holding boutiques that did little more than service a single client, such as Hyatt Hotels, then based in San Francisco. Much to management's credit, it viewed this Pony Express setup not as a national power—it was not, for example, strong enough to compete for business in local markets—but simply as the foundation for a crash building program to beef up Laventhol & Horwath's presence across the nation.

Playing accounting's version of catch-up ball, the firm moved heavily into mergers, joining forces with forty-one independent firms in three years (1968–71). L&H's objectives matched those of the local firms it acquired. Just as Horwath & Horwath and Laventhol, Krekstein had feared for their fate as marginal operations, its newest merger partners shared similar concerns. As such, L&H's pitch to combine forces in a truly national firm was appealing, and made for an enlightened move on the part of the acquired practices. By trading off the elusive benefits of independent entrepreneurship, the small practitioner gains entry to a substantial organization more capable of meeting the demands of a changing profession. This is a function not only of territorial penetration, but also of specialized services. As we have seen, the larger the CPA firm's client and capital base, the more it can invest in talent, technology, and continuing education. The greatest distinction between the nation's large and small accounting firms is not the number of partners on the payroll, but instead the depth of specialized services they offer. It's safe to say that regardless of a client's needs for consulting or financial services—from limiting taxes on repatriated profits to doing feasibility studies for automated steel mills—the top fifteen CPA firms can handle the engagement in-house, and handle it well. By rapidly expanding the client/capital base, mostly through mergers and acquisitions, a firm gains the wherewithal to invest in such practice components. This is vital for two major reasons: to retain clients as they expand in size and scope of operations and to profit from a more comprehensive array of financial (primarily consultative) services. With this in mind, L&H initiated a second round of thirty mergers beginning in 1980.

The product of this frenetic activity—a total of seventy-six mergers and acquisitions over seventeen years—is a surprisingly cohesive firm with 352 partners, 3,150 professionals, fifty-three domestic offices, and annual fee income of approximately $200 million. Although the first two merger cycles were followed by periods of disorganization and internal dissension, the establishment of uniform standards and procedures, and the recognition by the formerly independent players that they stood to benefit by assimilating into the system rather than clinging to their former methods of operation, helped to speed the transition from merger mayhem to relatively smooth, unified operations.

One of the most significant factors in L&H's success is that it has remained focused on a rather narrow set of founding ideals while simultaneously seeking broad expansion. This is not contradictory. In the creation of an enormous fast-food empire, McDonald's rarely lost sight of the principles—cleanliness, speed, and economy—espoused by founder Ray Kroc when his company was little more than a lowly burger stand with grand designs for the future. L&H—in the context of the accounting profession—has performed similarly, retaining the entrepreneurial outlook, the facility for dealing with seat-of-the-pants business owners, that distinguished the firm's principals since the turn of the century. Although L&H can now compete with the Big Eight on all but the monster audits and the most arcane practice specialties, it has continued to identify not with the *Fortune* 1,000, but instead with the closely held family-owned businesses that have always formed the bedrock of its practice. The difference is a matter of style, of outlook.

Seated around a conference table at L&H's Walnut Street headquarters in Philadelphia, the firm's management team of Jerry Rosenberg (operations), Ben Benson (marketing), Dave Arnold (MAS), Ernie Ten Eyck (audit, accounting), and executive partner Bernstein come off more like the principals in a family-owned garment house than national accounting practitioners. The choreographed behavior so common at Big Eight meetings is absent here. The impression is that of a group of men used to dealing with clients more on the basis of personal relationships than on tightly written procedures.

"We're in a better position to service midsized corporations—$10 to $100 million in annual revenues—than the Big Eight," says Benson, a former independent practitioner whose firm merged with L&H and became its Boston office, "because like our clients, we have an entrepreneurial outlook. From the day our people report to work here, we train them to be businessmen as well as accountants, to understand a client's market as well as his books, and that's what companies of this size need and demand.

"An example: Several years ago, I met with a new client that had just ended an unsatisfactory relationship with the Big Eight. The company was losing money, management didn't know why, and all its prior firm could do was offer a cost-cutting study for $50,000.

"As soon as I came aboard, I sat down with the two principals, who were always at each other's throats, to talk out the issues. It didn't take more than twenty minutes to identify the main problem. Yes, there were some losing operations that had to be pruned, some poor financial practices that had to be changed, but the real cause of red ink was the principals themselves. Precisely because they were always fighting, because no one was managing the company, it was adrift without effective leadership.

"My recommendation, which had more to do with psychology than accounting, was for the guys to split up, for one to sell out to the other, and for the business to have the benefit of a single chief executive. Happily, they took my advice, and to this day the surviving owner credits my advice with having kept the business alive."

Adds Jerry Rosenberg, a hard-boiled veteran of the accounting wars and an L&H veteran since joining Laventhol, Krekstein in 1952: "I was working out of our Wilkes-Barre office in 1972 when Hurricane Agnes hit, nearly wiping out one of my clients. He suffered terrible storm damage, to the extent that continued operations were in question. As a result, the guy went into a terrible depression and had to be hospitalized. Well, I didn't try to solve his problem with a calculator. No, I stood by his side, at his hospital bed, for two days, talking him out of his depression. I showed him that in spite of the damage there was hope, and that he could pick up the pieces. That's not an accountant's function of course, but it is indicative of the intimate relationships we have with our clients."

Certainly, L&H's claims to business moxie and to hands-on

client relationships are echoed throughout the Big Eight's small-business practice units. Bernstein freely admits this.

"We don't have a lock and key on any of the things we do. Certainly not. The truth is that in accounting, there's nothing really new under the sun.

"But where we do stand out is that we put greater stress on the business advisory role than many of our competitors. It's a matter of emphasis."

Robert Elliott, chief executive of Miami, Florida, based Levitz Furniture Corp., a $650 million New York Stock Exchange company, agrees. One of L&H's largest clients—and one atypical of its client base—the firm's comments are nevertheless interesting because it has grown with Laventhol & Horwath from a fledgling, family-owned venture to its current size.

"Laventhol and Horwath seems to be more interested in the business side of our operations—as opposed to the pure accounting issues—than other CPA firms I've had experience with," Elliott says. "They call now and then to discuss a business matter, to make a recommendation. Theirs is a real hands-on approach—much more so than the one I witnessed between Arthur Andersen and Montgomery Ward when I was a Ward vice-president.

"Levitz has made that extraordinary transformation from family-owned business to professionally managed public company, and Laventhol and Horwath has been with it throughout."

L&H sharpens its entrepreneurial focus with a clever marketing strategy centered on the real estate business. Although industry specialization is the primary marketing tactic at virtually every firm big enough to compete for substantial clients, real estate is an inspired choice for a firm of L&H's size and background. In spite of its enormous size and profitability, the real estate industry remains fragmented and entrepreneurial, in contrast to the airline, utility, and insurance businesses, which are concentrated in relatively few hands and are professionally managed. This distinction accounts for the fact that real estate is the last grand-scale market still serviced by a collage of varying-sized CPA firms rather than being dominated by the Big Eight. Another contributing factor is that real estate's major players—hundreds of independent developers, syndicators, and financiers—are bottom-line entrepreneurs who contract for accounting services based on professional capabilities, not prestige.

Howard Ronson, an immensely successful Briton who invaded New York's tight-knit real estate community in 1978 and has since become one of Manhattan's most prolific developers, is typical of the breed. Running a major real estate enterprise, HRO Associates, with a staff not much bigger than a coffee shop's, he relies heavily on top-notch accountants, lawyers, and leasing agents to manage his business on a daily basis. He wants and demands one thing, *performance,* and he pays to get it.

"I put in place the best professional firms experienced in every facet of my developments, pay them premium fees for as long as they perform up to the highest standards, and make it bloody clear that I'll fire their asses if they fail to live up to those standards. I care not if it's a big firm, a small firm, or in between. *Results!* That's what interest me."

Ronson's accounting firm, $50-million-a-year Kenneth Leventhal, is small by Big Eight standards, but it is the acknowledged leader in real estate practice and is widely credited as a "results-oriented shop." Competitive solicitations for the Ronson account, and they are likely to be more common than tenant complaints, will go unrewarded as long as Leventhal performs. Ronson the developer, Ronson the real estate entrepreneur, doesn't buy accounting services in the same way as the CFO at

The Accounting Wars

New York Life Insurance. To this hard-nosed Englishman, and to most of his real estate brethren, "Big Eight chic" doesn't amount to threepence.

Laventhol & Horwath, which boasts an impressive collection of real estate clients (including New York wunderkind Donald Trump, office building impresarios Olympia & York, and top tax shelter syndicator VMS), offers them a bountiful smorgasbord of specialized services:

- Economic feasibility studies comprising site analysis, market analysis, evaluations, and recommendations for proposed projects and financial analysis;
- Lease analysis and structuring for shopping center and office building developers and tenants;
- Financial projections that either forecast or illustrate project assumptions and data;
- Location studies that define site requirements for a project concept based on its marketing potential;
- Fiscal impact analyses to assist government in assessing potential benefits and costs to the community of a proposed project;
- Section 8/Section 11(b) economic feasibility studies to assist bond rating services in evaluation of mortgage bonds to finance government-subsidized housing;
- Design services that include studies of space requirements and use, space planning, and operational design programs;
- Highest and best-use studies to determine the most productive and profitable use for a particular site;
- Valuation studies to determine the economic value of an existing property based on its potential income;
- Energy management systems designed to evaluate, monitor, and control costs;
- Profit improvement studies to improve cash flow for distressed properties;

Too Big, Too Small: Competing with the Big Eight

- Accounting and financial systems, including electronic data processing, to control and monitor resources and programs and to evaluate operational effectiveness;
- Organizational and administrative studies of a real estate department or development company.

To maintain a high profile in the real estate community, and to reinforce its reputation as a source of information, Laventhol & Horwath acts as a majordomo of the industry, hosting two annual conferences for real estate syndicators (six hundred people each at $425 a head) as well as two general real estate conferences, publishes a real estate newsletter, and places partners on real estate panels including the Building Owners' and Managers' Association and the International Council of Shopping Centers. The net effect is to more closely identify the firm with real estate than any other CPA firm, save Kenneth Leventhal, which is much smaller.

Laventhol & Horwath's marketing strategy meshes perfectly with its position in the accounting marketplace: It is too big to be small and too small to be big. Although this appears to exclude the firm from key markets (the very big and very small), in reality it serves as a buffer in the more desirable middle market.* Should the sole practitioner hook into a fast-track client that explodes from a local retail shop to a regional menswear chain, his good fortune will likely end when the first banker or underwriter suggests a change of accountants. Next stop, a firm in L&H's class: big enough to impress the financial establishment but small enough, in the entrepreneur's eyes, to service what is still a modest-sized company. Once the client moves to L&H, it is likely to stay. The sole practitioner cannot

* One weakness here is in multinational practice, where the Big Nine have a decided advantage.

The Accounting Wars

hope to reclaim the client—it is clearly out of his league—and although the Big Eight will pitch for the business, entrepreneurs are unlikely to respond unless they are dissatisfied with their current level of service.

Which brings up another interesting point. By being too small to take on world-class audits—the likes of GM or GE—L&H is effectively shielded by the laws of the marketplace from the low-margin, commodity-type audits that are forcing the Big Eight to compete for business like purveyors of frozen pork bellies.* In dealing primarily with entrepreneurs—even those as substantial as the Pritzker family, best known as the owners of Hyatt hotels—the firm is locked into the emerging business/consulting sector that has taken up the slack of the declining Eisenhowers and puts a premium on high-quality accounting services.

"Our clients hang on our every word," Bernstein boasts, and although there is some hyperbole here, there is also an element of truth. Because the CPA to a $25 million firm serves not as the auditor—even if he does an audit—but instead as the chief financial officer, he is cemented into the firm like the first dollar bill taped to the wall. Management is not wont to dismiss him, as it will a *Fortune* 500 controller, on the basis of a competitor's lowball bid.

L&H's emergence as a merger magnet for smallish CPA firms has linked its destiny to the middle market—a fact that Bernstein, Rosenberg, Benson, et al. are quick to recognize as a beneficial by-product of the firm's evolution but which they are nevertheless tempted to trade for a bigger chunk of the *Fortune*

---

* There are two schools of thought on the issue of size. Some in the profession believe that bigger is infinitely better—that the future belongs to the behemoths. Economies of scale and the ability to offer the widest range of services through the strongest multinational network, they say, will be most important. This philosophy is evidenced by the possible merger of Price Waterhouse and Deloitte Haskins & Sells, which, if successful, will create the world's largest CPA firm.

1,000 audit market, which has evaded the firm over the years. In what must be viewed as a sign of the ferocious competition that permeates the accounting profession, these intelligent, affluent, otherwise level-headed men lust for the prestige, the visibility, the raw sex appeal of a six-figure audit. There's something irresistible about taking business away from competitors . . . about winning, winning, winning!

"Oh, we'll go after a *Fortune* 500 audit—even a *Fortune* 50—if we think we have a reasonable chance of landing the engagement," Bernstein says. "Every now and then the word gets out that one of the megacorporations is considering a change of auditors and that management would be open to our proposal. Our sources on the audit committee, who usually leak word of the imminent change, can tell us if we have a chance or if the Big Eight are locked in. Providing it's truly an open competition, we'll propose. In fact, we welcome the opportunity. But in most cases, it's all a charade. Management wants to appear open-minded, but it's completely biased in favor of the Big Eight."

Reflecting on his own words, Bernstein removes his eyeglasses and stares out across the conference table. As the conversation continues around him, he appears lost in thought, only to reassert his presence moments later, blurting out a comment that reveals the near-universal contempt for the exclusive fraternity at the top of the profession.

"I wish I could banish, eradicate, eliminate that damn term 'the Big Eight.' It's pernicious to so categorize professional firms. I'd like to wipe 'the Big Eight' from the English language." Again he pauses. "Or maybe just change it to 'the Big Ten.' Then we'd be included."

A common denominator that runs throughout big-time accounting is the preoccupation with each firm's standing vis-à-vis its local and national competitors. This refers not only to fees

The Accounting Wars

—the ever-popular "numbers race"—but also to reputation, credibility, and overall image in the business community. Israeloff Trattner, for example, wants to know how it stacks up against Margolin, Winer & Evans, a Long Island competitor, as well as Arthur Andersen, which retains a place within striking distance of Bob Israeloff's Valley Stream headquarters. Similarly, Laventhol & Horwath yearns to compare its real estate practice to that of Kenneth Leventhal and Coopers & Lybrand. Coopers, in turn, thirsts for all the grist it can gather on how its MAS staff rates against Peat, Marwick's.

Competitive intelligence is sought not for its ego value or because it makes for good gossip, but because it provides the raw data for effective marketing. Only when a firm is aware of its position in the marketplace, of its relative strengths and weaknesses, can it develop strategies to correct deficiencies and, perhaps more important, to seize opportunities.

"If we know that one of our Philadelphia competitors—be it a smaller firm or one of the Big Eight—is seen by clients and prospective clients as weak in taxes, well hell, that opens a door big enough for us to drive a truck through," says a Laventhol & Horwath partner who asked to remain anonymous. "By positioning ourselves as the premier tax boys, we can likely pick up a nifty chunk of business by default. Whether or not the competitor really is weak in tax or not isn't the issue: What matters is how he is viewed by clients. And if they see weakness, I see opportunity. Opportunity not only for the tax work but, once we're part of the family, for the audit, consulting, the whole shooting match.

"But remember, it all starts with the research. The starting point is knowing where you stand in relation to your competitors."

The marketing orientation that has swept through the accounting profession has sensitized most senior partners to the value of independent research. The old seat-of-the-pants judgment that once formed the basis for marketing strategies has given way to a more sophisticated approach.

"I once asked ten partners at Arthur Young why prospective clients should hire their firm," says market researcher Larry White, "and all ten of them responded identically: 'Because we're the accountant's accountant.'

"Well, what they didn't know is that their counterparts at virtually all of the other major firms responded the same way. Before they started commissioning market research, managing partners of the big CPA practices all believed their firms were viewed as the standard of excellence against which all others were judged. They've since learned that no single firm enjoys that preeminent image—certainly not on a national basis. Research has demonstrated that various firms are viewed as having various strengths in various markets—and it has pinpointed exactly who is strongest where."

The concern for image, perception, reputation—which often equals and in some cases supersedes the concern for professional standards—has given rise to a Larry White and made him a moderately influential figure in accounting. But who is Larry White? How did he come to be a factor in the profession?

"Back in the early seventies, when I was in charge of the University of Detroit's department of communications studies, I received a call from the newly appointed partner in charge of Arthur Young's Detroit office,"* White recalls. "It seemed he'd heard of my courses in business/marketing communications and inquired if I didn't know of a bright student who'd want to go to work for Young. As an aggressive partner with a mandate to build the firm's Detroit practice, he was eager to enlist people with sophisticated marketing skills.

"As it turned out, his plan was of great interest to *me*—I'd been eager to expand beyond academia—so I wound up going

---

* He has since left the firm.

to work for AY myself, serving as the PIC's lieutenant for marketing functions. Initially I was sort of an administrative aide, doing the detail work, the follow-through, on programs the managing partner initiated. My work on the firm's seminar program was typical: I provided some input for the speeches, helped prepare the guest list, and was on hand to see to it things progressed smoothly. But once I got some experience under my belt, once I had a better feel for public accounting, I started recommending ideas of my own. For example, I noticed that many of the partners were weak in personal salesmanship. They thought of themselves as professionals, and were thus wary of stepping into the salesman's shoes. But because the profession's new marketing orientation demanded a greater level of client contact, we had to find some way to get them over this phobia. My solution was to develop personal selling techniques that removed the fear factor, encouraged the partners to cultivate their clients, and in the process aided the firm-wide objective of practice building."

A bony, fresh-scrubbed midwesterner who still looks and dresses more like an academic than the entrepreneur he has become, White saw something in his first brush with public accounting that, as Bob Israeloff said, he could build on. That is, the big accounting firms' voracious appetite for marketing tools, for sales aids, for anything that could help them in the hotly competitive markets for audit, tax, and consulting. His brainstorm was to turn his once-scholarly pursuits into a highly lucrative enterprise serving the profession at large. Accounting was a market waiting to be tapped.

Leaving Young in 1975, White set out on his own, getting his feet wet as an independent marketing consultant. "My first major business contact, a Washington-based sales training expert, got me going by subcontracting to me parts of various marketing engagements he'd picked up, often in the accounting field. One of my first projects for him was to help develop a two-day sales training seminar he was putting together for A. M. Pullen, a midsized CPA firm.

"After that came a wide variety of assignments in a cross section of marketing disciplines. As my workload grew, I started making money, which was certainly gratifying, but even better was that I gained valuable experience and exposure. My network of contacts expanded, more and more people in accounting learned of my capabilities, and soon I had a going company —a growing company—with a bright future in a profession that really appreciated what I could do for it."

But what does he do for it? Has he contributed to the accounting profession's marketing sophistication? Or has he served up a placebo to a group of disoriented firms eager to play the marketing game but incapable of gauging whether they are playing it right or whether the services they are buying add anything to the bottom line? Whatever the answer, the customers are buying.

Today, Services Rating Organization (owned by White) boasts a staff of thirty-five, located in Birmingham, Michigan. Much of the firm's growth is attributable to its market-by-market research report, which claims to chart the local business community's perception of competing CPA firms in U.S. cities. Called Market Measurement Surveys, the reports are designed to show CPAs how they stack up against one another in key practice subdivisions. For example, White's MMS for Orlando, Florida, charts the market's perception of fifteen firms by the quality of their tax, audit, and consulting work as well as the fairness of their fees. Firm A finds that 27.1 percent of the respondents rated it "excellent" in auditing services, 2.9 percent rated it "fair"; competitor E was rated "excellent" by 44 percent of the respondents and "fair" by none; A was rated "expensive" by 20 percent and E by only 14 percent.

Although White balks at calling his Market Measurement Surveys syndicated research, this is precisely what they are.

The Accounting Wars

Boiled down to the fundamentals, he gathers information of likely interest to a group of firms hungry for competitive data and sells it for considerably less than it would cost these same firms to compile on their own. If the research sells well, the firms covered by it, or affected by the competitive environment it studies, effectively share the expense, adding a profit factor for the researcher.

Fees for the MMS range from $3,000 to $5,000, depending on the market, with New York and Los Angeles being higher. Although White is close-mouthed about some of his research techniques, claiming this to be proprietary information, we do know that the bulk of the research is done by telephone interviewers operating out of White's Birmingham office. About half are part-time, but most hold degrees in a cross section of disciplines. White claims his interviewers limit their conversations to senior executives, controllers, chief financial officers, or business owners of the respondent firms, as well as referral sources, such as attorneys and commercial loan officers.

Although it is puzzling why busy CFOs and CEOs would take the time to reveal personal thoughts on long-standing relationships to unknown interviewers, White's clients appear to have full confidence in his reports.

"Whenever we've used White, we've found that his reports reflected precisely what we ourselves knew about the market," says Main Hurdman's Dick Levine. "He was right on target."

Interestingly, Laventhol & Horwath's Ben Benson reports nearly identical findings: "He confirmed what we already knew about our position in the various markets. I can't say that we learned anything new from the research, just that our perception of where we stood was right."

White's marketing tactics are really quite clever. Rather than focusing his sales efforts exclusively at the headquarters level, he peddles Market Measurement Surveys to the local practice offices, knowing, from his Arthur Young days, that this can be the most productive route.

From White's viewpoint, the guys in the field—the local managing partners—view the main office as a bureaucracy bloated with overhead, so if word comes out of Chicago or New York or wherever the executive office is located that the local practice should buy this or that program, chances are the partners in charge will resist it. They'll view it as wasteful and will do what they can to avoid participation.

On the other hand, if the local PICs buy the very same program, if the decision to acquire it is theirs alone, they'll embrace it as a sound investment.

But there may be another factor at work here. When the Ben Bensons and the Dick Levines of the profession—the guys in the national marketing posts—buy the MMS, they often do so not for the benefit of the findings, which they claim to know already, but to prod PICs to improve their performance in weak markets.

"You tell a partner in charge that he should be doing more to gain exposure and he'll tell you everything's okay, we're doing fine, don't bother me," Benson says. "But when you can wave the market research in his face, you have an objective confirmation of your claim that his office is not up to snuff with the competition. You use it as a people-management tool."

White's market surveys are only one part of an integrated product line. His research reports, which in a sense diagnose business ailments (poor image in this or that market or practice subspecialty) are sold with a self-contained cure-all.

The reports come in three components, White explains. There's the generic research report, the client relations survey (an enhancement of the market survey, including ratings on the firm from a sample of its clients in the market area), and a one-half-day workshop explaining the results to the partners

The Accounting Wars

and managers and indicating what they can do to make their firms more successful in the marketplace.

"Quite often, sales training is the missing link, and that's a service we provide to increasing numbers of our clients. I think it's of enormous value. A business—any business, including an accounting firm or a law firm—has to be in a position to sell. This means tending to four key marketing activities: working with present clients; working with third-party relationships (other professionals, bankers, insurance brokers); working with general image (public relations); and working with key prospects (hit list). By focusing on all of these business-building components, the firm positions itself to get the most productivity from its selling efforts. But laying this groundwork is only stage one. To compete in public accounting today, the partners and associates have to sell on an individual level, and we help them with that as well. Learning the finer points of salesmanship is probably one of the hottest developments in the profession today."

Long popular with business equipment manufacturers—the Xeroxes and the IBMs of the world—sales training has come late to accounting but it has come, nevertheless, with a vengeance. As the CPA firms jockey for competitive advantage, and as they seek to reposition themselves for the more lucrative engagements in a changing America, they have come to recognize that the marketing effort must extend beyond the firm level to the individual partners and senior staffers. Much as Bob Israeloff requires his colleagues to break bread with bankers every few weeks and much as Tom Presby's staff holds forth in Touche Ross's private dining room, the profession is moving en masse to an appreciation of salesmanship as an indispensable tool of the accountant's practice.

"Gone are the days when we could leave the selling to those of our partners who, by dint of their personalities, were best suited for the wining and dining that often goes with winning new clients," says the managing partner of a midsized CPA firm. "Now the Big Eight are moving in on us and we're moving in on them, and the competition's getting hotter than a pepper pot. While it seemed, at first, that the battles would be won by the firms that did the best job in professional practice, advertising, public relations, and industry specialization, I'm not so sure of that anymore.

"As important as these endeavors are, and my God, you can't run a major firm today without them, we've all learned that marketing can only flesh out clients. Our partners have to then go out and sell, they have to close on new business, and the competition's so wide open now that everyone on staff has to participate.

"But for God's sake, no one ever taught an accountant how to sell. In fact, I have the suspicion that a goodly number of my colleagues entered this profession precisely because it promised to insulate them from selling. And much as that may have been true as little as ten years ago, it sure as hell ain't today. I'm not queasy about admitting that we've hired a consultant for salesmanship, whose only job is to go from office to office turning accountants into salesmen."

Turn CPAs into salesmen? Is it really that easy? Can determined introverts be led, often kicking and screaming, into "salesmanship seminars" only to emerge three hours later as newly minted Lee Iacoccas? The small band of salesmanship consultants now working within the accounting profession—some on a contractual basis, others as full-fledged partners—say yes indeed, the closet-case auditor can be transformed, à la Cinderella, into the Ed McMahon of accounting. All it takes, they insist, is an understanding of the principles and techniques of salesmanship.

But conversations with a number of accounting's sales consultants reveal a group more similar to Sunday-morning television ministers than CPAs. Their definition of selling is a

The Accounting Wars

condescending, manipulative approach that is so transparent as to be irritating and counterproductive.

An exchange between the author and a sales trainer working for a Big Eight firm went like this:

MARK STEVENS (MS): Making a salesman out of an introvert seems to be a form of personality modification. I'm skeptical that that can be accomplished in a seminar.

SALES TRAINER: I perfectly understand your view on this, Mark. In fact, it's quite perceptive on your part. Let me congratulate you on that. Our only difference is a semantic one. You say modification, I say education. We're teaching people to sell; we're not changing their personalities. Doesn't that make sense, Mark?

MS: If a person feels uncomfortable initiating conversations, attending social functions, asking others to buy services he or she is selling, and if that person has felt that way for ten, twenty, thirty years, or more, can learning these techniques really help them feel differently?

SALES TRAINER: I'm impressed with the way you stick to your opinion. I can see you have a real mind of your own. And by God, Mark, I agree with everything you are saying. What you must keep in mind, however, is that you're referring to "feelings" and I'm referring to "thoughts." Even if the person feels uncomfortable with certain types of interaction, we can train him to think away those bugaboos and free himself from past limitations. It works, Mark. People can be anything they really want to be—they can accomplish all that they're determined to accomplish.

But not everyone agrees.

"*Mr. Rogers* . . . have you ever seen the kids' show *Mr. Rogers*?" asks a Big Eight partner who has attended sales training seminars. "The way he talks to my three-year-old is the way these sales consultants speak to us and it's also the way they expect us to speak to clients.

"Well, that's naive bullshit. You can't say to a tough-minded entrepreneur or a controller, 'Well . . . aren't . . . you . . . smart . . . as . . . a . . . whip. I . . . am . . . certain . . . you . . . will . . . want . . . to . . . avail . . . yourself . . . of . . . all . . . of . . . the . . . fine . . . services . . . we . . . can . . . offer . . . to . . . your . . . very . . . fine . . . company, Mr. Wonderful.'

"Jesus, all I've come away with from these seminars is that the people supposedly teaching us to sell have probably never sold anything in their lives except their own services."

There's no denying that the trainers' techniques tend to be simplistic and heavily weighted with motivational slogans that make for nice classroom pointers but are of questionable value in real-world client negotiations. What's more, manipulative techniques are unbecoming for professionals widely viewed as trusted financial advisers.

"You've heard of sleight of hand," says one sales trainer. "Well, I teach sleight of word. By that I mean saying something that the client thinks is in his interest but is really in yours. The choice of the right word alone can make the difference.

"Consider this: You want to sell a cash management program to a major client who's already complaining about your fees. He says, 'I'd like to sample your cash management package, but the budget's stretched to the limit.'

"Typically, the accountant would go on the defensive, saying everyone has to earn a living and the fees are already rock bottom. But that approach is off base. I'd suggest the CPA respond to the statement about the budget limitations this way: 'I'm pleased you brought that up because my intention is to cut your expenses rather than increase them. I'm not as interested in earning fees for myself as I am in helping you manage your cash better. Your interests are my primary concern.'"

And the moon is made of cream cheese. Clearly, clients would view this Mr. Rogers-ism as slick double-talk if not worse.

Larry White claims his approach "builds self-confidence and thus makes the person a more competent and effective salesman. It is important to structure the conversation so that the client will reveal his concern, his opinions. This information can then be used to present a sales proposition in a way that will be attractive to him.

"Take a Main Hurdman partner who's out there proposing to a small business. The business owner says, 'I'd like to work with you, but I'm afraid a firm of your size is not going to take a relatively small client like us very seriously. You're too darn big.'

"Typically, the Main Hurdman guy would respond that his firm has a special department assigned exclusively to servicing smaller businesses. But that's not the best answer, because it's really a defensive posture. Instead, I suggest responding in a way that forces the client to air his concerns. Faced with the complaint that Main Hurdman is too big for the client, I'd say 'Yes, we are one of the world's largest accounting firms. Why does that concern you?' As you can see, I've prompted the client to provide me with the ammunition I'll need to convince him that our firm is best suited to serve his company's interests."

Much as there are skeptics to this approach, there are also true believers. Dick Levine, very much a pragmatic marketer, insists that White's techniques work: "Larry's greatest strength is that he understands the accounting profession. He knows that many CPAs are afraid of salesmanship because they think they have to hit a home run every time they go out to pitch a client. But Larry shows them how to adjust their expectations to match their capabilities. They learn they can hit singles, they can drive runs in, they can assist others."

Which sales techniques work for some CPAs and not for others may not be as important as the fact that accountants are being taught lessons that would make the profession's founding partners turn in their graves.

"A Volkswagen dealer once taught me, quite inadvertently, a selling lesson that I pass on to all of my clients," says a sales trainer active with Big Eight and second-tier firms. "After taking me out for a spin in a brand new shiny yellow Beetle—a ride I thoroughly enjoyed—he took out his order form and started writing up the sale. When I made it clear that he was jumping the gun, he said, 'I know you like the car, what's holding you back?'

" 'Safety,' I answered.

" 'Safety? Please explain.'

" 'I'm a bit wary of buying a rear-engine automobile. If I get into a head-on collision, God forbid, I'll be a goner.'

"The dealer, who up until this point feigned ignorance of my concern, firmly grasped my shoulder. Looking into my eyes, he said, 'Do you have any idea of what it feels like to have a thousand-pound engine sitting on your lap! The front engine's not a safety feature: It's a death trap!'

"Well, you know something, that guy made a sale. He told me just what I wanted to hear. No, even more important than that, he gave me a good rationale for buying something instinct told me was not a wise choice. Were that dealer just a body in the showroom, he'd have said goodbye to me empty-handed. But because he was a *salesman* he went home that day with a $500 deposit in his register and another order on the books.

"The same magic can work for accountants. All they need is knowledge of the selling principles and the confidence to put them to use."

Open and shut case? Not quite. CPAs willing to model themselves on automobile salesmen will find that the turn of a phrase or the readiness to take the offensive will no more assure a sale than a rub of a "lucky" rabbit's foot. Marketing professional services is a complex process that relies more on trust and confidence than on simplistic formulas.

Even the sales gurus themselves can come up empty-handed. One trainer admitted: "During a break in a seminar I was conducting, I went to a pay phone to call a prospective client. After hearing my pitch, he told me he wasn't interested and hung up. I was struck by the irony of it all. There I was teaching others how to sell and my own client was giving me the brush-off."

7

Book Cooking, Numbers Juggling, and Other Tricks of the Trade

Not all the competition in accounting is over who does what best. Increasingly, clients are won and lost on the basis of a less noble criterion: Who is most willing to sacrifice professional standards for audit fees. In accounting's version of musical chairs, clients dissatisfied with their audit, which, theoretically, should produce virtually the same findings regardless of who performs it, shop the market for firms more willing to see things through their own eyes than through Generally Accepted Accounting Principles (GAAP).

"It's not a very savory story, not for American business or the accounting profession," says Glen Perry, former chief accountant of the Securities and Exchange Commission's Enforcement Division. A Peat, Marwick partner who served from 1982–84 as the SEC's in-house snoop for corporate fraud, Perry operated, in his Washington days, from a disheveled D.C. cubbyhole littered with lopsided stacks of top-secret documents, annual reports, and newspaper clippings. His mission: to un-

The Accounting Wars

cover corporate book cooking, numbers juggling, and related indecencies. In the course of his investigation, he came to see a direct relationship between management fraud, accounting flimflams, and the pressure to produce an ever more bountiful bottom line.

"Companies play games with their financial reports for any number of reasons, the most common being the intense pressure on corporate management to produce an unbroken stream of increasing earnings reports. Well, if operating results don't comply with that objective, management may try for an accounting solution. In other words, they'll figure out some sort of ass backward way to fiddle with the books so that the numbers come out the way the stockholders and the analysts expect them to—and the way the CEO damn well insists that they do.

"The scenario goes like this: Company A, displeased with its earnings, cooks the books to come up with a more palatable financial report. Accounting Firm B is told to approve this book-cooking scheme. When the CPAs refuse, which many of the reputable firms will do, Company A may fire B and call in B's competitors to take on the engagement.

"Although the first, second, and even tenth firm invited to assume the engagement may refuse, when the music stops there'll likely be a new CPA firm sitting by the client's side, accepting the client's financial machinations or finding some other way to accomplish similar results."

Perry's terrible ten of accounting frauds—ploys used to misrepresent corporate financials—include:

Recognition of revenues before they are realized;
Recognition of operating leases as sales;
Inclusion of fictitious amounts in inventories;
Improper cutoffs at year end;
Improper application of LIFO;

Book Cooking, Numbers Juggling, and Other Tricks

Creation of fraudulent year-end transactions to boost earnings;
Failure to recognize losses through write-offs and allowances;
Inconsistent accounting practices without disclosure;
Capitalization or improper deferral of expenses;
Inclusion of unusual gains in operating income.*

In the case of questionable audits—those failing to uncover fraud or other material misrepresentations—Perry points to five major shortcomings:

Scope restrictions: e.g., agreeing not to confirm certain receivables;
Incompetence: e.g., not having the level of training or experience necessary to take on the engagement;
Auditing by conversation: e.g., taking the word of management without independent verification;
Not critically evaluating transactions: e.g., not noting provisions of a contract that cause it to be nonbinding on one or both parties;
Lack of objectivity and skepticism: sometimes auditors get confused between doing the right thing and keeping their clients happy [emphasis added].†

While admitting that CPA firms are partially responsible for audit failures, Perry insists that the vast majority of audits are performed according to the highest standards, and that more of the blame rests on the client side. Central to his thinking is a belief that the pressures of the executive suite, always considerable, are multiplied exponentially in periods of economic turmoil. As companies struggle to prosper in a difficult period—or

---

* From the SEC's Enforcement Activities, *CPA Journal*, April 1984, page 9.
† Ibid., page 12.

The Accounting Wars

to retain the image of prosperity—the temptation, the urge, the compulsion to cook the books become, for some, irrepressible. In many cases, top management creates a climate that makes fraud acceptable, if not unavoidable.

"Middle managers who cook the books don't always do so to fool the boss. Rather, they also do so to please the boss. . . . The corporate environment leading to middle-management fraud is often created by top management. This is most often done by creating unrealistic budgets followed by excessive pressure to meet or exceed such budgets. This is commonly referred to as management by objectives. In these circumstances, should top management share the responsibility when middle managers commit frauds? There is a fine line between good aggressive management and an environment in which it is probable that fraud will be born."*

Says SEC commissioner James Treadway: ". . . [W]e have seen outright 'cooked books' involving well-known commercial companies. Heinz and McCormick are two examples. A common aspect of these cases is that they arose in a corporate atmosphere which tolerated or encouraged reporting profits, even if they did not exist. That atmosphere was caused by four factors: (1) aggressive and arbitrary demands by top management for the achievement of unrealistic profit goals; (2) a highly decentralized corporate structure, with virtually autonomous divisions; (3) poor communications between top managers who unilaterally and arbitrarily set the profits and the divisions which were supposed to produce the profits; and (4) the failure or absence of adequate internal controls and a failure by certain headquarters to oversee adequately the accounting practices of the divisions.

"In the resulting atmosphere, middle- and lower-level managers came to have the attitude that outright falsification of

---

* Ibid., page 12.

books and records on a regular, ongoing, pervasive basis was an entirely appropriate way, sanctioned by senior management, to achieve profit objectives. The employees who participated in undermining the financial statements frequently believed they were acting in the best interest of the company, sometimes admitting that it was all a 'team effort.' In these cases, the wrongdoing was startlingly direct and simple: prerecognize revenue; falsify or totally concoct inventory; ship without invoices or issue invoices without shipping; and play games with a variety of expenses."

Referring to the Heinz case, Treadway says: "The methods used by the divisions to achieve the demands of world headquarters, and undermine the integrity of the financial statements in the process, were simple. Invoices were solicited from advertising agencies in a current period for services to be rendered during the succeeding period. Shipping invoices were pulled to prevent processing. A shipping moratorium was declared for the last week of the fiscal year and already-issued invoices redated to reflect shipment in the new year."

The SEC's complaint against McCormick, Treadway notes, "alleged that the Grocery Products Division, McCormick's largest division, improperly inflated current earnings. Recognition of promotional allowances due customers was improperly deferred from one period to a future period, and the division did not account for other expenses—primarily advertising—for a current period until a future period. In addition, the division accounted for goods ready for shipment as sales in the current period, even though they were not actually shipped until the succeeding period. To conceal these activities, false statements were made to auditors, two sets of expense records were kept and auditors were permitted to review only the fictitious records, and shipping invoices and advertising bills were altered.

"McCormick had the same type of decentralized corporate structure as Heinz. Special counsel concluded that the pressure

The Accounting Wars

by distant, top management for greater profits contributed to the situation and that those who directed the improper practices believed that the *practices were the only means to achieve the unrealistic profit objectives of central corporate management* [emphasis added]."[*]

More often than either side would like to admit, clients and CPAs view the financial statements as documents subject to flexible treatment.

"Every few years, it seems as if a new generation of corporate managers, and perhaps *accountants and attorneys*," Treadway notes, "arrive on the scene who are convinced that they have discovered the new way to create profits from thin air and who regard the integrity of financial statements as an inconvenient interference."

Says a CPA-turned-stock-analyst for a Wall Street brokerage firm: "The scenario goes like this. Comes year end and top management needs another fifteen cents per share in earnings to meet Wall Street's projections. What happens? Often—very, very often—the controller or chief executive calls in the accountants and says: 'I need fifteen cents a share, and I need it badly. Find a way to get it. Trim this or that expense. Accelerate this or that revenue. Do whatever the hell you have to do and do it quickly and discreetly.'

"Well, you can bet your Boy Scout ring that the CPAs will find that fifteen cents—maybe seventeen cents just for good measure."

Unethical? Fraudulent? Misleading? Not necessarily. Or so say the auditors.

"If you're talking about finding fifteen cents out of total earnings of sixteen cents, then there's likely something improper going on," says a Big Eight managing partner. "But an additional fifteen cents on per share earnings of five dollars, that

---

[*] Treadway speech, November 3, 1983, pages 6–7.

Book Cooking, Numbers Juggling, and Other Tricks

can be entirely appropriate. You have to remember that many of the factors that make up the corporate financials are judgment calls. Take the tax reserve; if a client has a $30 million tax reserve, we may find, quite legitimately, that $27 million is adequate. There's flexibility in these determinations and there's nothing at all wrong with the accountant's making use of that flexibility to compute the earnings. Nothing wrong at all, providing he believes the client has a valid point."

Winning clients in today's competitive markets demands that even the most respected and conscientious firms position themselves as creative practitioners, willing to take a "flexible" rather than a play-it-by-the-book approach. This is especially true in tax practice, where the CPAs' mandate is to save their clients dollars otherwise earmarked for the federal treasury. While this is generally accomplished by steering through legal loopholes in the tax code, aggressiveness can move beyond the threshold of acceptability to creating deductions that are far more questionable.

In one controversial case, the IRS brought suit against Ernst & Whinney for allegedly manipulating claims for the investment tax credit (ITC), a charge E&W denies.

The drama began in the spring of 1982 when a computer analysis of IRS corporate audits (in the Southeast) revealed a disturbing pattern of what were deemed to be illegitimate claims for the ITC. While the law allows companies purchasing production equipment to take a percentage of the purchase price as a credit against taxes, IRS rules specifically exclude most airconditioning and heating units and other nonproductive items. But the audits found that many corporations were camouflaging credits for nonproductive equipment simply by renaming building parts to connote productive uses. "Knock-out panels" turned out to be brick walls and "environmental control systems" were simply air conditioners.

At first the IRS was baffled. Similar ploys were used by

companies having no business relationships, no apparent means of communicating. Only by discussing the case among themselves did IRS agents find the common denominator the computer analysis had missed: All of the corporations had availed themselves of Ernst & Whinney's so-called Investment Tax Credit Study, a service ostensibly designed to ferret out legitimate ITC credits. But the IRS, which considered the credits anything but legitimate, sought a court order directing E&W to cease offering the tax service and charged the Big Eight firm with "a pattern and practice" of "wrongful classification of items which plainly do not qualify and the use of false, misleading, and deceptive labeling so as to obscure questionable items from audit recognition."

E&W's vice chairman for tax, Herbert Lerner, responded this way in a speech to the AICPA's Federal Tax Division: "Taxpayers and their advisors, of course, are often at odds with the Service on matters of interpretation of the tax laws. And responsible professionals are obliged to and do take an adversarial role on behalf of clients—the ITC study area being no exception for this purpose. Consequently, when we prepared ITC study reports we took reasonable basis positions as to eligibility of property, allocations of costs, etc., and we were not surprised when certain ITC issues were raised on examination. In this connection, it should also be understood that IRS agents often disallow reasonable ITC claims based on language alone. To counter this tactic by the IRS, experience has shown that it is wise to include a descriptive word or statement in a report, as to why the ITC claim is made or justified. Moreover, a given claim is less likely to be automatically disallowed by the IRS if it is properly labeled in the report as a 'movable' partition (rather than just a partition), a 'detachable' railing, an 'accent' light, a 'privacy' partition, or a 'modular accoustical' ceiling. Labeling or nomenclature has thus become an element of completeness in an ITC study report. Of course, nomenclature aside, the ultimate correctness of a given item for ITC purposes does not turn on labels, but rather is based on the substantive ITC provisions. We know that and the IRS knows it as well."

Court battles on the issue have led to victories and defeats for both sides. The IRS, at first rebuffed by the courts in its efforts to bar E&W from continuing to offer the ITC study, won a subsequent appeal and has also won early-round decisions on its right to subpoena the names of all E&W clients who've made use of the service.* The final outcome on both issues (still on appeal), and the effect they may have on tax practices, may not be known for years.

Just as client companies are struggling to reposition themselves in a changing America, so too are their accountants scrambling to expand, to reshape their practice mix—to add partners, managers, real estate divisions, computer consultants, tax shelter teams, sales trainers, multinational networks, China connections, and virtually every other service that can be sold by a man or woman in a blue business suit. A billion-dollar professional firm's appetite for new business is voracious—$100 million a year just to achieve a modest 10 percent growth. The pressure to keep the furnace stoked, to keep partner earnings rising along the same upward curve that Wall Street demands of the *Fortune* 1,000, serves as a mighty temptation to those on both sides of the CPA-corporate relationship to take an aggressive stance on taxes, to cook the books, or, equally repugnant, to bless a client's dirty tricks. Although the vast majority of CPAs cling to their principles, the temptations persist and some do succumb.

"You're always trying to remain independent, and in the day-to-day course of events you can, but when there's a problem, when you clash with your clients, that's when the whole independence issue can rise up and smack you in the head," says a

---

* All decisions as of September 1984.

The Accounting Wars

Houston-based Big Eight audit partner who asked to remain anonymous. ("Not for what my clients will think but because my colleagues will have my head for speaking my mind.") "If you object to a client's treatment of a financial transaction, or if you insist on a qualified audit opinion, that client who never before talked fees with you, except when you were first hired, takes you to lunch, calls you at the office, calls you at home, and talks fees, fees, only fees. He suddenly feels the need to remind you, virtually around the clock, that he's paying your salary, and your manager's salary, and your staff's salary, and your secretary's salary, and wouldn't it be wise to agree with his accounting treatment or agree with his opinion that your qualified opinion is not really a good idea after all.

"Well, that client's really suffering from delusions of grandeur. In a big firm like ours, his threat to walk isn't going to have a dire effect on all of those people he fancies himself supporting. We'll all still be here, soaking up other engagements if he goes elsewhere.

"But, this much said, any honest CPA will admit that he doesn't want to lose that client. And he knows that if he refuses to go along with the client's demands, it's probably bye-bye baby. Maybe not immediately, but in six months or sixteen months he'll likely get the axe. The client will invent some subterfuge for making the change, but everyone will know the real reason.

"Most of my colleagues learn to live with client losses, to accept them as the price of professionalism, but others get in the client's bed and spread their legs."

When a firm holds to its principles—refusing to give in to client pressure and for that reason losing the engagement—chances are good that a competitor will claim the spoils. Knowing this may prompt certain clients to shop for opinions much as they would for computer systems. Jim Treadway points to the case of two state-chartered, state-insured savings and loan associations, which he believes illustrates this.

"Southeastern Savings & Loan Company and Scottish Savings and Loan Association entered into a merger agreement and filed related proxy materials with the commission. During 1981, both institutions had received deposits from the sale of all-savers certificates, insured market rate certificates, and various certificates of deposit which they in turn sought to invest in long-term liquid instruments to lock up favorable yields. Upon the advice of the same financial adviser, an investment banking firm, each invested in *15 percent and 16 percent GNMA** certificates. The institutions were concerned, however, that any increase in interest rates would cause a decline in the market value of the GNMA certificates and expose the institutions to losses if they had to sell the GNMA certificates to generate cash to satisfy customers' withdrawals of deposits. As a protective measure, the associations sought to hedge their positions in GNMA certificates by selling futures contracts for U.S. Treasury bonds.

"In the summer and fall of 1982, interest rates dropped rather than increased. The market value of both GNMAs and Treasury bonds increased, but Treasury bonds increased in value more than the GNMAs because the market anticipated that the high-interest-rate mortgages underlying the GNMAs would be prepaid at an earlier date due to the availability of cheaper mortgage money. That perception caused the market to value the GNMA certificates as a relatively short-term instrument. Fearing prepayment of the GNMAs, both institutions sold their 15 percent and 16 percent GNMA certificates and purchased 8 percent through 12.5 percent certificates. Almost simultaneously, they closed out their Treasury bond future

---

* Securities offered by the Government National Mortgage Association.

contracts at large losses and hedged the new GNMA positions with GNMA futures contracts.

"Both institutions deferred recognition of the net losses realized from closing out the Treasury bond future contracts. Instead, they added the loss to the cost of the new GNMA positions, planning to amortize the amount of losses over a twelve-year period. Thus, the losses were not recognized currently in the financial statements filed with the commission. *Each association had extensive discussions with their auditors over several months, seeking concurrence in this accounting treatment. Failing to obtain such concurrence, each discharged their auditors and engaged a new firm that agreed with them on the deferral of the losses.*

"In the administrative proceeding, we only sought a corrective restatement of the financial statements. Despite the absence of fraud allegations, this case nonetheless highlights the inaccuracies which can result when corporate managers take the attitude that an *accounting treatment that 'dresses up' a company's financial statements is acceptable if they can only browbeat their auditors into acquiescence or, failing that, find another auditor who will acquiesce.* That attitude is the direct opposite of the concern corporate managers should have about the integrity of financial statements. . . .

"The Southeast-Scottish case also highlights again the insidious and potentially destructive practice of 'shopping' to find an accounting firm willing to support an extreme position. When a company has taken an accounting issue, as both institutions did, all the way to the national level of a major accounting firm and has been rebuffed, despite threats to discharge the accounting firm if it did not accede, questions about the good faith of the issuer and its management are inevitable if the case comes to the commission. And if the succeeding auditor blesses a practice rejected by its predecessor, questions about that auditor are likely to arise. Granted, room exists for disagreement on close questions, but where a practice is clearly contrary to established accounting literature, blessing such a practice in the face of a considered opinion to the contrary inevitably will cause inquiry into both the issuer and the successor accounting firm." (Emphasis added.)

Looking out on the stark D.C. landscape visible from his comfortable and spacious office, Treadway, a big man with a round, almost boyish face, sighs the weary sigh of a man fighting a battle that he knows, consciously or otherwise, he cannot win.

"You tend to see a proliferation of audit shopping among companies in precarious financial condition or in troubled industries. With the former, an audit client about to get a qualified opinion sees the switch of auditors as a 'quick fix' of its immediate and often devastating problems. In most cases, however, it's less of a fix than a further complication—a tighter knot of misleading actions.

"In the latter, like many quarters of the savings and loan industry, there is a mass effort on the part of the firms involved to seek a paper solution to very real and very stubborn business problems. The s&l's have more transactions than you can shake a stick at. Any accounting treatment that can get some bad debts off the books and produce instant income is worshipped. When an accounting firm puts out the word that it will look kindly on such a treatment, its phone rings off the wall. I can assure you of that."

One of the most infamous audit failures of recent years, the so-called O.P.M. fraud, was replete with charges of audit shopping. The case dates back to the early 1970s, when childhood friends and brothers-in-law Mordecai Weissman and Myron Goodman founded O.P.M. Leasing Services (the initials stand for "other people's money"). The premise, typical of the then promising computer leasing industry, was to borrow money, use the funds to buy computers, and then lease the hardware at lucrative rates. If all went according to plan, the computers would be used to secure the loans and the lease payments would go to the lenders. A highly leveraged operation with bright profit potential.

But Weissman and Goodman, raving egotists with a penchant for lavish offices and palatial homes, sought to speed the company's growth by reducing lease rates and assuring customers they would take back obsolete units. The former pushed O.P.M. deep into the red—later investigations revealed the company was never profitable—and the latter opened a black hole as a new generation of IBM computers was announced in 1977.

To keep the company afloat, O.P.M.'s founders needed a fresh infusion of cash, which, in Catch-22 fashion, they could not get if the company's true financial condition were known. To get around this, Goodman and Weissman used the same leases as collateral for more than one loan (this fraudulent practice dated back to the company's earliest years), and created fictitious leases for nonexistent computers, which the lenders believed they were financing. According to a report by a court-appointed trustee,* Goodman sought to further enhance the illusion of financial well-being by shopping around for a "flexible" accounting firm—one that would certify financial statements that painted a rosy picture of O.P.M. and did not detect the lease frauds. In 1976, he turned to Denver-based Fox & Co.

At first, "Fox drafted financial statements showing large losses and negative net worth. Then, the report states, an enraged Mr. Goodman told a Fox audit partner for O.P.M., to 'get back to the grindstone and try to figure out a way to show a profit.' "† He used what the "report calls a 'series of question-

* Appointed for O.P.M.'s subsequent bankruptcy proceedings.
† *New York Times,* May 1, 1983, page F4.

able accounting techniques' to produce 'materially false and misleading' and 'indefensible' financial statements. They showed profits and a positive net worth for 1976, and later for 1977 and 1978. Meanwhile, O.P.M.'s losses rose."*

Fox was accused of turning "red ink into black simply by booking in the first year all the lease income that would be paid over the life of the machines. Hence, the $60,000 profit generated in a six-year deal would be booked as income as soon as it was inked." †

The full impact of Fox's techniques could be seen when Price Waterhouse was hired by the bankruptcy trustee to redo the books.

"The Fox-certified report for the period ending December 31, 1976, shows O.P.M. with a positive net worth of $724,273. And things were going to get a lot better."** Under the Fox method, "O.P.M. in 1977 showed net income of $1.3 million and retained earnings of $2.2 million. Restated by Price Waterhouse under GAAP standards, income becomes a loss of $9.4 million and retained earnings turns into a deficit of $13.7 million." ‡ Similarly, "Fox method" net income for 1978 is $1.7 million, compared with PW's restated $17.8 million loss. §

O.P.M.'s massive fraud, which finally unraveled in 1981 when a fictitious lease to Rockwell International was discovered by a Rockwell executive, resulted in ten- and twelve-year jail sentences for Weissman and Goodman respectively, and a mean, puffy black eye for their auditors. But Fox's troubles were not limited to the O.P.M. case alone. Equally damaging were

* *New York Times*, May 1, 1983, page F4.
† *Forbes*, April 25, 1983, page 38.
** Ibid.
‡ Ibid.
§ Ibid.

The Accounting Wars

audit controversies involving Saxon Industries and Alpex Computer.*

In a complaint against Fox, the SEC alleged that the firm "examined and reported on the 1979 and 1980 financial statements of Saxon Industries, Inc. . . . and the 1981 financial statements of Alpex Computer Corp. . . . that Fox issued unqualified accountants' reports concerning the above-mentioned financial statements, and that such accountants' reports were false and misleading. . . .

"In connection with Fox's examinations of Saxon's 1979 and 1980 financial statements, the Complaint alleges that Fox aided and abetted Saxon's material overstatements of revenues, net income, and assets, and material understatements of liabilities in those financial statements . . . that Fox recklessly failed to comply with GAAS† in that it did not obtain sufficient competent evidential matter to afford a reasonable basis for an opinion regarding Saxon's financial statements. . . . Fox recklessly failed to verify the inventories of Saxon and failed to detect fraudulent inventory entries in Saxon's books and records. Fox also allegedly did not adhere to GAAS in failing to analyze the underlying documentation concerning the sales of equipment subject to operating leases and failed to detect the improper recognition of revenue and understatement of liabilities relating to such transactions. . . .

"Fox recklessly allowed Saxon to limit the scope of its 1979 and 1980 audit examinations by delaying the commencement of the on-site audit, by restricting physical access to records and prohibiting conversations with all but a few Saxon employees,

---

* According to Edmund Coulson, the SEC's Deputy Chief Accountant, the Saxon and Alpex cases have been settled with the companies signing consent orders, but a third case involving Flight Transportation Corp. is still in litigation (as of October 1984).

† Generally Accepted Auditing Standards.

Book Cooking, Numbers Juggling, and Other Tricks

and by providing insufficient facilities for Fox auditors to perform their work. . . .

"In connection with Fox's examination of Alpex's 1981 financial statements, the Complaint alleges that Fox aided and abetted Alpex's material misstatement of revenues, operating losses, net income, current liabilities, working capital, and stockholders' deficit and Alpex's failure to disclose material related-party transactions in such financial statements. In this regard, the Complaint alleges that Fox's audit was not conducted in accordance with GAAS and that Fox recklessly failed to adhere, in numerous instances, to professional standards relating to the acceptance of new clients, audit planning, audit supervision, and audit review."*

The SEC's complaint sought an order requiring a special review committee† to examine "the manner in which Fox conducts its audit practice with respect to those clients whose financial statements reported upon by it are required to be filed with the Commission (SEC audit clients), that the Committee's report be submitted to the Commission staff and filed with the Court, and that Fox adopt and implement any and all recommendations the Committee may make."**

---

* SEC litigation release 10022, June 8, 1983.

† Known as the Pollack/Stringer Committee, named for its two members, a former SEC chairman and a former Deloitte Haskins & Sells managing partner.

** In what must be viewed as a lapse in the accounting profession's highly touted program of self-regulation, Fox's quality controls were blessed in a 1980 peer review by Price Waterhouse, which stated: "The system of quality control for the accounting and auditing practice of Fox & Company for the year ended May 31, 1980, was appropriately comprehensive and suitably designed for the firm, was adequately documented and communicated to professional personnel, and was being complied with during the year then ended to provide the firm with reasonable assurance of conforming with professional standards and the membership requirements of the Section" (refers to the AICPA's SEC Practice Section). On the plus side, however, PW did note that documentation of Fox's audits could be improved in key areas, including "inquiry into existence of possible illegal acts."

The Accounting Wars

Most threatening to the firm's financial condition, the SEC prohibited Fox from taking on *new* SEC client audit engagements until all of the committee's recommendations were accepted and a follow-up review, to be conducted a year later, confirmed their implementation.* In short, the SEC's complaint made for roundhouse condemnation of a major CPA firm. The charge, boiled down to its essence, was that this accounting practice is currently ill-suited to function as a full-fledged member of the audit community; Fox & Co. must correct serious deficiencies, cannot be entrusted with new clients, and is on probation until and unless it makes substantive changes in its standard of practice.

Because of the double whammy of highly publicized audit failures and the SEC actions against it, Fox was unlikely to write much new business with or without the commission's ban. But the more serious threat, according to some of the profession's most astute observers, was the potential for mass defection by Fox's existing partners and clients. To this school of thought, chief executives, wary of guilt by association, would abandon Fox rather than diminish the credibility of their financial statements. But this may be inaccurate. A major client hemorrhage has not occurred.

Still, like news of a hanging in a country town, rumors of Fox's demise continue to buzz throughout the accounting profession. When CPAs gather—especially those in the Big Eight and Second Eight—the gossip often touches on Fox's prospects for long-term survival.†

"Clients don't like to be stampeded into auditor switches,"

---

* A report on Fox's progress in satisfying these recommendations filed January 1, 1984, was accepted by the SEC, thus freeing Fox to accept new SEC clients.

† A possible merger with Alexander Grant & Co., under discussion as this book went to press, would do much to strengthen Fox's practice. But Bob Kleckner, Grant's executive partner, refused to say whether the Fox name would be retained by the consolidated firm.

Book Cooking, Numbers Juggling, and Other Tricks

says one CPA, overheard at an accounting seminar. "They also don't like to sever relationships without having time to prepare themselves for a change. That's why Fox has been able to hold onto as much of its business as it has. But I don't think the partnership should engage in any long-term fee projections. Not yet. Unless my intuition, based on twenty-seven years of experience in this business, fails me, Fox's troubles aren't over yet."

And this from a Big Eight managing partner: "We keep hearing reports that clusters of Fox partners may break away, perhaps to form their own firm. Should that happen on a major scale, Fox will be seriously damaged. Some public companies may not stay on board—and if they depart, small clients are likely to follow suit."

Bill Dent, Fox's tough-talking director of professional practice, bitterly contests this: "Hell, we do $100 million in fee revenues a year and SEC practice is maybe 5 percent of that. We could lose all of our SEC clients and still survive—more than survive, we'd be in fine shape. The bulk of our clients are entrepreneurial midsized companies that may care somewhat about our firm's involvements with various legal actions, but they're far more concerned with their own businesses and with how we service them on a day-to-day basis."

He has a point. While *Fortune* 50 controllers may be sensitive to their auditor's standing in political and financial circles, this is of far less concern to emerging businesses too preoccupied with their own survival to fret about their accountant's latest go-round with the boys in Washington. To entrepreneurs, the accountant's performance is of primary importance, and Fox's staff does appear to be capable and well informed.

While Dent refuses to discuss the SEC's complaint, claiming "all the issues are in litigation and the attorneys don't want me to comment," he roars "bullshit" to charges that Fox made itself available to audit shoppers and writes off predictions of the firm's demise as "our competitors' fantasies."

He also points to the committee report on Fox, which failed to find the pervasive malpractice some may have expected. Instead, the report paints a portrait of a fundamentally honest firm guilty of little more than weak controls in setting and reviewing professional standards. Although it suggests that "Fox's auditing policies and procedures could be further strengthened in some respects, including certain matters relating to the identification and evaluation of audit risks, reliance on internal control and on management's representations . . ." the committee made clear that it was "favorably impressed by the competence and dedication of Fox's Director of Professional Practice . . ." and by "the coverage, objectivity, and candor of the Fox Inspection Team reports that we reviewed. . . ."

Considering Fox's troubled reputation before the committee issued its report, the findings can only be seen as a shot in the arm.

Charges of audit failure and audit shopping—which have plagued most of the big firms at one time or another—are tied to another, more fundamental issue: whether the SEC's limited powers, widely viewed as little more than a slap on the wrist, can prevent or even seriously discourage fraudulent practices.* For the most part, the agency relies on intimidation and the court of public opinion to prompt corporations and individuals to comply with the nation's securities laws. Its two major types of actions, administrative proceedings and injunctions, can enjoin corporations from continuing practices deemed to be in violation of the securities laws; but neither can seek fines or jail sentences. What's more, the vast majority of cases are settled

* The SEC cannot launch criminal actions but can refer cases to the Justice Department for this purpose.

without litigation, with the corporation's signing consent orders agreeing not to violate the securities laws but not admitting or denying guilt. But Jim Treadway, for one, believes it may be necessary to adopt harsher measures against those "willfully and extensively falsifying corporate records, lying to auditors, and coercing vendors into covering up their practices ... improperly applying accounting principles, making numerous false disclosures concerning the accounting principles which were applied, and repeatedly violating generally accepted accounting principles."

For these hard-core cases, Treadway proposes such options as (1) a restatement of the prior years' financial statements; (2) the appointment of new directors acceptable to the commission, thus diluting incumbent management's control; (3) heightened responsibility of the audit committee, further diluting incumbent management's control; (4) a review of certain accounting practices; and (5) perhaps even retention by the audit committee of its own accounting firm, acceptable to the commission, as an adviser.*

"That's a far cry," he says, "from merely a prohibitory injunction, even one coupled with a restatement."

But does it go far enough? Although corporate management shudders at the prospect of outside interference, especially the brand that emanates from Washington, this is not exactly the fear of God. A far more effective deterrent would be a shift in SEC actions from the institutional to the individual. By holding executives rather than their companies liable for book cooking, the commission would make it more difficult for corporate management to blend into the woodwork of institutional suits, to pay for their legal defense with corporate earnings, and to repeat illicit practices without fear of significant loss to pocketbook or reputation. To some, it is a disturbing paradox that those most

* All these forms of "ancillary relief" may be requested by the SEC; whether or not they will be implemented is up to the courts.

responsible for misleading financial statements—statements which can injure a long list of innocent bystanders, including investors—should be the only ones to escape virtually free of retribution. Were those corporate executives found responsible for fraud to be routinely singled out and referred to the Justice Department for uncompromising criminal action likely to result in jail sentences, it is safe to say that there would be a concerted effort by the full battalion of *Fortune* 1,000 CEOs to tighten internal controls, to forbid numbers fudging, and to prohibit any and all attempts to "slip one past the auditors."

SEC chairman John Shad has noted that penalizing institutions rather than individuals can actually short circuit the drive for honest and accurate financial information.

"Punishing corporations made it more difficult for them to hire top-quality executives who were concerned about the image and reputation of the companies with which they became associated.... *Shareholders are harmed, rather than helped,* when their companies are sanctioned for the acts of unscrupulous executives [emphasis added]." But he also adds that the issue of whom to punish, the corporation or the individual, "is not an either/or issue. Rather, the question is how to best serve investors. Depending on the facts of the case, investors are sometimes best served by sanctioning corporations, and at other times executives, or both."*

In its actions against the accounting profession, the SEC typically censures individual practitioners rather than entire CPA firms.

"It has always been accepted here that unless there is a systemic breakdown, seeking an injunction against an entire firm, rather than the culpable individuals, reflects unfairly on that firm," Treadway says. "So we've generally taken the institutional approach vis-à-vis accountants.

* John R. Shad, *New York Times,* March 4, 1984

Book Cooking, Numbers Juggling, and Other Tricks

"Does the injunction against individuals have any real impact? Is it a real deterrent or a slap on the wrist? I can tell you that the debate over those questions is as intense in this agency as it is outside of these walls. But the fact is that our statutory authority is limited to injunctions, plus possible ancilliary actions, and I believe that in most cases, this is strong and appropriate medicine. The censuring of a CPA carries a stigma that is anathema to professionals and that can be very damaging to his practice and career.

"When we go beyond individual actions—in those extraordinary circumstances where there is evidence of a systemic breakdown—the injunction against an entire firm can have very severe repercussions. In the Fox case, for example, we were warned that an injunction against the firm would jeopardize its continued existence. But we acted anyway. The magnitude of the wrongdoing demanded dramatic action. And we took it."

For a profession accustomed to bureaucratic meddling, a more ominous threat may come from dramatic action of another kind. That is, clients' attempts to shift culpability to their auditors—not for accounting deficiencies but instead for the clients' own shortcomings. As some in the profession fear, companies whipsawed by the marketplace will use their accountants as convenient scapegoats.

To some, this was at least partly responsible for Chase Manhattan Bank's abrupt dismissal of Peat, Marwick, its auditor for fifteen years, soon after a major scandal rocked the bank and business community at large.*

The blow came with the failure of Penn Square Bank, an aggressive Oklahoma City–based lender active in the South-

---

* Chase was paying Peat about $3 million a year in fees at the time the relationship was severed.

west's energy business. Through the late seventies and early eighties, Penn Square grew in tandem with the booming oil and gas industry by lending to local companies and remarketing participation in the loans to other financial institutions. "Penn Square made some $2.5 billion in participation loans that were sold to other banks, including such giants as the Continental Illinois Bank and Trust Company of Chicago and the Chase Manhattan Bank of New York. They relied on Penn Square's judgment that the loans were sound."*

The remarketing procedure, common in the banking business, was as easy and as profitable as printing money, as long as borrowers continued to prosper, take out loans, and pay them back. But the pendulum swung the other way as the start of the eighties saw the energy business decline and then nearly collapse. When the bottom fell out in 1982, Penn Square, which only four months before had received an unqualified audit opinion from Peat, Marwick, went belly up and was closed by federal regulators. Chase and a long list of creditors were left holding a bag of worthless "participation loans." Innuendos concerning Peat's handling of the audit swirled around the case, including allegations that the audit firm's partners held substantial loans with Penn Square at the time the audit was conducted. Peat officials testified before a House subcommittee investigating banking practices that "a group of the CPA firm's partners borrowed $2.3 million from Penn Square before the bank became a Peat, Marwick client in December 1981. Penn Square arranged to sell the loans to other banks that weren't Peat, Marwick clients, but one $300,000 real estate loan that was sold to another bank was later returned to Penn Square during the Marwick audit." †

Chairman of Peat's international partnership and former domestic managing partner, Tom Holton, vehemently denies any

* Kenneth B. Noble, *New York Times*, November 1, 1983, page D6.
† Lee Berton, *Wall Street Journal*, May 9, 1984, page 18.

wrongdoing and shuns responsibility for Penn Square's collapse.

"As to our work on the audit, we have nothing to apologize for. The economy changed drastically and the loan went bad. You can't predict an economic reversal of that magnitude."

The "reversal" produced heavy losses for Peat's premier banking client, Chase Manhattan, which was forced to write off about $200 million in Penn Square participation loans. In the same year, Chase was rocked by an even more disastrous event, the collapse of Drysdale Government Securities, a trader in government instruments. When the small New York firm failed to make interest payments of $180 million—owed to parties from which it had borrowed securities for its trading activities—its default threatened to precipitate a crisis in the delicately balanced financial markets. To prevent this—and to preserve the integrity of the system—Chase, which acted as a clearinghouse for the securities Drysdale borrowed, made good on the interest payments. When the dust cleared, the bank reported losses of $285 million.

The Penn Square and Drysdale affairs shared two common elements. In both, Chase found itself burned by scandals in which its business associates—Penn and Drysdale—were engaged in questionable practices and for which Peat, Marwick failed to provide warnings of imminent disaster.

But the question is, Was Chase's auditor remiss, or did the fault lie with the bank's own practices? By firing Peat, was the bank shifting blame to a scapegoat rather than admitting management's poor judgment in sizing up its business partners and in setting its lending criteria? "Penn Square grew like a weed in part because it was doing some real wild things," says Robert W. Casey, managing editor of the *American Banker,* a trade newspaper. "I mean that place was like *Animal House.* Other banks would buy participations for what they were told were drilling rigs but were actually for race horses. I don't know if an auditor is supposed to uncover this kind of thing, but I'd say that it's fair to conclude that the banks that were taken for a ride were remiss in conducting their own investigations—in knowing what they were buying."

Although Holton is clearly reticent about accusing Chase of anything—it is indiscreet for the managing partner of a Big Eight firm to be mouthing off about former clients—he nevertheless hints that Peat got a raw deal. Talking in the slow, plodding drawl that is his trademark, he intimates that the bankers shied away from accepting responsibility for a disappointing year and an unhappy series of events. For the record, however, he refuses to speculate on the reasons why Peat was axed.

Chase's public comments on the audit switch are no more enlightening. "We just wanted a fresh look," says a bank spokesman, "but that's no reflection on Peat, Marwick. They served us well." One would have to assume, then, that the Chase rewards satisfactory service with a pink slip.

"If you read Chase's love-letter press release about Peat, Marwick, Mitchell, you'd have to say they were good enough to be fired," snipes a Big Eight bank audit partner. "You tell me how that makes sense. Of course it doesn't. The fact is that when Chase bit the bullet, I knew they'd take it out of someone else's hide. And how does Chase spell scapegoat? P - E - A - T - M - A - R - W - I - C - K. Chase was responsible for some awfully bad banking practices, but it was much easier to blame Peat than to admit to in-house responsibility for the losses."

But that's only one side of the story—and perhaps a defensive one at that, coming from another bank auditor. The truth is that Penn, which had been under surveillance by the controller of currency for two years before its collapse, was cited for fraud by government regulators. Although auditors generally disclaim responsibility for detecting fraud, one school of thought —and Chase is likely in this camp—holds that Peat should have done a better job of sniffing out the troubles and alerting its clients to the potential repercussions.

Book Cooking, Numbers Juggling, and Other Tricks

"Peat's axing was a housecleaning effort on Chase's part," says one Big Eight managing partner who watched the proceedings from the sidelines. "I think the bank felt they might be sued, they might want to sue a third party, and they didn't want to be encumbered with an audit firm that was tangled up in the charges and countercharges.*

"Was Peat a scapegoat? I don't think so. But its work was no worse than that of many auditors still engaged by bank clients. That's the way it goes in this business. Contrary to popular opinion, things aren't entirely rational in the world of accounting. Not by any stretch."

As an indication of the crazy quilt nature of the audit market, Chase's choice to replace Peat—Price Waterhouse—was also involved in a highly publicized audit controversy, this involving AM International.

Once a profitable manufacturer of graphics products and information processing systems, AMI experienced a drastic decline in its business in 1981. Sluggish marketing, a controversial acquisition program, and mounting long-term debt pushed the corporation to the brink. Hoping to reverse the company's fortunes, the board of directors recruited a new chairman,† Richard Black, whose assignment was to engineer a turnaround. The changing of the guard was trumpeted as an end to AMI's troubles and the beginning of a return to solid growth and profitability. But about a year after taking his place in the

---

* Chase subsequently filed suits against six of its former officers for their handling of the Penn Square loans, and against Arthur Andersen for the Drysdale losses (Andersen was Drysdale's auditor). The Andersen suit, settled in October 1984, netted the bank a payment estimated at $45 million.

† To replace Roy L. Ash, former director of the Office of Management and Budget under Presidents Nixon and Ford, who resigned from AMI in 1981 after serving as CEO for four years.

corner office, Black filed a $3 million* lawsuit against the company and its former auditors, Price Waterhouse, claiming he'd been hoodwinked into buying 300,000 shares of AMI stock.

Black contended that financial statements prepared by AMI's previous management and blessed by Price Waterhouse induced him to pay $11.25 a share for AMI's stock only to see it nose-dive to $1.65 at the time of his resignation. Before his departure, Black fired PW and installed Arthur Andersen, who promptly confirmed Black's claims that AMI's financials were misstated and notified the SEC that it would delay AMI's annual report until revised numbers could be prepared. Price Waterhouse, for its part, wrote off the charges as a calculated plan to bolster Black's case.

So who are we to believe? The investing public, the financial community at large, is left with two rather unappealing choices: that Price Waterhouse botched an audit so badly that new management felt compelled to sue, or that Andersen, in confirming Black's claims, was looking to win points with its new client. Just which, if either, is true may never be known, but the specter of two prominent CPA firms casting aspersions on one another further diminishes the integrity of the audit process.

According to the SEC, AM International misrepresented its financial statements. Although AMI settled the complaint (as it was issued on May 2, 1983) without admitting or denying any wrongdoing, the SEC announced that it was continuing its investigation of the firm's financial dealings. The original complaint, covering AMI's 1980–81 fiscal year, charged: "AMI misrepresented to its shareholders and the public its consolidated financial conditions and results of operations by improperly and arbitrarily making adjustments to certain of its allowance and accrual accounts and to its gross profit, attribut-

---

* He subsequently settled with AMI for $1.7 million.

ing certain expenses and charges to periods other than those to which the expenses and charges were attributable, and inflating revenues and results of operations. Moreover, according to the Complaint, AMI failed to record on its books and records material amounts of adjustments to its results of operations which were necessary to present properly consolidated results of operations. . . .

"As a result of the above-described courses of business, *AMI's consolidated financial statements were materially false and misleading in that results of operations, assets, and shareholders' equity were overstated, liabilities understated, and statements of changes in financial position were misstated.* Moreover, various notes to AMI's consolidated financial statements were false and misleading concerning, among other things, AMI's accounting policies, interim results of operations, unusual income, acquisitions, bank loans and long-term debts, and the income and financial condition of AMI's finance subsidiary." (Emphasis added.)

SEC investigations linked AMI's chicanery to the now familiar performance pressure.

"At some point during the first quarter of its 1980 fiscal year, AMI learned that most of its divisions were reporting results of operations which were significantly below budgeted performance levels. At or about that time, AMI increased the level of its review of its divisions, and throughout the remainder of the 1980 fiscal year was in continual contact with the divisions concerning their operations. During the course of the 1980 fiscal year, AMI's financial position deteriorated, and its management then applied increasing pressure on the divisions to meet performance goals. Such pressure consisted of, among other means, threatened dismissals, actual dismissals, and ad hominem attacks on certain of the divisions' senior management. This pressure was, in turn, applied by the divisions' senior management to middle management. These pressures were motivated, in part, by the desire of AMI to have a public offering of its securities in the fall of 1980, and the belief that a pretax profit of $10 to $12 million for the 1980 fiscal year was necessary in order to proceed with the offering.

"During the 1980 fiscal year, in response to the pressure applied by AMI, various divisions of AMI engaged in widespread and pervasive accounting irregularities as discussed herein in order to present results of operations which conformed to budgeted performance objectives. Throughout the 1980 fiscal year, AMI's corporate headquarters learned of many instances of accounting irregularities employed by its divisions. Despite this knowledge, AMI continued to pressure its divisions to meet projected operating results."* †

If such tactics ran through all levels of the corporation, why were the auditors unable to detect it? The question is one PW's Joe Connor clearly finds distasteful. "That case is tied up in litigation and I won't comment on any specific charges," he snaps. "But I will say this. That report was accepted by the new management that came in after we were dismissed. Because it lays all the fault for the company's ills with the former management, I'd have to say it's a self-serving document. Price Waterhouse is prepared to vigorously defend itself in this case."

Connor's point may be well taken. Much as CPAs can be scapegoats, they can also be innocent victims caught in the crossfire of corporate animosities.

Charge and countercharge. Suit and countersuit. Win one, lose one. Accounting's version of musical chairs. Consider this from the front page of the *New York Times* Sunday business section of May 13, 1984:

* The SEC report.
† AMI, which eventually sought court protection to reorganize, emerged from Chapter 11 in September 1984.

Book Cooking, Numbers Juggling, and Other Tricks

When Accountants Miss the Mark

TOUCHE ROSS

November 1983—The S.E.C. censures Touche Ross for failing to use "generally accepted auditing standards" in its examination in the mid-1970's of the financial statements of Litton Industries, a big defense contractor. The agency also censures the firm for accounting irregularities in its 1978 audit of the Gelco Corporation. Touche Ross neither admits nor denies the charges.

COOPERS & LYBRAND

August 1982—The S.E.C. charges both a partner and a manager at Coopers & Lybrand with conducting a deficient 1979 audit of the Security America Corporation, a Chicago insurance holding company. Later, Security's chief subsidiary is forced into liquidation. Without admitting or denying the charge, the two accountants settle the case with the S.E.C.

ARTHUR ANDERSEN

July 1983—Warren Essner, a former senior partner at Arthur Andersen, is indicted for having issued a false financial statement about the bankrupt Drysdale Government Securities Corporation. He had reported that Drysdale was formed with a net value of $20.5 million—a statement the Justice Department's lawsuit contradicts. The Government case says Drysdale had been begun with $150 million in liabilities.

The question is, Do today's headlines announcing this SEC action or that audit failure dissolve into tomorrow's reports of war in Lebanon, of nuclear confrontation, of panic on Wall Street? Does anyone outside of the accounting profession or the SEC care about these cases? In an imperfect world, does anyone except a naive idealist really expect a peace treaty to last a lifetime, an audit to be inviolate? Can anyone really expect perfection? Can accounting firms? Their clients? Investors? The public?

"An undeniable fact of life in these very turbulent 1980s," says a Second Eight marketing director, "is that we live in a litigious society. This firm, this profession, does a very capable job under what are often difficult circumstances. But there will always be lawsuits. There will always be complaints and allegations and controversies. You can't let it stop you. You have to learn to live with it."

In public accounting, the more things change, the more they remain the same.

8
Who Does What Best

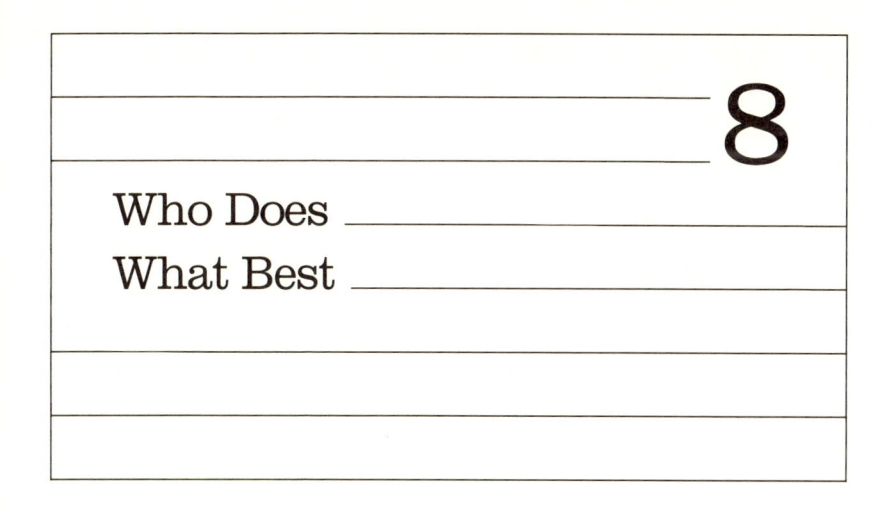

The endless debate in accounting circles over who does what best draws sharp opinions from CPAs, college professors, bankers, and attorneys. But the one group whose ratings carry the most weight—the controllers, chief financial officers, and CEOs instrumental in appointing and dismissing the twenty or so top accounting firms that compete for their business—rarely voices its thoughts in public.

The following survey, which makes no claim of scientific accuracy, is based on the author's interviews with corporate managers of various-size companies (others, doing similar research, might come up with different rankings). Although most of those who talked with the author were biased in favor of their current accounting relationships, virtually all indicated that these relationships were based on reviews of competitors' capabilities. Some were newly matched with their CPA firms, some enjoyed long-standing relationships. Some used a single CPA firm for all major services; others employed several firms for

The Accounting Wars

varying practice specialties. Most expressed satisfaction with their CPAs; others expressed the belief that there were better practitioners but were reluctant, for any number of reasons, to sever existing relationships.

Most Attentive Client Services

1. Kenneth Leventhal
2. Seidman & Seidman
3. Arthur Young
4. Price Waterhouse
5. Deloitte Haskins & Sells

Best Tax Practice

1. Coopers & Lybrand
2. Arthur Andersen
3. Peat, Marwick
4. Price Waterhouse
5. Laventhol & Horwath

Strongest Worldwide

1. Price Waterhouse
2. Arthur Andersen
3. Main Hurdman
4. Peat, Marwick

Highest-Quality Audits

1. Arthur Young
2. Ernst & Whinney
3. Deloitte Haskins & Sells

4. Price Waterhouse
5. Alexander Grant

Most Original and Creative

1. Coopers & Lybrand
2. Arthur Andersen
3. Touche Ross

Most Profitable

1. Kenneth Leventhal
2. Arthur Andersen
3. Price Waterhouse

Best Managed

1. Price Waterhouse
2. Deloitte Haskins & Sells
3. Arthur Andersen
4. Arthur Young

INDEX

accounting firms:
  consulting as future role for, 99–100
  mergers and, 100
  rankings of, 26–27, 251–253
  sole practitioner, 191–193
  see also Big Eight; Big Nine; Second Eight; smaller firms
Alexander Grant & Co., 42–47, 253
Alpex Industries Corp., 234–235
AMC Jeep, 81–82
American Can Co., 6
American Institute of Certified Public Accountants (AICPA), 30
  Financial Forecasts and Projections Task Force of, 158
  Future Issues Committee of, 12
AM International, 245–248
Arnold, Dave, 198
Arthur Andersen & Co., 39–40, 48, 101, 246, 249, 252–253
  regulatory atmosphere as concern of, 90
  structure of, 49–50
Arthur Young & Co. (AY), 179–180, 252–253
  marketing and, 207–208
  structure of, 51–52
  on tax shelters, 140–141
audit failures, 232–236
audits, 1–3, 94
  fraud in, 232–236
  low bid contracting of, 1–2
  "shopping" for, 230–233
  shortcomings in, 221–222
  tax shelters and, 141, 146

Bache Halsey Stuart Shields, 95, 100–102
bankers, investment, 122–126, 128–129
Benson, Ben, 198–199, 210
Berkowitz, Harvey, 182
Bernstein, George, 195, 198, 200, 205

254

Index

Betts, George, 82, 85
Biegler, John, 59–61, 83, 86–87
Big Eight, 205
　Big Nine vs., 25–26, 56
　China and, 59, 83–84
　competition for, 18–19, 177–206
　fees of, 186–187
　former government officials in, 116
　member firm mergers and, 47–48
　multinational accounting and, 37–41
　public trust in, 158
　ranking of, 27
　small-business practice units of, 199–200
　tax shelters and, 168, 177–178
　unprofitable clients tolerated by, 186–187
Big Nine, 25–26, 203n
　federated firms in, 50–51
　integrated firms in, 49–50
　network firms in, 51–52
　ranking of, 26
Black, Richard, 245–246
Boschma, Paul H., 28
Bowman, Art, 53
Burton, Sanford, 179
business:
　capital and, 4–5, 98–99
　changes in, 1–6
　government relationship with, 6
　national agenda proposed for, 6–7
　unpredictability in, 97–98

Casey, Robert W., 243–244
Chase Manhattan Bank, 241–245
chief financial officers (CFOs), 20, 204
China, People's Republic of (PRC), 7–8, 57–91
　accounting profession in, 58–61, 77, 82
　Big Eight and, 59, 83–84
　bureaucracy in, 63, 86–87
　capitalism in, 84–85
　DH&S in, 81–83
　foreign corporations in, 59–60, 73, 81–82, 85–90
　high-technology companies and, 60
　industry in, 81–83
　interpersonal communication in, 77–78
　management techniques in, 60–61, 83–84
　oil companies and, 60, 73, 86
　opportunities in, 60–61
　personal ties as important in, 63
　PMM in, 76, 86
　political changes in, 83–86
　PW in, 7–8, 57–81, 86–90
　TR in, 76, 82n, 86
　trust as important in, 62–63
　U.S. corporations in joint ventures in, 85–86
China Daily, 84
Chinese Foreign Enterprise Tax Law, 59, 61, 64–77
　affiliate taxability in, 74–76
　approval process for, 65
　articles of, 66–71
　as collage of foreign tax systems, 65
　consolidated earnings in, 73, 88–89
　flat vs. progressive rate for, 76–77
　Hammer suggestions and, 73–77, 88–90
　intracompany charges and expenses in, 73–74, 89
　omissions from, 71
　sample return for, 72
Chinese National Offshore Oil Corporation, 86
Citibank, 192
clients, 179–180, 183–186, 204
　accountant strength and, 179–180
　base of, as market, 190–191
　expectations of, 146

255

Index

clients (*cont.*)
　fraud and, 220–222
　loyalty of, 55–56
　unprofitable, 186–187
Cody, Roxanne, 149–150, 152–153, 169–170
Cohen Commission, 158
competitive intelligence, 205–207
Conkling, William H., 24–25, 36–37
Connor, Joseph, 5–7, 248
Coopers & Lybrand (C&L), 249, 252–253

Daimler-Benz, 31–32
Dean Witter Reynolds, 95, 100–102
Deficit Reduction Act of 1984, 140
Deloitte Haskins & Sells (DH&S), 101, 109, 252–253
　China and, 81–83
　client list of, 109
　image of, 109–110
Dent, Bill, 237–238
Deutsche Treuhand, 24–25, 31–32
Dorgan, Byron L., 147

earnings, personal, 128–129
Egger, Roscoe L., Jr., 135, 145, 150, 161
Eisenhower companies, 3, 9–10
Elliott, Robert, 200
Ernst & Whinney, 225–227, 252
European accountants, 21–22
　impact of KMG on, 56
Exxon, 35, 87–88

fees, 183–185
　for audits, 1–3, 94
　for Big Eight vs. smaller firms, 186–187
　for European clients, 22
　for financial consulting vs. investment banking, 128–129
　for Marketing Measurement Surveys, 210
　for partners, 111
　in tax shelters, 175
　for TR hot-line service, 119
　Wall Street and, 93–94
Feinglass, Mitchell, 176
Financial Accounting Standards Board (FASB), 30
financial consulting, 93, 99–129
　banking vs., 122–126, 128–129
　borrowing and, 122–123
　complexity of, 117–119
financial reports, 220–225
　judgment in, 224–225
　losses concealed in, 229–230
　profits misrepresented in, 222–224
financial services industry:
　cyclical swings in, 113
　strategic planning in, 112–113
Forbes, 25–26
Fortune, 54
Fox & Co., 232–238
fraud, accounting, 220–222, 230–239
　audit "shopping" and, 230–233
　client initiation of, 220–222
　individuals vs. corporations responsible for, 239–241
　penalties for, 238–241

Ganner, Tom, 60–61
Generally Accepted Accounting Principles (GAAP), 219
Generally Accepted Accounting Standards (GAAS), 234–235
Goerdeler, Reinhard, 24, 28, 31
Goodman, Myron, 231–233
Gregory, Grant, 8, 95–100, 102–103
Groveman, Howard, 42
Guide for Review of a Financial Forecast (AICPA), 165–167
Gu Mu, 83–84

Hall, William, 39–40
Hammer, Dick, 57, 63–66, 71–80, 88–90

Index

Chinese tax law and, 63–66, 71–77, 88–90
on life in China, 78–80
Hankes-Drielsma, Claude, 122–124, 127
Heinz case, 222–223
Hickok, Richard, 20, 22, 31–32, 42–47, 52–54
Hogan, Al, 120
Holton, Thomas, 5, 242–244
Horwath & Horwath, 195–196
hot lines, 117–121
Hurdman, Frederick, 23

Iacocca, Lee, 5
image, 11–15, 109–110
in multinational accounting, 34–40, 52–54
industry, capital and, 4, 98
Internal Revenue Service (IRS), 135–142, 151–156
behavior of, 151–156
coal mine tax shelters and, 137–138
Ernst & Whinney sued by, 225–227
film tax shelters and, 136
prefiling notification required by, 154
Rule of 78s and, 152–153
sample letter from, 155
tax shelter valuation and, 150
TEFRA and, 140–142
uncertainty encouraged by, 151–154
International Accounting Bulletin, 40, 90
investment tax credit (ITC), 225–227
Israeloff, Bob, 178–194
buy-out finances and, 182–183
early career of, 178–180
professional standing of, 188–189
Israeloff Trattner & Co., 178–194
buy-out strategy of, 181–183
client base as market for, 190–191
client relationship with, 183–186
fees of, 183–184
late fee payment and, 184–185
marketing tactics of, 189–191
paraprofessional division of, 191
referral system and, 189–190
self-promotion by, 188–189
as small business specialists, 183–184
success of, 187–189
uniform standards at, 193–194

Jack, Margaret, 58, 61–64, 66
Jahrling, Robert, 35
Japan, 4, 37
Johnson, Milan, 100–101, 105–106

Kaye, Bob, 117–120
Kenneth Leventhal, 201–202, 252–253
Kibler, Nelson, 116
Kleckner, Robert, 42–47
Klynveld Kraayenhof & Co., 24–25, 40–41
Klynveld Main Goerdeler (KMG), 24–42, 52–56
client list of, 38
consistency of, 18
formation of, 24–25
image of, 34–38, 52–54
Main Hurdman in, 24–25, 28–34, 41–42, 47
member firm mergers and, 47
member firms of, 25
organization of, 27–29, 48–53
Kullberg, Duane, 90

Lafferty, Michael, 56
Lafrentz, Ferdinand William, 22–23
Laventhol & Horwath (L&H), 178, 194–206, 252
client reliance on, 204

257

Index

Laventhol & Horwath (*cont.*)
  formation of, 195–196
  founding ideals of, 197–198
  growth and mergers of, 196–198
  hands-on approach of, 198–200
  middle market and, 203–205
  real estate market and, 200–203
  specialized services of, 202–203
Lee, B. Z., 13–14, 146
Lerner, Herbert, 226
Levine, Dick, 20, 30, 33–34, 210, 216
Lill, Ed, 103–104, 109–110
Lin Rong-sheng, 76–77, 89

McCormick case, 222–224
McGregor, Jim, 81, 86
Macy, Tom, 126
Main, Frank Wilbur, 23
Main Hurdman & Cranstoun (MH), 15, 17–18, 22–26, 28–34, 41–47, 252
  domestic market position of, 23–24, 41, 46
  formation of, 22–24
  Grant merger considered by, 42–46
  in KMG, 24–25, 28–34, 41–42, 47
  marketing strategy of, 33–34
  on tax shelters, 142
management consulting, 111–113
Manley, John, 116
marketing, 11–12, 189–191, 206–218
  competitive intelligence and, 206–207
  sales training and, 212–218
  strategy for, 33–34
  techniques in, 214–217
Market Measurement Surveys, 209–211
mergers and takeovers, 4, 10, 100
  of accounting firms, 47–48, 196–198
microcomputer consulting, 14–15
Milde, Simon, 10

Moxley, David, 95, 102–103
multinational accounting, 7–8, 17–91
  accounting firm "families" favored in, 20
  China as important in, 60
  client loyalty in, 55–56
  competition in, 18–22
  consistency of, 21, 34–35, 90–91
  European firms in, 21–22
  image in, 36–40
  member firm mergers and, 47–48
  quality of, 17–18, 21, 55
  regulation and, 90
  tradition and, 34–36
  transnational business environment and, 36–40

New York Times, 84, 248–249

O'Connor, Walter F., 19–20, 38–39, 47–52, 55–56
oil companies, China and, 60, 73, 86
O.P.M. Leasing Services, 231–233
Oppenheim, Appel, Dixon, 121

Padolin, Leonard, 139–140
Palmer, Russell, 8, 95, 104
Peat, Marwick, Mitchell & Co. (PMM), 19–20, 48, 55–56, 252
  in China, 76, 86
  international practice of, 55
  Penn Square Bank and, 241–245
  structure of, 49–50
Peloubet, Lewis, 28
Penn Square Bank, failure of, 241–244
Perry, Glen, 219–222
Presby, Tom, 92–95, 100, 102–120
  recruiting by, 104–106, 115–116

258

Index

"slam-dunk" approach of, 107
  as TR Financial Services head, 103–120
Price Waterhouse & Co. (PW), 7, 31–32, 40, 252–253
  AM International and, 245–246, 248
  China and, 7–8, 57–81, 87–90
  as Chinese intermediary, 86–87
  Chinese tax law and, 59, 61, 64–77
  Exxon and, 87–88
  structure of, 49–50
  worldwide practice of, 17–18, 35
Price Waterhouse & Partners, 122–127
  bankers vs., 122–126
  conflict issue and, 125–126
  formation of, 122–123
  PW relationship with, 122–123, 126–127
  services of, 123–124
Prudential Bache Securities, Inc., 148
Prudential Insurance Companies, 100–101, 105
Public Accounting Report, 26–27
Putnam, Robert P., 23

Raby, William, 134–135
real estate, 9–10, 200–203
referrals, from banks, 186–187, 189–190, 192
regulation, government, 90
  see also Securities and Exchange Commission
regulatory consulting, 115–116
Ronson, Howard, 201–202
Rosenberg, Jerry, 198–199

sales training, 212–218
  effectiveness of, 213–215
Salomon Brothers Inc., 121
Saxon Industries, Inc., 234–235
Scottish Savings and Loan Association, 229–230
Sears Roebuck, 100–101

Second Eight, fees of, 186–187, 190
Securities and Exchange Commission (SEC), 234–241, 246–249
  AM International and, 246–248
  Fox & Co. and, 234–237
  powers of, 238–241
  strengthening suggested for, 239–240
Seidman & Seidman, 15, 163–171, 252
services, accounting, 12–15, 197
Services Rating Organization, 209–212, 216
  marketing by, 210–211
  research reports of, 211–212
services sector, 3–6, 8–10
Shad, John, 240
Shebairo, Richard, 137
small business, 7, 183–184, 199–200
smaller firms, 177–206
  client relationship with, 179–180
  competitive intelligence and, 205–206
  consistency of, 193–194
  discrimination against, 192–193
  fees for, 186–187
  growth of, 193
  specialized services and, 197
  tax shelters and, 168, 177–178
  unprofitable clients and, 186–187
smokestack industries, 6–7, 22
Société Cooperative, 39–40, 48
sole practitioner firms, 191–193
Southeastern Savings & Loan Company, 229–230
Spiro, William, 149, 152, 158–159, 161, 169–171
standards, professional, 219–221, 227–228, 234–250
  independence and, 227–228
Stein, Harvey, 192
strategic planning, 112–113

259

Index

Tax Equity and Fiscal Responsibility Act of 1982 (TEFRA), 139–142, 174
taxes:
  affiliate liability for, 74–76
  international trade and, 65–66
  Wall Street and, 110–111
  see also Chinese Foreign Enterprise Tax Law
tax shelters, 13–14, 130–176
  abusive, 135–136, 140–150
  accountant's letter for, 157–172
  attorney's opinion in, 172–175
  audits and, 141, 146
  Big Eight vs. smaller firms and, 168, 177–178
  in coal mining, 137–138
  CPA fees in, 175
  CPA firms as catalysts for, 156–161, 175–176
  CPA input on, 169–171
  CPA responsibility for, 141–145, 158–172
  creation and marketing of, 146–147
  as deferrals, 130, 145–146
  definitive statements difficult for, 146, 149–156, 165–175
  described, 133–135
  film production and, 135–136
  guarantees lacking for, 132–133
  high-multiple write-offs in, 136, 145
  as investment incentives, 134–135, 147
  as misnomer, 144–145
  mortgages as, 133–134
  prefiling notification for, 154
  Rule of 78s and, 152–153
  syndication cost in, 147–150
  syndicators and, 147–152, 156–161
  TEFRA and, 139–142
  valuation of, 150
technology, high, 3–4, 60
  capital and, 98–99
  management and, 7

Ten Eyck, Ernie, 198
Thompson, John A., 28
Thomson McLintok, 41
Thyssen-Bornemisza, 40
Touche Ross & Co. (TR), 15, 25, 249, 253
  aggressiveness of, 121
  in China, 76, 82n, 86
  financial consulting and, 93, 99–121
  local office territories in, 106
  management of, 95–96
  Prudential and, 100–101, 105
  structure of, 51–52
  Wall Street and, 8–9, 102–103
Touche Ross Financial Services Center, 103–121
  Audit Group of, 109–110
  client style imitated by, 117
  cost of, 108
  financial advisory services of, 114
  generalist practice at, 107–108
  hot line of, 117–121
  local office territories and, 106
  Management Consulting Group of, 111–113
  recruiting for, 104–106, 115–116
  regulatory consulting by, 115–116
  reorganization advisory services of, 114–115
  Tax Consulting Group of, 110–111
trade, international, 7, 65–66
Trattner, Dick, 182
Treadway, James, 222–224, 228–231, 239–241
Treasury Department, U.S., 171–172

Union Carbide, 28–31

Vagliano, Alexander, 123
VMS Realty, Inc., 148

Index

Wall Street, 8–9, 92–121
   fees and, 93–94
   management consulting and, 111–113
   taxes and, 110–111
Wall Street Journal, 62
Wall Street Planning Group, 102, 107

Wanniski, Jude, 84
Weissman, Mordecai, 231–233
Wellerer, Charles, 159
White, Larry, 207–212, 216
   background of, 207–208

Zimmerman, Jules, 52